Centro Torinese di Psicoanalisi

W. R. BION:
BETWEEN PAST
AND FUTURE

Centro Torinese di Psicoanalisi

Other volume of Selected Contributions from the International Centennial Conference on the Work of W. R. Bion:

Bion's Legacy to Groups, edited by Parthenope Bion Talamo, Franco Borgogno, and Silvio A. Merciai

W. R. BION: BETWEEN PAST AND FUTURE

Selected Contributions
from the International Centennial Conference
on the Work of W. R. Bion

Turin, July 1997

Edited by

*Parthenope Bion Talamo, Franco Borgogno,
Silvio A. Merciai*

Foreword by

Léon Grinberg

London & New York
KARNAC BOOKS

The Editors' special thanks go to Francesca Bion and Nicola Bion Vick for their kind assistance with completing this book.

First published in 2000 by
H. Karnac (Books) Ltd., 58 Gloucester Road, London SW7 4QY
A subsidiary of Other Press LLC, New York

British Library Cataloguing in Publication Data

A C.I.P for this book is available from the British Library

ISBN 1 85575 187 9

10 9 8 7 6 5 4 3 2 1

Edited, designed, and produced by Communication Crafts
Printed in Great Britain by Polestar Wheatons Ltd, Exeter

www.karnacbooks.com

Parthenope Bion Talamo died on 16 July 1998 in a tragic car accident, together with her younger daughter, Patrizia, who was only 18.

This book, along with its companion title, *Bion's Legacy to Groups*, concludes several years of work dedicated to the study, clarification, and dissemination of the thoughts of her father and culminating in the *International Centennial Conference on the Work of W. R. Bion*, held in Turin, Italy, 16–19 July 1997. Parthenope acted not only as its President, but also as a gentle host to the many participants from all over the world. Although she was very tired when she opened the Conference, she was smiling and excited—and this is the way we remember her.

Work on the manuscript was almost finished when Parthenope died. One of us [S.A.M.] completed the final editing, in no way changing or revising what we had done and shared. This is why, for example, we have left the original dedication to our spouses, Luigi, Mariella, and Mirella.

We feel indebted to Parthenope for all that she taught us and for what we learnt together with her. She created a special atmosphere among us, emphasizing W. R. Bion's core idea that to be a psychoanalyst implies a willingness to maintain a full sense of freedom when thinking, feeling, theorizing, and being curious and aware of one's ignorance.

We deeply miss our beloved friend Parthenope. This book should be read as her legacy and as our grateful homage to her. In producing it, we would like to share our mourning with all colleagues who met her and came to know and love her.

F.B. & S.A.M.

To Luigi, Mariella, and Mirella
for their patience and help
before, during, and after

CONTENTS

EDITORS AND CONTRIBUTORS   xiii

FOREWORD   xix
   Léon Grinberg

Introduction
   Parthenope Bion Talamo, Franco Borgogno,
   & Silvio Arrigo Merciai   1

1 Random reflections on Bion: past, present, and future
   POSTSCRIPT (January 1999)
   Francesca Bion   11

2 Laying low and saying (almost) nothing
   Parthenope Bion Talamo   20

3 Considerations on some of W. R. Bion's ideas
   Deocleciano Bendocchi Alves   27

4   The sick syllogism: the fear of dying
    and the sacrifice of truth
        Emanuele Bonasia   45

5   Searching for Bion:
    Cogitations, a new "Clinical Diary"?
        Franco Borgogno and Silvio Arrigo Merciai   56

6   Whom was Bion addressing?
    "Negative capability" and "listening to listening"
        Haydée Faimberg   79

7   Sexuality as a narrative genre or dialect
    in the consulting-room: a radical vertex
        Antonino Ferro   91

8   The primordial mind and the work of the negative
        André Green   108

9   Bion's "transformations in 'O'"
    and the concept of the "transcendent position"
        James Grotstein   129

10 Thinking aloud about technique
        Isabel Luzuriaga   145

11 A dreamlike vision
        Alberto Meotti   155

12 The theoretical and clinical significance
    of the concept of "common sense" in Bion's work
        Gianni Nebbiosi and Romolo Petrini   164

13 The fundamental role of the Grid in Bion's work
        Rosa Beatriz Pontes Miranda de Ferreira   178

14   What is thinking—an attempt at an integrated
     study of W. R. Bion's contributions
     to the processes of knowing
         Paulo Cesar Sandler   200

15   The various faces of lies
         Elizabeth T. de Bianchedi, Claudia Bregazzi,
         Carmen Crespo, Elsa Grillo de Rimoldi,
         Silvia Grimblat de Notrica, Delia Saffoires,
         Adela Szpunberg de Bernztein, Alicia Werba,
         & Rosa Zamkow   220

REFERENCES   237

INDEX   253

EDITORS AND CONTRIBUTORS

DEOCLECIANO BENDOCCHI ALVES graduated in Medicine from the University of Brazil and was a resident physician at Hospital das Clinicas of the University of São Paulo; he holds a degree in the theoretical and practical psychoanalysis of adults as well as children and adolescents at the Institute of Psycho-Analysis of the Brazilian Society of Psycho-Analysis of São Paulo. He is a training analyst of the Sociedade Brasileira de Psicanalisis of São Paulo. He holds study groups on the reading of *Cogitations* and *A Memoir of the Future* by W. R. Bion with São Paulo psychoanalysts and psychoanalytical students. He has published many papers on clinical psychoanalysis. The author attended courses, seminars, supervisions, and conferences given by W. R. Bion in Brazil in 1974, 1975, and 1978.

FRANCESCA BION is the widow of W. R. Bion. She worked with him closely on his books and papers and has edited all the books that have appeared posthumously.

PARTHENOPE BION TALAMO, PH.D., the eldest daughter of W. R. Bion, was born in England, where she went to school; she then read philosophy in Italy, at Florence University. She worked in full-time private practice as a psychoanalyst near Turin, Italy, being a member of the Società Psicoanalitica Italiana and of the International Psychoanalytical Association. She also had some experience in group therapy and supervised the initial stages in setting up a non-residential therapeutic community in Florence for psychotic and borderline patients. As well as editing and translating many of W. R. Bion's books and papers into Italian and preparing the Bion Centennial Conference together with a group of colleagues led (and spurred on) by Silvio A. Merciai, she wrote several psychoanalytical papers, some on Bion's work.

EMANUELE BONASIA is a psychiatrist and a supervising and training analyst at the National Institute of Training of the Società Psicoanalitica Italiana. Interested in the comparison between theoretical models, he is also the author of a number of papers on the subjects of separation and death anxieties. He lives in Turin, where he is Scientific Secretary of the Turin Centre of Psychoanalysis and works in private practice as a psychoanalyst and psychotherapist, particularly committed to short-term dynamic psychotherapy.

FRANCO BORGOGNO, PH.D., is Professor of Clinical Psychology at Turin University and training and supervising analyst of the Società Psicoanalitica Italiana. He is the author of a book about the problems of observation in psychoanalysis and many papers about psychoanalytical technique and historical issues (the more recent ones on Paula Heimann and Ferenczi). He is in private practice as a psychoanalyst in Turin.

HAYDÉE FAIMBERG, M.D., is training and supervising analyst at the Paris Psychoanalytical Society and former Vice-president of the International Psychoanalytical Association (IPA). She initiated in 1994 a Standing Conference on Psychoanalytical Intracultural and Intercultural Dialogue at the IPA. She has contributed chapters to several books; one of the hypotheses she proposes in her work is that certain unconscious alienating identifications, which condense three generations, are discovered in every analysis and links those identifications to a "narcissistic dimension of the Oedipal configuration".

ANTONINO FERRO was born in Palermo and lives and works in Pavia. He is a member of the International Psychoanalytical Association and a training analyst of the Società Psicoanalitica Italiana, of which he has also been the Scientific Secretary. He is the author of a book on the technique of child analysis as well as a book on the theory of technique in adult analysis, both of which have been translated into several languages. His particular interests are in the field of severe pathology and in that of child analysis. He is Past Professor of Child Psychotherapy at the University of Milan. At present he is in private practice and also holds supervisions in several institutions.

ANDRÉ GREEN lives and works in Paris, where he is a training analyst of the Paris Psychoanalytic Society. He is also former Director of the Paris Psychoanalytic Institute, Past President of the Paris Psychoanalytic Society, Past Vice-president of the International Psychoanalytical Association, and former Professor, Freud Memorial Chair, University College, London. He is the author of a great number of papers and books that have been translated into many languages; among these are *The Tragic Effect* and *On Private Madness*.

JAMES GROTSTEIN, M.D., is Clinical Professor of Psychiatry at UCLA School of Medicine and training and supervising analyst at The Los Angeles Psychoanalytic Society and Institute and at The Psychoanalytic Center of California, Los Angeles. He is the author of 223 contributions to the literature and author, editor, or co-editor of six books. He is in private practice in West Los Angeles.

ISABEL LUZURIAGA, Spanish-born, lived in England and Argentina between 1937 and 1976 for political reasons and returned to Spain in 1977. She has a degree in Education and Philosophy from Buenos Aires University and underwent psychoanalytical training in the Asociación Psicoanalítica Argentina, Buenos Aires. She is Full Member and Training Analyst of the Asociación Psicoanalítica Argentina and the Asociación Psicoanalítica de Madrid. She holds Seminars in Buenos Aires and Madrid and is also a Child Psychoanalyst in both associations. She is author of a number of papers and books on psychoanalysis.

ALBERTO MEOTTI is training and supervising analyst of the Società Psicoanalitica Italiana and is Professor of Philosophy of Science at the University of Pavia. After taking degrees in law and philosophy, he has devoted himself from 1964 onwards to clinical psychology and psychoanalysis. His main interests and research are reflected in his papers on clinical psychoanalysis, on the scientific character of psychoanalysis, on the contributions of psychoanalysis to the overcoming of the crisis of empirical sciences, on the identity of the psychoanalyst, on the use and relevance of theories in psychoanalytic practice, and on the influence of internal groups on individual maturational development. Recently his research on clinical psychoanalysis and its technique has focused on the problems of unconscious transmission between generations and on unconscious organization and functioning of groups.

SILVIO ARRIGO MERCIAI, M.D., is an Associate Member of the Società Psicoanalitica Italiana. He works as psychotherapist and psychoanalyst in private practice in Turin. He acted as the Secretary of the International Centennial Conference on the Work of W. R. Bion. He is currently the Webmaster of some innovative psychoanalytical sites on the Internet and is a member of study groups dealing with long-distance health services and psychological services on the Net.

GIANNI NEBBIOSI, Ph.D., is an individual and group psychoanalyst. He is co-director of the ISPS [Institute for Psychoanalytic Self-psychology and Relational Psychoanalysis], a member of the Italian Council for Psychoanalytic Self Psychology; training analyst at the NIP [National Institute for the Psychotherapies, New York], Corresponding Member of the ICPC [Institute of Contemporary Psychoanalysis, Los Angeles], and a member of The International Association of Group Psychotherapy. He has published a number of papers in several languages. With Parthenope Bion Talamo, he translated Bion's last work, *A Memoir of the Future*, into Italian. He lives and works in Rome.

ROMOLO PETRINI, M.D., is a psychiatrist, and an individual and group psychoanalyst. He is an associate member of the Società Psicoanalitica Italiana. A former President of the Centro di Ricerche Psicoanalitiche di Gruppo "Il Pollaiolo", Rome, he lives and works in Rome.

ROSA BEATRIZ PONTES MIRANDA DE FERREIRA, a mathematician and a psychoanalyst, is a full member of the Brazilian Psychoanalytic Society of Rio de Janeiro. She is an expert on W. R. Bion's "Grid" and holds a long-term study group on it.

PAULO CESAR SANDLER, master in medicine, psychiatrist and psycho-analyst, is a training analyst in the Brazilian Psychoanalytic Society of São Paulo. He has translated many of W. R. Bion's books and papers into Portuguese and has written numerous papers and books both on W. R. Bion's work and on his own.

ELIZABETH TABAK DE BIANCHEDI, a medical doctor and psychoanalyst, is a full member of APdeBA (Buenos Aires Psychoanalytic Association), with training analyst and teaching functions in this institution. She was associate secretary for Latin America of the Executive Council of the International Psychoanalytic Association from August 1993 to July 1997 and was co-author, with Drs. Léon Grinberg and Darío Sor, of *Introduction to the Work of Bion* (1973) and *New Introduction to the Work of Bion* (1992), books that have been translated into French, Italian, German, Swedish, and Japanese, among others. She is also author and co-author of a large number of published papers on Klein's, Meltzer's, and Bion's ideas and an active participant in human rights activities in Argentina.

FOREWORD

Léon Grinberg

In August 1968, there was great excitement as the date of Bion's arrival in Buenos Aires grew near, following his acceptance of our invitation to come to Argentina for the first time. For my part, I was looking forward to meeting him personally, having until then only seen him briefly from a distance at several Congresses. I remembered the many hours devoted to reading and discussing his books and articles by a study group of young analysts that was under my guidance at the time, and our efforts to endeavour to understand his thinking. I awaited his arrival in the hope that our doubts might be dispelled. The picture I had of Bion from books was that of a very original thinker, who accepted our invitation despite the fact that our Society lacked the prestige of the American or European ones. At the airport, where I went to receive him, I encountered a tall, portly gentleman of very serious demeanour, but who, to my surprise, turned out to be extremely

---

A personal recollection of Bion, written especially for this book [Editors' note].

affable and rather shy, and who spoke to us in a most unaffected and friendly manner.

His first conference aroused great expectations, and I recall that the assembly-room in our Society was crammed with analysts and students, many of whom, though they had little or no knowledge of his theories, arrived with preconceived ideas and an *a priori* critical attitude. Only a small group, as I have already mentioned, had attempted to delve more deeply into his ideas. In this first conference, Bion began by presenting a clinical case, covering aspects of his own technique.

I cannot be certain whether it was in this first conference or in a later one that an unfortunate, but moving, incident occurred. One of our training analysts, who had been suffering from arteriosclerosis and certain accompanying mental disorders that had led to his abandoning the practice of psychoanalysis, surprised everyone by being present and by making certain untimely critical remarks in most immoderate terms, reflecting his perturbed state of mind. A tense silence ensued while some colleagues helped him out of the room. At first there was some concern that the criticism had upset Bion, as he remained silent and thoughtful for a few moments. However, he promptly said that he wished to pay tribute to someone, who, "in working with something so terrible as the human mind", had become yet another victim within the psychoanalytic community. The outburst of prolonged applause that greeted Bion's words clearly reflected the admiration that those present felt for such an understanding, generous, and human response.

We also benefited greatly from his seminars and supervisions. There was a considerable reversal of opinion as regards his personal esteem and his analytic capacity. Praise was abundant, and after his departure his ideas continued to be discussed at scientific meetings.

Shortly after arriving in Buenos Aires, he had observed that what impressed him most was the number of book-shops in comparison to Los Angeles (he had only just moved to that city). He had a striking passion for books, as revealed in his use of quotations in both his writings and his oral deliveries. Having mentioned his love of books, I cannot resist the temptation to relate a personal anecdote. On one occasion when he came to dinner, he went straight over to the bookcase to examine the titles of the books. One of the English volumes caught his attention, and he picked it up for a closer inspection. It was *The Maggid of Caro*, a biographical account of the mystical life of the famous scholar and kabbalist, Joseph Caro, who was born in Toledo but later emigrated to Israel, at the time when the Jews were expelled by the Spanish Inquisition. I had received the book as a gift from the Israeli Ambassador to the United States on one of my visits to New York; it contained a dedication and, for other personal reasons, was of special sentimental value to me. The whole scene was played out in a few minutes. Bion's interest in the book was evident from the way he was leafing through it and from his remarks about the Kabbala. I felt that, were I to present it to him, it would make a splendid token of my admiration for him; but, at the same time, I was finding it difficult to do so. Bion, concentrating as he was in reading a few paragraphs, was apparently unaware of my dilemma at that moment. Suddenly, however, he turned to me and said: "Don't worry, Grinberg, I won't ask you to give it to me. I would be grateful though if you would let me borrow it over the weekend to read it in the hotel." Needless to say, my surprise was enormous, and we both burst out laughing. Here, once again, Bion's reaction showed both his intuitive ability and his human capacity for understanding and considering others.

As stated above, I had been studying Bion's writings over a period of years while co-ordinating a group of young analysts, some of whom would later collaborate with me as co-authors of our book, *Introduction to the Work of Bion* (1975). It was striking how often Bion related his concepts to other disciplines pertaining to general sciences. We were particularly interested in ascertaining his theoretical position, although naturally we knew that his ideas were based primarily on Freud, in particular on the "Oedipus complex" and the "Two Principles of Mental Functioning", and on Kleinian theory, especially on the importance of internal objects, the paranoid–schizoid and depressive positions, and projective identification. Yet, we were also impressed by the originality of his hypotheses and their development through time. We came to the conclusion that his theory was basically a theory of the capacity to "think emotions". We also came to believe that the relationship between his theory and clinical work was analogous to that between pure and applied mathematics. When Newton developed his laws of motion, he introduced some abstract notions such as mass, force, and absolute space, assuming that they possessed certain properties within the conceptual framework of his theory. In similar fashion, we realized that Bion's theory of thinking and thought was also a conceptual framework within which were to be found preconceptions, conceptions, concepts, and alpha-elements.

At that time, as now, criticism of psychoanalysis was rife, chiefly among epistemologists who rejected its scientific status and objected to its dualistic doctrine (mental and physical substances viewed as two separated types of entity). According to them, science has demonstrated the monist doctrine: all that we refer to as "mental" is associated with the brain and its functions. Here we raised the question as to where Bion stood in relation to dualism or monism. Around that time we learnt that the philosopher Bertrand Russell had put forward the idea of neutral monism, which held that the essential nature of reality is neither mental nor physical but, rather, a combination of both. Mental and physical events or properties thus stem from the way in which this ultimate substance is structured. Subsequently, Russell and Moore suggested that sensation would potentially be waiting to become sensory, from which it follows that sensation has a prior existence. At this point, I would now propose this thesis as a model for comparison with Bion's hypothesis regarding the existence of a "thought without a thinker", or, in other words, thoughts waiting for a thinker to think them. It may also be equated with his analytic technique of working "without memory, desire or understanding", in order to await the "evolution" of O and the emergence of intuition.

In one of his last works, Bion (1987b) employs the term "self" to encompass what he calls body, mind, and a "mental space" for subsequent ideas that may eventually develop. He notes that the philosophical expression of this approach is monism. According to him, the analyst should be sensitive to the whole of the person of the patient—that is, to both his physical and emotional aspects. To illustrate this idea, he quotes the following lines by Donne (*Progress of the Soul*):

> Her pure and eloquent blood . . . spoke in her cheeks, and so distinctly wrought, that one might almost say, her body thought.

Our last meeting took place at his home in Los Angeles on the occasion of an intimate dinner at which only Bion, Francesca, my wife, and I were present. The evening turned out to be an unforgettable one lasting several hours longer than planned. Once again we realized the extent of Bion's interests and his acute sensibility. Without doubt, his knowledge of the natural sciences and the humanities enriched his thinking, while, in turn, his clinical findings and his original theorizing contributed to, and will continue contributing to, the expansion of the psychoanalytic universe.

The importance of the seed that Bion bequeathed to those of us who have taken nourishment from his ideas is that it enabled us to think not only Bion's thinking but also those thoughts of our own for which we could not previously be thinkers.

W. R. BION:
BETWEEN PAST
AND FUTURE

Introduction

Parthenope Bion Talamo, Franco Borgogno,
& Silvio Arrigo Merciai

Only the Ship of Fools is making the journey this year.

W. H. Auden, "Atlantis"

This anthology can be thought of as being the natural offspring of the International Centennial Conference on the
Work of W. R. Bion, which was held in Turin, Italy, in July
1997. It is its "natural" offspring not so much in the sense of illegiti-
mate—though some of the papers have been slightly revised from
the original presented version, making use of the stimuli furnished
by the Conference itself, and so could be said to have an unknown
plurality of parents—but in the sense that as the Conference was a
transient occasion, the desire to leave some more tangible sign of
its existence was "naturally" very strong.

We decided that the book was to represent as nearly as feasibly
possible the atmosphere that resulted from the intermingling of:

(a) the original formulation of the Conference philosophy as expressed right from the start in the call for papers (i.e. not to

1

celebrate Bion's thought, but to give room to all who have continued his work with an independent way of mind: very much a work-in-progress affair, with the possibility of presenting ideas that may not have been fully worked out or tied up to other parts of psychoanalytic theory—Bion's or other people's—with which they might seem to have a natural affinity);

(b) the development of the above during the preparatory months, as more and more people contributed advice and ideas, especially via the Internet mailing list—a kind of open group working through the possible meaning of the Conference itself;

(c) the realization of our dreamt philosophy, the Conference itself, that is to say, the resulting mix of our intentions, other people's interpretation of them, and the actual outcome.

This obviously means that the criterion for the inclusion of papers in this collection is a subjective one (though, on the other hand, who has ever seen a human being do things for objective reasons— i.e. other people's—and still feel that their own capacity, great or small, for creativity, is satisfied?). We three pooled our individual feelings, and, basing ourselves on what we each felt about the Conference, while still warmed by the heat (metaphorical and, unfortunately, also physical) of the event itself, made our choices on the basis of an emotional adherence to the spirit of the Conference as *we* understood it. This perception of the "quiddity" of the meeting itself (to use Joyce's term)—the realization of what had, up to the opening of the Conference, only been a partially shared and barely verbalizable set of fantasies and phantasies—was an extraordinarily important experience for all three of us and, we believe, was shared in different ways by nearly everyone at some point during the four days. It was indeed a scientific meeting with a significant emotional component, which was perceivable at the time and which we have tried, if possible, to transmit via this book: our desire to think, keeping mental freedom and openness and preserving "wild thoughts" as such.

* * *

We feel that the Conference—and also this book—are faithful reflections on the development of psychoanalytical thought following on the stimuli provided by Bion's work. He was not the founder of a "new" school of psychoanalytical theory but was very firmly embedded in Freudian theory and ways of thinking: thanks to the detailed analysis and further study of many of his intuitions which this book provides, it should be possible to integrate them more thoroughly into the Freudian cultural heritage.

The chapters of the book have been organized using an intentionally neutral criterion—that of the alphabetical order of the authors' surnames (with the exception of the first two chapters, which are by way of a more personal introduction to Bion)—so as to leave the reader free to invent his own non-sequential reading, a creation of his own pathway through the book. This choice mirrors the almost "do-it-yourself" atmosphere of the Conference itself, at which, while subject to the inevitable limitations of reality, people could choose from among the several ongoing panels those threads that they wished to follow up.

Most of the authors deal with Bion's later work as well as with the earlier—a new departure compared with the many (even fairly recent) writings on Bion that did not take the second half of his production into account, as well as a certain persistent tendency to discount his later work as irrelevant or not serious. Almost all the authors are psychoanalysts, and the differences in language reflect both different approaches to different parts of Bion's writings and also, probably, different styles of psychoanalytical culture in different countries.

* * *

The Foreword by Léon Grinberg is almost more of an "introduction to Bion as a person" than a survey of the book's chapters, and is in itself much in keeping with the spirit of the Conference, at which personal reactions to the stimuli furnished by Bion's ideas were much to the fore. It is followed by Francesca Bion's recollection of W. R. Bion, which touches mainly on his individual characteristics, and by Parthenope Bion Talamo's short chapter, which tries to bridge the gap between "my father" and "W. R. Bion", making an attempt to show how his personality had certain stable features that suffused both his private and his professional life.

Four movements and three "contrapuntal episodes" go to make up Deocleciano Bendocchi Alves's symphony, a sort of poetical tale or personal echo of an autobiography inspired by Bion and his work. In order to appreciate this chapter, the reader is required to make the same effort of refinement and close listening as the author has made, and to participate in the affectionate aesthetic experience of not knowing right from the beginning what the paper's theme will be. Instead, he is asked—as happens every day in our professional lives—to be available for hearing, for listening, in short, for dreaming.

"Human reasoning"—and specifically psychoanalytical reasoning—are taken severely to task by EMANUELE BONASIA in "The Sick Syllogism", in which he discusses what he feels to be the fundamentally unsatisfactory results of all theories, philosophical and psychoanalytical, when it is a question of coming to terms with the reality of one's own death. He states that the anxiety, which he terms realistic, connected with the inevitability of our own end "has, to a great extent, been denied in psychoanalysis, through the defensive employment of different theories, which include those of castration anxiety and the death instinct". After a brief discussion of the main aspects of Freud's and Klein's theories in this field, the author suggests that Bion did develop some conceptual tools useful in thinking about death, namely the concept of the psychotic part of the personality, transformations, invariance, catastrophic change. Bonasia uses these concepts to develop the idea of lies about death as based on a hallucinatory transformation, particularly in the fields of myth and religion, and links this up with a sort of primary, basic resistance to analytical work.

FRANCO BORGOGNO and SILVIO A. MERCIAI take a specific aspect of Bion's development as an analyst as their subject. Without feeling hampered by having to "belong" to a given school of analytical thought or "depend" on some specific clique subscribing to a limited field of theory, they follow up Bion's development, comparing him to other analysts (Winnicott, P. Heimann, and, above all, Ferenczi) who bravely fought against the use of jargon in the representation of psychoanalytical experience, trying, as they went along, to free themselves from the ideological components of thinking and from the socialized narcissistic defences that feed the latter. From this standpoint, the authors—while commenting on Bion's entire output as an analyst—focus their attention on *Cogitations* in particular, suggesting that it can be read as a sort of new "Clinical Diary" à la Ferenczi, showing us both the link between the writings of the London Bion and those of the American one, which is, so to speak, closer to us in time, and the dramatic change that took place in his psychoanalytical position around about 1967. The authors emphasize the relevance of this change, stressing the great extent to which it was prepared and matured, slowly and not without contrasts and suffering. This led Bion to part company to a certain extent with the Kleinian group to which he had principally referred until then. Indeed, he gradually formulated theoretical and technical positions that were increasingly autonomous and independent, more centred on listening to the patients' individual specific voices and more authentically open both to his own thoughts and emotions and those of the patient during the analytical encounter.

Remembering a week's work with Bion during the summer of 1968, HAYDÉE FAIMBERG identifies Bion's principal message as a critique of the position of the analyst as regards knowing and coming to know. This is a position that narcissistically blocks the session that "has not yet come to pass". Referring to previous papers of hers, the author ties up her thought on "listening to listening" (1981, 1996) with the "negative capability" of which Bion speaks and discusses the Freudian concept of *Nachträglichkeit* from an original stance. According to Faimberg, Bion is *classical* in the sense that Calvino gives to this term—namely, that a classic produces a new meaning at each reading for every reader. He is a classical *psychoanalyst*, therefore, since by choice psychoanalysis deals with what is new, different, unconscious, in its attempt at releasing the process of knowledge and comprehension from alienating ideologies and identifications.

The chapter by ANTONINO FERRO does not deal with sexuality as such, but, as the title declares, with sexuality in the consulting-room, with all the tales that gradually characterize the analytical couple's experience being a metaphor for it. It is a metaphor of the meeting of two minds and of the qualities that characterize its basic attitude—producing transformation and thought or not doing so.

The author reflects on what it is in the session, which furthers the burgeoning thought of the patient. In an original way he melds Bion's theories with those of other authors, introducing his own intriguing concept of "balpha"-elements, neither beta nor alpha, which imply a lack of "alphabetization" with which the analytical couple has to deal by making the balpha-elements visible so that they can be digested and become elements of thought.

ANDRÉ GREEN, after a brief introduction in which he remarks amusingly on his credentials for having been invited to give the opening main lecture of the Conference, programmatically entitled "The Primordial Mind and the Work of the Negative", states the architectonics of his paper: "Bion's work can be divided into two categories: the first represents his attempts to build a new psycho-analytic theory which would not only be an extension of Freud's work or even of Klein's, but a contemporary new formulation of psychoanalysis starting from an entirely different point of view." This new formulation is that of psychoanalysis as a scientific de-ductive system, whereas the second category is that of Bion's "psy-choanalytic science fiction". Green suggests that we apply Bion's own model to his thinking and wonders what we can learn from the experience of reading him: Green himself has picked out the theme of the primordial mind as the main path to follow in his study of Bion, and he illuminates most clearly the roots of Bion's thinking in Freud's. This pathway leads him to a very important discussion of the "negative" and shows how in Bion's work this concept has been deepened to include two different types of nega-tive—"nothing" and "no thing", whose differentiation has very far-reaching consequences.

JAMES GROTSTEIN, one of the most affectionate and inspired stu-dents of Bion's work, read a stimulating main lecture at the Con-ference and wholly revised it for this book, starting from the suggestions offered by the floor discussion that followed his pres-entation. His chapter, even if somewhat affected by the limited space available in the book, offers the reader an illuminating ver-tex not only on Bion's *episteme*, but also on Bion as analyst and thinker. The main focus is, nevertheless, the concept of O (one of the most controversial and discussed themes in Bion's work, and possibly a frequently misunderstood one) and the suggestion of a "transcendent position": on this matter, the author strictly adheres to "psychoanalytic and epistemological vertices even when ap-plied to mysticism itself". "O", he says, "is one's reality without pretence or distortion. This reality can be a symptom, the pain of viewing beautiful autumn leaves, gazing upon the mystique of the

Mona Lisa della Gioconda, contemplating the horror of Ypres (for Bion), trying to remember Hiroshima, Nagasaki, Auschwitz, or Vietnam, or resting comfortably beside one's mate trying to contemplate the exquisiteness and ineffability of the moment. Transcendence is the mute 'Other' that lies 'just beyond, within, and around' where we are. It is the core of our very Being-in-itself. As I shall hypothesize, the mystic or genius is that aspect of us which is potentially able to be at one with transcendence as O—but only after we have 'cleared' with P↔S and D. *The mystic, according to Bion, is one who sees things as they really are—through the deception or camouflage of words and symbols."* Grotstein not only offers us a comprehensive framework for understanding the so-called mystical dimension of Bion the analyst and thinker (quoting from philosophers such as Kant and Heidegger, and from psychoanalysts, such as Klein and Matte Blanco), but he also puts forward the idea that the transcendent position could be seen as a significant move "beyond" Freud's and Klein's main theories and as an interpretation of the analytical process, which is at one and the same time both classical and modern.

As Isabel Luzuriaga points out, the title of her chapter ("Thinking Aloud about Technique") represents the contents exactly: the author's emotional experience with Bion as an internal object, while she reflects about her work with her patients. The author describes in detail how Bion's theory of container and contained has modified both her analytical attitude and her technique. In a Kleinian way, she underlines how, in the light of Bion's classical papers of the 1950s and 1960s, the principal difficulty in using oneself in order to understand the patient lies in having to keep in mind the different aspects present in the session (healthy and ill, libidinal/vital and death-dealing/destructive, neurotic and psychotic) all at the same time without excluding or undervaluing any one part in favour of another.

Alberto Meotti, in his interesting chapter on *A Memoir of the Future*, "A Dreamlike Vision", explores the possible meanings and intentions of Bion's last major oeuvre. He suggests that Bion proposes in the Trilogy "a sort of dream full of images, a kind of manifest content that could be the anticipation of a latent controversy that might involve in the future the collapse of a substantial part of present knowledge and the development of new psychoanalytic theories". The author's philosophical background emerges in his further suggestion that Bion has drawn on the servants of Hegel's *Phenomenology of Spirit* as a sort of model for the most innovative members of the group, who have to labour in the background with the most obscure matters in order to humanize the latter and make them generally accessible and useful. In his clarifying exploration and discussion of this difficult text, Meotti illuminates the reasons why Bion may have felt that the dreamlike vision was the most appropriate for his presentation of his ideas, and he touches on the very sombre side of Bion's theorizing on aggressiveness and destruction.

GIANNI NEBBIOSI and ROMOLO PETRINI's chapter clarifies and deepens our understanding of Bion's concept of "common sense", illustrating its central position in Bion's work in general. The authors highlight the dual definition that Bion gives of "common sense" (meaning the correlation between sensorial perceptions in the individual and also that "sense" which is common to all the members of a group), teasing out the important implications of this concept in clinical experience, with particular reference to the analyst's position, communication, and interpretative activity. The authors' standpoint can be thought of as being in many ways relational, and in this sense they suggest links between Bion's thought and that of authors who have studied the subject of attachment and have worked in the field of infant research.

We are indebted to the devotion of ROSA BEATRIZ PONTES MIRANDA DE FERREIRA for the preservation and recent publication of Bion's 1963 paper entitled "The Grid" (Bion, 1963b). The fruits of her continued study, backed up and permeated by her own mathematical training, of this important paper, carried out over many years, together with a lively, friendly group of students and colleagues in Rio de Janeiro, are presented here. This is an extremely clear discussion of the structure of the Grid and the theories connected to it in which the author goes back and forth between the many scattered references in Bion's own work to weave together a richly textured fabric of theories, showing how the latter mesh together and lead out of each other. In the interesting section that shows practical uses of the Grid on clinical material, the author brings out several subtle points, such as, at the beginning of Section V, the need for the language of achievement to be couched in

Category C terms. The last section, which seems a mere "outline" of Bion's work, furnishes a great deal of food for thought as one struggles to tease out the implications of the subdivisions and caesuras that Rosa Beatriz has chosen to highlight.

PAULO CESAR SANDLER deals in his contribution with the core problem of thinking and attempts to help us focus more on thinking than on thought—expanding one of the more penetrating intuitions of Bion's theory. Through the constant emphasis and practice of paradox and brilliant, somewhat surprising suggestions as a way of keeping our minds free and open, the author suggests that the digestive model and the reproductive one of the thinking activity should be integrated and consolidated in a working model for our comprehension of the analytical session as well as of life itself. We hope the reader can feel the same sense of "sane" confusion and richness of stimuli to be worked through, when reading his chapter, as we felt when editing it for the book. Actually, this book was prepared to stimulate free thinking, as we share the author's idea that "Thinking allows a marriage of the person with his or her inner reality, instinctual needs, and real possibilities and limitations—the person as he or she really is. With the aid of thinking processes one is able to reach some partial knowledge of who one is in reality. To know, to think, to live, and to love are inseparable facts, made separate by failures in thinking."

The last chapter of the book, written by a group of Argentinian analysts led by ELIZABETH TABAK DE BIANCHEDI, who is well known, together with Léon Grinberg, for her pioneering work on Bion's theories, discusses the development of Bion's thought about lies and truth and illuminates the shift in his position as to the nature of truth from a more Aristotelian view to a more Platonic/Kantian one. The authors tease out, in a passionate and moving way, the distinctions between lies and falsity with reference to the truth; they reflect on the implications of their ideas with regard to both mental functioning and mental health and illustrate their points with telling clinical vignettes.

CHAPTER ONE

Random reflections on Bion: past, present, and future

Francesca Bion

Accurate according to Chinese calculation, one hundred years ago Bion had reached the age of seven and a half months. We cannot know what his pre-natal life was like, but his mother must surely have suffered many anxieties and difficulties in the hostile and, by our present-day standards, primitive conditions of north-west India in the late nineteenth century. Women in that situation needed to be strong and courageous, both physically and mentally. How would any of us nowadays cope with years of extreme heat, isolation, the proximity of wild animals, poisonous snakes and spiders, no emergency medical help, primitive sanitation, no refrigeration, no telephone. . . . I could go on, but I begin to frighten myself.

Frederic Bion, his father, was a pioneer, a man of courage, an irrigation engineer, a builder of dams, who had a close relationship with his Indian colleagues and workers.

Perhaps the thought that in England her son would be protected from the dangers of life in India made their parting, when he was eight years old, more tolerable for his mother. But did she know how longingly he would think of "home" while suffering the miseries of prep school?

Fortunately, his parental inheritance endowed him with the fortitude he needed and displayed throughout his life. He also possessed the qualities essential in a truly civilized human being—tolerance, restraint, curiosity, and a capacity for sympathetic concern for the individual. He became as much of a pioneer and empire builder as his father had been, improving the quality of life by turning the parched land of the mind into fertile soil.

We are fortunate to enjoy here and in *Bion's Legacy to Groups* some of the fruits of the many years' work and experience of those who have been influenced by Bion, both personally and through his writings. This kind of communication is essential—without it the work becomes as ephemeral as our lives. To quote Bion:

> If we cannot communicate with our contemporaries, we are even less likely to be able to communicate with our successors. If this communication cannot be made, the future development of analysis is imperilled and the successful discoveries made so far could be lost to the world. [*Cogitations*, 1991, p. 173]

As this is not an analytic session, we can with impunity indulge in remembering the past and expressing our hopes, fears, and desires for the future while enjoying the challenges and rewards of the present.

Bion hoped that his work provided a positive stimulus to thinking about and understanding the human psyche, but he did not regard his contribution as more than a very small drop in an exceedingly large ocean. Nevertheless, that drop can create far-reaching disturbances. Some of those caught in the turbulence may decide never again to leave the reassurance of stable, dry land beneath their feet, but others brave the waves and find the challenge well worth the struggle. Bion was well acquainted with the painful nature of thinking—as he said in Paris in 1978: "I don't like thinking . . ." but "it is very important to dare to think or feel whatever you do think or feel—never mind how much it is not scientific." So it was no surprise to him to encounter this dislike in others.

Although he did not welcome hostility (a "quiet life" is always a seductive phantasy), he accepted it as an unavoidable part of the job. However, he was impatient with, and intolerant of the clashes, splits, and struggles for precedence within institutions; he thought them a sad waste of valuable time. And he certainly wanted to distance himself from the opposing forces that aimed, on the one hand, to thrust upon him the role of a messiah or deity and, on the other, to stress his failings and defects, even his madness.

He often quoted from *Ecclesiasticus* (XXXVIII, 24): "The wisdom of a learned man cometh by opportunity of leisure"—the verse continues, "he that hath little business shall become wise." In this age of "busy-ness", of ever-increasing technological wizardry, of speed and noise, it becomes almost impossible to hear ourselves think. In spite of the introduction of more and more sophisticated labour-saving devices, there seems to be less and less time for leisure, for luxuriating in reverie, for re-charging our mental batteries, for converting experience into wisdom. How are we to become wise when so much emphasis is placed on cleverness, on building increasingly complex substitutes for thought? Where does wisdom come on a scale measuring success? Will putting a space probe on Mars make us wiser? Science fiction has already become science fact, but what has happened to concern for the individual? Is it being smothered by this apparently unstoppable flood of machines as substitutes for people? I often fear so.

I have been asked how Bion had the time to write so much. He had formidable mental stamina and the single-minded approach of an explorer to his work, but to achieve that he needed to be freed from as many of the distracting, time-consuming concerns of everyday life as possible—to name but a few: correspondence, accounts, income tax returns, travel arrangements, and the limiting of calls on his professional life. He had to be mentally fresh enough each day to do the best possible work with his patients (and to stay awake at evening meetings!). Almost all of his writing was done during weekends and vacations.

As I came to know him and his needs, I undertook more and more of the tasks that would have diverted him away from creative thinking and writing. He believed that the human unit is a couple; as he said: "All human beings are imperfect creatures. So there are two imperfect beings and the problem is whether these two halves make one whole or not." We two were fortunate in becoming one whole; it was a fulfilling, rewarding, and precious experience, alleviating the fundamental loneliness of the individual.

It was a struggle to persuade him to spend time on professional correspondence, though this usually required only rapid, brief dictation or merely a suggestion to "say such-and-such". Nor did he welcome a request from me to read through my edited typescripts of his books. Even work on *A Key to A Memoir of the Future* (Bion & Bion, 1981), which was, after all, part of the main book, had its stormy moments, principally because it entailed re-reading the text. But he was always ultimately contrite. "How do you stand it?" he would ask. The answer was obvious.

He confided in me his doubts and fears, his feelings of inadequacy, but he loved his work and would not have changed it for any other. When he was writing or sunk in deep thought, I learnt not to interrupt him except in an emergency—such as announcing, "Dinner is served". I never tried, "The house is on fire", but if his phlegmatic response to the Californian earthquake in 1971 was any indication of what, for him, constituted an emergency, I fear it would have been ineffective.

The main body of his theoretical work was produced prior to our move to Los Angeles in 1968, but the work that followed during the next twelve years was also of great importance. I have spoken elsewhere of his reasons for leaving England; he did *not* leave in order to retire from the practice of psychoanalysis, nor as a money-making exercise, nor to spend a sybaritic existence in the Californian sunshine. The writing he did between 1968 and 1979 had a vigorous, illuminating, refreshing quality in keeping with his new surroundings; a sense of release made possible the autobiography and the three books of *A Memoir of the Future* (1975, 1977a, 1979). I do not believe that they would have been written had he remained in England. The breadth of his vision in The Trilogy is breathtaking: it spreads before us his life's experiences, insights, loves, hates, fears, and hopes in a staggering display of verbal *son et lumière*; it weaves past, present, and future into a vivid and highly disturbing tapestry.

Six months after arriving in California, Bion was asked to work for two weeks in Buenos Aires—the beginning of his continuing relationship with South America. Here he encountered yet another

culture, one with European roots and a Latin flavour in its liveliness. He felt at ease with the people and was thrilled by their
music. He always treasured the recording given him by the five
Abalos brothers, who performed for his benefit. The account of the
show given in his honour can be found in the published letters, *The
Other Side of Genius* (1985a). The work he did in Buenos Aires had
lasting and wide-ranging benefits, notably the publication of *Introduction to the Work of Bion* (Grinberg et al., 1975). Almost thirty
years later, I am happy to say that two of the authors of the latter
work—Dr Grinberg and Dr Tabak de Bianchedi—were present at
the Conference.

When Bion died in 1979, I thought my life was over, but I
discovered that although I was bereft of his physical presence, he
left behind a large part of himself, which continues to be very
much alive. The love and support of my growing family have been
a blessing and a gift; I am proud of their successes in their various
professions. We are, of course, sad that "Grandpa" knew only one
of his six grandchildren.

I have been favoured with good health and (so far) a clear
mind, enabling me to edit seven more publications of Bion's work
since his death. It has been a deeply satisfying labour of love. The
two most recent books were published in time for the Turin Conference, thanks to Cesare Sacerdoti's drive and enthusiasm, and to
the highly concentrated and skilled work of Eric and Klara King of
Communication Crafts; we are grateful to them for the punctual
and healthy delivery of the *War Memoirs* (1997)—so apt an addition to this centennial year.

Special thanks and congratulations are also due to those—and
especially to Silvio A. Merciai—who made the Turin Conference
not only possible but also a successful and memorable occasion. I
would have liked also to express my thanks to Parthenope, but she
assured me that she "did very little"! I know how much effort,
determination, and sustained optimism in the face of many difficulties have been invested for over two years in this achievement.

The future, as far as Bion was concerned, began in 1979 and has
continued in a way of which he would have approved: he has *not*
been elevated to sainthood, nor has he been "loaded with honours
and sunk without a trace". His work has endured as a valuable

part of the body of research into the intricacies of the human mind. The following quotation could well have been written about himself:

> We are familiar with Freud's attempt to build up a system; we are also familiar with the fact that he felt that he had not completed his system or what he was capable of. The problem has to be passed on, delegated to his survivors, the inheritance passes to others who might be called his professional family, his professional colleagues. [*Taming Wild Thoughts*, 1997, p. 49]

Finally, a valuable word of warning from the last year of his life: I have quoted this elsewhere, for I believe it merits frequent repetition.

> Comparing my own personal experience with the history of psychoanalysis, and even the history of human thought . . . it does seem to be rather ridiculous that one finds oneself in a position of being supposed to be in that line of succession, instead of just one of the units in it. It is still more ridiculous that one is expected to participate in a sort of competition for precedence as to who is top. Top of what? Where does it come in this history? Where does psycho-analysis itself come? What is the dispute about? I am always hearing—as I always have done—that I am a Kleinian, that I am crazy. Is it possible to be interested in that sort of dispute? I find it very difficult to see how this could possibly be relevant against the background of the struggle of the human being to emerge from barbarism and a purely animal existence, to something one could call a civilized society. . . . I think it might be useful if we were to remind ourselves of the scale of the thing in which we are engaged, and whereabouts a little niche could be occupied by ourselves. [*Cogitations*, 1992, p. 377]

Postscript
(January, 1999)

I add these lines at the beginning of 1999 in a very different frame of mind from that of July 1997. We, the Bion–Talamo family, have all suffered grievously since the catastrophe that befell us—by a cruel and perverse irony—on the first anniversary of the opening of the Turin Conference: July 16th.

So many people recall those four days of meetings, both professional and social, with immense pleasure and have been left stunned and incredulous by the loss of a respected and loved colleague and friend, together with her lovely younger daughter, so full of sparkle and academic promise, who in her thinking and reasoning showed a maturity beyond her years; she had a vibrant sense of humour—like her mother—and often amused us all with her gift for impersonation.

Parthenope arrived in Florence in 1963 at the age of eighteen after the restless and unhappy years of adolescence. She had not seemed to experience any intellectual stimulation from her years at school and showed no particular sense of direction. Fortunately, access to a wide range of books from infancy onwards—mentioned in her paper, "Laying Low and Saying (Almost) Nothing"—provided the stimulus needed by her enquiring and fertile mind, setting up a store from which grew her future outstanding and productive work.

In Italy she felt "at home" and during her years at university and subsequent analytic training she underwent a transformation: she blossomed, matured, and found fulfilment in her marriage, family, and the psychoanalytic work, for which she was ideally suited. Her study of philosophy enabled her to form well-judged and balanced opinions; coupled with her natural sensitivity and an exceptional intuitive capacity, it was an ideal foundation on which to build a deep understanding of herself and her patients.

Her writings of the 1980s and 1990s will be published in due course. Her numerous papers are a pleasure to read; her style is clear, lively, penetrating, and mercifully free from jargon. Her disciplined thinking and mental stamina are clearly demonstrated in "Sleep as a Way of (Mental) Life", an account of her treatment of an exceptionally difficult case.

During our visits to Italy in the 1970s she acted as interpreter at Bion's seminars. I was astonished at the amount she could retain and then translate, instead of the usual interruption at the end (or even in the middle) of every sentence to which he was more accustomed. (Throughout her life she possessed a retentive memory bordering on total recall.) Her grasp of his ideas and familiarity with his style of delivery put her in a unique position; it is rare to find a translator who is not only verbally but also mentally on the same wavelength as the speaker. Her many translations of Bion's writings can therefore be counted on to represent accurate, intuitive transformations of the originals.

Parthenope knew that the label, "Bion's daughter", would not make her position an easy one—comparisons would inevitably be made. But she was courageous and not easily intimidated; in spite of her love and admiration for her father she was able to detach herself from the role of "daughter" and bring her own personality and insight to her analytic work. I saw in her so much wisdom and tenacity that I recognized as inherited—learnt?—from her father.

Less than a year ago, in February, she spent a few days with me here in Oxford. We tracked down as many books as possible containing Bion's annotations, which I then photocopied. Two weeks later, on February 27th (her birthday) she began to write the book that had been simmering in her mind for some years: *Bion and His Books—Pathways to the World of Bion.* The first words, "Today, at the age of 53 years, I start to write my book on the life and work of my father, W. R. Bion", are now infinitely sad ones. We know there is no one who can write that book in the way she would have done; it is yet another tragic loss.

Nevertheless, we are grateful for the lives of Parthenope and Patrizia and for the gifts they left us. Our feelings are reflected in these lines:

> There will be voices whispering down these ways
> The while one wanderer is left to hear,
> And the young life and laughter of old days
> Shall make undying echoes.

Geoffrey Winthrop Young, 1909

Oxford
January 1999

CHAPTER TWO

Laying low
and saying (almost) nothing

Parthenope Bion Talamo

The Tar-baby said nothing, and Brer Fox, he lay low.

Pritchard, 1925

Don't jump to conclusions, Griselda.

Molesworth, 1877

Perhaps I ought to start with a brief introductory note on my use of language: one of my friends—Silvio A. Merciai—noticed quite a few years ago that, when speaking in public about W. R. Bion, I tend to oscillate (rather disconcertingly, I gather) between referring to him as "Bion" and referring to him as "my father". At the time we rather laughed it off and went on to more serious matters. But I have done a little thinking about it since then, and I have come to the conclusion that this is not so much an indication of a serious, pathological "split" as a natural outcrop from whichever field of thought it is that I am engaged on at the time. By this I mean that if I am thinking of him as I remember him personally—and when I was a child, he was just "Daddy", and in fact was not yet a psychoanalyst anyway—I tend to use a more familiar term, but if I am thinking about his theoretical or clinical writings, then I tend to refer to him as "Bion", which seems to me to be normal in a scientific paper. Since today I *do* intend to speak about his theoretical work, but approaching it via memories from a long time ago, I will no doubt move from one usage to another. You have been warned!

The two quotations that I have chosen as a starting point come from children's books that my father either read to me when I was a rather small child or gave to me when I was a little older. They were the first things that came into my mind while I was rather idly wondering whether there might be traces in his private, personal life, that would show some sort of coherence with his later writing; things that perhaps illuminate his character, a certain type of philosophical attitude towards life in general, which could have merged in with his later rigorous thinking. An Italian proverb, "*Il buon giorno si vede dal mattino*", meaning that later events are foretold by their first burgeonings, illustrates what I am trying to describe. I am not really talking about extra-analytical sources for his thinking (the analytical sources were first and foremost Freud [Bion Talamo, 1997]) because at the moment I am more interested in trying to capture something of the overall flavour of his personality as it emerges from a glance at one aspect of his general reading. Reading was a very important part of our family life, as my father read to us children in the evenings at weekends, and Francesca did so too during the week. We three children became rather precocious and dedicated readers, having complete freedom to read all the books in the house. There was no sort of censorship, unless paternal advice: "If a book bores you, put it down" could be taken as such. Until the much later move from California to Oxford, there was never a specific room worthy of the title of library, so we simply had books everywhere, which implied that access was very easy—to the lower shelves, at least.

Let us turn to the more scientific side, after this apparent digression. The base camp, so to speak, from which I intend to make a few forays consists of the following writings by Bion: *Notes on Memory and Desire* (1967a), some later comments on the same ideas in *Cogitations* (1991), together with the references to his clinical technique and the theorization on this subject, which are scattered through many of the published clinical seminars that he held in different countries (1973, 1974, 1978, 1979a, 1980, 1987a, 1994).

There is a very great difference between the style of *Notes on Memory and Desire* and the later seminars, but, although the latter are much more discursive, they are only apparently less rigorous, and the main ideas remain the same. These can be briefly summarized: the analyst should rid his mind (perhaps, for the sake of political correctness, I ought to say "its mind", but this seems to be going rather too far with analytical neutrality) of extraneous, permeating thoughts and emotional states. He should actively try to get rid of conscious searching for memories of the patient, such as "what on earth was the dream that this person told me in the last session, and to which reference is now being made without giving any clue about the contents or context?" as he should also rid himself of desires, of whatever sort, such as wishing for the end of the session or week, or hoping that the patient will get cured, or even *desiring to understand.*

I will come back to these points later.

The first quotation comes from one of the Uncle Remus stories, "The Wonderful Tar-Baby Story", which is part of the saga of the unending struggle between Brer Rabbit and Brer Fox, his sworn enemy. In this particular story, Brer Fox makes a sort of statue of tar mixed with turpentine and sets it in the road along which the rabbit will be passing. The tar-baby, of course, does *not* reply to Brer Rabbit's polite greeting. So Brer Rabbit punches, kicks, and butts it with his head—to teach it a lesson in good manners— getting completely stuck in it, all four paws and his head too, while Brer Fox lies low, and the tar-baby goes on saying nothing. As a matter of fact, the two lively characters in the story must also have "run" together somewhat in my mind, as I remember my father misquoting it as "Brer Fox, he lay low and he said . . . Nothing." Naturally, I may be wrong about its being *his* misquotation (although he frequently did misquote, just slightly, adopting and adapting phrases to his own need), and it may simply be mine. The pertinent aspect of this, in any case, is that I now tend to think of Bion as an analyst partaking a little of the characteristics of all three figures—the fox, the tar-baby, and the rabbit. (This might be said to be a sub-set of his internal group.)

For example, Bion's comments on alpha-elements in *Cogitations* (1992) make it quite clear that there really were moments when he felt "stuck", like the rabbit, and that he was only able to get clear of the morass by thinking very deeply about his own emotional and intellectual reactions to the atmosphere in the consulting-room. (Not to be confused with the idea of using one's countertransference, which he liquidates rather scathingly in *Bion in New York and São Paulo*, 1980, pp. 16, 37.) Furthermore, one gets the impression from several people who had been in analysis with him that he must, at times, have seemed rather like the tar-baby too, saying almost nothing, or perhaps nothing at all. And as for the fox? Well, from my childhood memories of him, I can imagine my father "lying back" in the rocking-chair in his consulting-room and just waiting to see and to feel his way through what was about to happen—although not with the malicious intentions of the fairy-tale fox.

The complex concept of working without memory or desire links up, in fact, with the idea of trying to purify your mind, letting what is inessential sediment somewhere and drain away, so that you could have the "laying low" without the sneaky or violent element . . . although it is interesting to note that analysands with paranoid streaks frequently comment that they cannot stand the analyst's silence precisely because it does feel malicious and threatening to them, as though they were being spied on with evil intent. Another aspect of "laying low" can be seen in the firm decision not to fall in with the analysand's unconscious ploy of seducing the analyst away from the present moment—for example, as I said earlier, by mentioning a previous dream while being very careful not to give the analyst even the slightest of hints about its contents. This can be dealt with on the spot, to my mind, by interpreting—or simply mentioning—the fact that the analysand seems to be desirous of distracting attention from what is going on now. One may also be fortunate enough to be able to detect the dominant emotion that is suffusing this way of speaking, as the analysand may already have given hints through other phrases or his behaviour as to which emotion is the principal one. It is sometimes possible to tell whether he is feeling envious of the analyst, or reluctant to "come into" the session at all—he might have been late for it, or given the impression of "dawdling"—or whether he is just trying out the analyst's capacity to remember him and not get him muddled with someone else. This latter attitude, then, might come either from doubts lying behind feelings of omnipotence ("You couldn't possibly forget *me!*—or could you?") or else from despair at ever being able to make any sort of impact on anyone. This possibility was brought home to me by a very depressed patient who was absolutely amazed on discovering that I actually did remember things that had been said to me even years back, without any muddling with others. From this analysand's point of view, it was a question of discovering in my mind a vital container, whereas from mine, the episode involved the emergence of alpha-elements, working as selected facts to illuminate a whole series of events in such a way that the latter make "new sense".

The other points that arise in connection with "laying low" include simply sitting and waiting, with the negative capability (Bion, 1970, pp. 124ff) involved in this stance, not striving after answers of any sort. It is interesting that Bion mentions understanding as being one of the things that one must not actively seek and the "cure" of the patient as another. To his mind, *any* extraneous desire is damaging to the analyst's capacity to concentrate on the present situation, but I would add that these two desires in particular are perhaps worse than others since they open the floodgates of the analyst's own anxiety about his ability, and anxiety is not a useful companion in the consulting-room, unless it arises from the reception of conscious or unconscious communications from the patient.

The second quotation comes from a book about a little girl staying in a strange house full of all sorts of curiosities, through which she is accompanied on nocturnal explorations by the cuckoo from the cuckoo-clock, who tries to persuade her to stop making logical (or illogical) leaps in her reasoning processes. This, I feel, is a particularly strange quotation to have come into my mind in the context of the early phase of "musing" over the preparation of this paper, and I might have thrown it out as not being relevant, were it not for the fact that intuition in a session (and not only the analyst's) has to be backed up by hard rational thinking. So though one's intuitive flash—the spontaneous presentation to one's conscious mind of an alpha-element—may seem perfectly correct, it is not enough, on its own, to serve as an interpretation, although it will probably merge with other things, including a private (to the analyst) process of reasoning about the other parts of the mosaic of fragments that this alpha-element "makes sense of", to form the base for an interpretation.

Another facet to this quotation is naturally Griselda's curiosity about the enticing things in the house, which the cuckoo tried to keep "open" and "alive" by not coming to precipitous conclusions, encouraging the little girl to go on observing. This seems to me to tie up with Bion's ideas on the stifling of curiosity by premature answers, as in the quotation from Maurice Blanchot that was "bestowed" on Bion by André Green and as exemplified by the second column of the Grid. This particular column sometimes seems rather less useful as an idea against which to check your own interpretations as well as the analysand's remarks, but in fact the attacks on the furthering of the thinking–feeling process are a fundamental aspect of analytical exchange, and the possibility of their subtle occurrence should always be kept in mind. In my early days as an analyst, I coined the phrase (in that sort of private language that one develops as one thinks about one's own work): "'stop it' interpretations", which referred to those that made analysands suddenly "dry up" in an unpleasant fashion, as though they had been shamed or bullied into silence, and I think that such interpretations had a great deal to do with my own unconscious countertransference. Analytical experience and attempts at putting into practice the discipline advocated by Bion "without memory and desire" have greatly improved this slight tendency on my part, which was certainly an attack on both the analysands' and my own curiosity.

Speaking of curiosity, it is noticeable how Bion's treatment of the subject has moved slightly from the Freudian–Kleinian base of almost exclusive concentration on the oedipal contents that arouse curiosity to a greater interest in the mechanisms and uses (and misuses) of curiosity itself.

In any case, I feel that these two quotations, together with the backgrounds of the stories from which they come, can give us an inkling about Bion's general philosophical attitude to life—not so much his "formal" philosophical leanings, which were neo-Kantian as much as anything else, but in the sense of his way of taking things. This attitude certainly included a capacity for "not jumping to conclusions", which he developed more as he grew older, even reaching the point of eliminating conclusions alto-gether, as towards the end of his life he spoke of interpretations themselves as being not only transient (Bion, 1980, p. 16)—staging-posts on the way to somewhere else—but also as being in a certain sense "too late". By the time the analyst reaches the point of formu-lating an interpretation, which indicates the conclusion of a process of thought that has come about between analyst and analy-sand, he is talking about a state that is *already past*; the analytical couple has already moved on. So no interpretation can be a conclu-sion. I may add that my father did not think much of death as indicating one either—it was merely an end, and as such, not par-ticularly significant. *His* idea of a suitable epitaph for his tomb was "Snuffed Out", but none of us in the family felt that we quite agreed.

In fact, the remarkably lively and numerous attendance at the Centennial Conference itself, with nearly 650 people participating, seems to belie the fantasy of his ideas having been "snuffed out", although for some years after his death—about a decade, I would say—very little notice was taken of his work at all.

Conclusions

Bion's writings on the theory of technique are aimed at helping analysts to be free of preconceptions and so freer to think. All his discussions of this subject suggest, in one way or another, that we discipline ourselves to be patient, not to jump to conclusions, not to stifle our imagination and curiosity. The general idea behind pa-pers and seminars that sometimes seem to the reader to be unpleasantly prescriptive and even frustrating is simply that we should try to provide ourselves with the best possible conditions for thinking, because, as analysts and analysands and as ordinary human beings too, such conditions are a fundamental necessity. This was one of the basic, rigorous convictions that underlay Bion's thinking and way of being—so much so as to lead him to encourage his children (in a bland way) to become familiar with such concepts from an early age.

CHAPTER THREE

Considerations
on some of W. R. Bion's ideas

Deocleciano Bendocchi Alves

A psychoanalytic fantasy:
almost a dream in four movements

Once again I am using some lines from a poem by Carlos
Drummond de Andrade (1983), called "Fragilidade", to illustrate
what I shall be developing:

> This verse, only an arabesque around the essential
> element—inaccessible.
>
> No longer the desire to explain, multiple words
> going up in a beam, the spirit that chooses, the eye
> that visits, the song made of depurations and
> depurations, the delicate shape of a crystal of
> thousands of pure and clean sighs.
>
> Nothing else but an arabesque, only an arabesque.
>
> It embraces things, without reducing them.
>
> [p. 177; translated for this edition]

First movement

When we admire certain masterpieces, we feel that they strike us with an inexplicable, inaccessible, and lasting fascination. When I first saw the French tapestries of the sixteenth century showing the Unicorn, more than fascinated, I was intrigued and curious, trying to understand their mysterious meaning. There are two sets of these tapestries. One, at the *Cluny Museum* in Paris, is entitled *La Dame à la Licorne*; the other, *The Hunting of the Unicorn*, hangs at the Cloisters, in New York. I shall focus my comments on the set that is in Paris. At every visit, my attraction to their beauty is renewed, and the meaning I have been giving them becomes more and more clear to me. I will make some comments about the tapestries. There are six in total. The first five show pictures whose meaning is easy to grasp: they represent the senses—sight, hearing, touch, smell, and taste. The sixth panel—and also the most beautiful—has an inscription that is self-explanatory: *A mon seul Désir*.

Aesthetically speaking, the six tapestries are characterized by a common richness of elements, which are distributed on the cloth, forming an elaborate and masterful arrangement. Over a colourful background, entitled "a thousand flowers", which characterizes a style, a kind of island appears where the main characters are located: the Lady, the Unicorn, the Monkey, and the Servant and some other animals (lion, rabbit, birds), as well as trees. The composition suggests a dream realm in which a woman and a mythological animal—to which extraordinary powers have been attributed since ancient times—are put together to stimulate our imagination, in an environment full of mystery and magic.

The sense of sight—which is the theme of the first panel—is represented by the Unicorn looking at itself in a mirror firmly held by the Lady. On the panel concerning the sense of hearing, the Lady plays a song on a portable organ, which is given to her by another woman. On the panel about the sense of taste, there is a little monkey with a candy in its mouth while the Lady chooses another candy, among many in a basket. On the fourth panel, the little monkey, sitting on a stool, is smelling a carnation stolen from a small basket while the Lady also holds a carnation, taken from the basket, which is presented to her by the Servant—who apparently is not paying any attention to what is happening around her.

The sense of touch is the theme of the fifth tapestry; it is represented by the soft touch of the Lady's left hand that rests, smoothly, on the Unicorn's horn while it firmly holds a spear in the other hand. On the first and fifth panel, the Unicorn is an active participant of the allegories. On the other three panels, the Unicorn is also present, looking at the scene represented by the Lady, the Monkey, and the Servant.

The sixth tapestry—the richest in details—is magnificent. The Lady puts a necklace back into a jewellery box, which is held by the Servant, while the Unicorn is looking at them. The three main figures are under a tent, at the top of which is written "A mon seul Désir". This necklace can also be seen in the other tapestries around the Lady's neck. So I conclude, like other scholars have done, that the Lady—due to a natural and genuine inclination—chooses to adopt a superior and grave behaviour. This inclination would be lost if, through sensorial gratification, the Lady became a slave of her desires. Putting aside the necklace, she stresses her renunciation of passions and submits herself to her "free will" only. She goes from the sensorial reality to the psychic one.

Second movement

L'enfant et les sortilèges is an opera by Ravel, with libretto by Colette. The verses of the poem are very meaningful. Melanie Klein had also used the poem as a starting point to one of her works, "Infantile Anxiety Situations Reflected in a Work of Art and in the Creative Impulse" (1929).

The story is about the vicissitudes of a six- or seven-year-old boy. The boy is in his room doing his homework, sitting at his desk. Lazily, he bites the pencil, scratches his head, and sings to himself: I don't want to do my lesson; I want to walk in the garden; I want to eat all the cakes in the world, to pull the cat's tail, to poke the squirrel, to pull out the parrot's feathers; but what I want most is to punish my mother. Then he is caught red-handed by his mother, who opens the door and asks him if he has already finished his lesson. Realizing he has done nothing, his mother becomes angry and punishes him: he may not leave his room until dinner-time, and he will only get stale bread and tea without sugar for lunch. The boy puts out his tongue at her, and she, roughly, replies: "Watch your manners, think about your lessons, and most of all think about how sad your mother is." The boy is full of anger and has a tantrum. He screams, jumps on the furniture, and breaks the cup and the teapot, throwing them on the floor; he pulls the cat's tail; he hurts the squirrel, which, free from the cage, escapes through the window; he takes the tongs from the fireplace and spreads ashes and embers over the rug; he throws the kettle on the floor; he tears the pendulum out of the clock. With the tongs as a sword, he tears the wallpaper, splitting a couple of lovers; he spills ink on the table; and he throws books and notebooks into the air, screaming loudly.

Suddenly, the mistreated objects come alive in a swirl that involves everything. They dance, sing, and take revenge on the boy. A little man comes out of the book and starts tormenting the boy by asking him mathematical problems. All of them are now terrifying objects; they have become chasers. Frightened, the boy runs for cover in the garden that surrounds the house. But, under the moonlight, even the garden is alive and threatening: insects, frogs, squirrels, lizards, and the wind conspire against the boy and attack him. The animals surround and threaten him; they discuss which one of them is going to hurt the child. Afraid, in his loneliness, surrounded by the animals, the boy stammers out: "mother". One squirrel, which was going to attack him, is hurt and runs in front of the boy, who takes his scarf off and bandages the small animal. The other animals step back; they are surprised by the child's behaviour. They see that the boy is also hurt. The animals leave, repeating the word "mother" and saying that now the child is a "good boy". At this moment, the boy raises his arms and cries "mother". The magic is over; everything goes back to normal, and the child is hugged by his mother. He is calm and protected.

This marvellous poem, written by Sidonie Gabrielle Colette [1873–1954], describes aspects of a child's emotional life with rare sensitivity, showing a deep insight. It is a poetic description of the interaction between paranoid–schizoid and depressive positions: the initial frustration, hatred, fragmentation, paranoid anxiety, acting out, hallucination, guilt, and reparation. The moment at which a selected fact arises and makes coherent everything that was dispersed is evident: the boy stammers "mother", and everything becomes organized and goes back to its place and to its normal features. The fear is substituted by guilt and making amends. The child goes back to the mother's breast.

Third movement

Years ago I went through a personal ordeal that kept me bedridden for six months. For forty-five days I could not even move in bed without help, and at that time I underwent three surgical operations. I was helped by my family, friends, and a nurse, who took very good care of me and gave me all the necessary help for survival.

During that period, I was able to observe myself in a very special way since I was alone most of the time, first in hospital and then at home. Being all by myself, my senses were sharp to what was happening around me and in my body. I needed to pay attention to the experiences that happened fast and sometimes in a surprising way. I also had a good knowledge of how my digestive and circulatory systems worked and the care I had to take with the respiratory system so as to avoid lung problems. Six months later, as my health improved, I had to walk again. I needed the help of a physiotherapist who supported me and taught me to walk again because my muscles were atrophied. For the second time in my life, I realized how a baby feels in the cradle, depending on its mother's care to be fed, washed, and moved. I was very aware of the correlation between the ingestion of the food and the intestinal movements and other particularities of my body. I felt lonely with my feelings and thoughts and also about the decisions I had to make (some of them very serious) about my health and life. I felt lonely in my limitations and in the consequent feelings of frustration. I was entirely dependent. I was an adult who depended on others to survive. I felt lonely while I was being taken care of. I felt frustrated, but I had to count on my possibilities of finding ways to deal with my discomfort and limitations.

Some nights, I only dozed, and others I slept and woke many times. There were nights when I did not know whether I had dreamt or had had hallucinations. It was a repetitive feeling in sensorial terms, but with different emotional nuances. Over my room window I saw a white banner, of different sizes, looking like a cloud or a mist, faintly lit up and slightly torn. It made me frightened, anxious, and uneasy, but many times I felt comfortable looking at it. These feelings used to change according to the night. Awake, I tried to think about this experience: the visions and my feelings. One day, I remembered my psychoanalytical sessions by association. For a time, my psychoanalyst treated me at his house, due to health problems. I used to go there at sunset and could see the evening light coming through the curtain. At the most intense emotional moments, everything around me disappeared, and only a white spot remained like a mist in front of me. This memory, associated with other knowledge that I have about myself, made me think that my dreams or hallucinations were a psychoanalytical session in which, detaching myself from the sensorial experience, I could notice something more intimate and deeper; something that gave me support, although I could not put it into words. I was depending on material help, and even on people's understanding, but at the same time I was conscious of my solitude. I was conscious of a painful external reality, but in contact with myself, feeling alive and trying to work out the experiences I was going through. The white spot represented I and **Myself**.

Awareness of solitude is developed throughout a lifetime. The human being is both dependent and completely alone. Awareness of solitude and its implications of being separate, in psychic terms, as well as the feeling of personal freedom and authority puts you in contact with the more real and genuine part of yourself.

Fourth movement

I am going to present clinical material from a psychoanalytical session. The patient is a male who works in trade. He lives with his parents and has been my patient for years.

As soon as he enters my office, he says he is not happy with his work. He has a fixed salary, but it is frustrating to look for buyers. He also feels that the job does not allow him to develop. Then, he tells me a dream. I will try to tell it as closely as possible to what I heard. *He sees himself standing, unable to move, stiff. Suddenly he hears a sound and starts to move. Then he is on the telephone, telling his mother that he is alive and awake. After a pause, he says that he sees blood in his bed—a lot of blood after having intercourse with his fiancée. He thinks she has had a haemorrhage during the sexual act. He becomes anxious and starts washing the sheet: he rubs it many times until the sheet is clean. It is not a difficult task. He remembers that he washed the sheet in his mother's bath-room.* He associates this fact with a piece of news he had read in the newspaper about a young football player who was moving to another country with his wife and two small children. He thinks about how brave that player is, although much younger than he. The man takes life seriously. The patient reports that his fiancée has told him that she has not had her period yet. It seems that she has miscalculated her fertile period, and they have had sex without any contraceptives. Then he remembers that his fiancée has asked him to meet her very early in another part of town to take her home. He answered that she could take a taxi or the underground. She complained and said that she was frustrated, but he did not feel like either waking up early or waiting for her if she were late. He felt he was being rude at that moment.

Later on, the patient says he is rude and impatient with his mother. He also says that he first masturbated in his mother's bathroom; but he always used to leave everything very clean, being very careful not to leave any evidence of his sperm.

The narration of a dream is an acceptable and understandable method in psychoanalytic communication. In any other situation, it would be strange as an expression of a present emotional experi-ence. The interpretation and meaning of this report would vary, according to the group to which an occasional reader belongs. For example, it would depend on that person's knowledge of psycho-analysis, and, even so, on his or her sophistication and education. In many groups, this dream would be seen as a premonition of a future event, with different connotations of fortunate or unfortu-nate facts. A member of any scientific group could consider it an indication of stupidity. To psychoanalysts, it would not be a sur-prise if the dream were an indication of oedipal material. The analysand and his psychoanalyst saw the dream as an expression of curiosity about the emotional experience that had occurred during the night before the session and related to another emotional experience during the session. The analyst gave a personal interpretation, which was shared by the analysand and was meaningful to both of them. So the dream, together with other information emerging in that session, seems to indicate that certain alpha-elements were constantly interlinked. Therefore, the alpha-function (dream-work-alpha) turned the emotional experience into material from which it is possible to learn, giving alpha-elements for dream-thoughts or for a correlation with common sense. The given interpretation was that the patient's hatred of reality makes him feel incapable of being responsible for his states of mind. In its place, a parasitic and, therefore, hallucinated liaison is established with the breast. The analysand accepted this version of his emotional experience. At that fleeting and transitory moment, the understanding of the facts was meaningful to the psychoanalyst and to the analysand. It would not be meaningful either to other individuals or to those who do not belong to the psychoanalytic group. I shall go back to certain topics inherent in this interpretation.

A question arises at this moment: why have I associated these reports with the movements of a musical composition?

MYSELF: Since the beginning I have thought of a symphony.

I: Symphony?

MYSELF: Symphony means a set of sounds, a perfect harmony (Honegger, 1976). It also means a musical piece—instrumental, as opposed to those pieces composed for human voices. It worked as an overture to great vocal music. Will this overture communication be helpful to a transformed and wider vision of psychoanalytic work?

I: I don't know. I feel frustrated trying to pass on my experience . . . and I can only write about it. . . . I notice I am imitating W. R. Bion in his book *A Memoir of the Future*.

MYSELF: I am not responsible for the effect or for the reactions to what I have written. I am full of doubts and uncertainties. My ideas go . . .

I: There is a paragraph in *Cogitations* that aroused my reflections:

This at once raises the question, what is common sense?—a problem that has received inadequate attention because without modern psychoanalytic technique and theory, it is impossible to make any useful approach to the question, or perhaps even to realize that a most significant phenomenon lies embedded in the term, which is itself a striking emanation of common sense. [p. 9]

In my work I have been observing, mainly with analysands who have been in analysis for years, that some aspects that are important for the development of awareness of the uniqueness of each individual have emerged. The development of the intuitive process in the psychoanalyst is also important, first resulting from his personal analysis and then, of course, increased by his life and working experiences. Psychoanalyst and analysand are permanently confronting each other in the psychoanalytical session, each one using his own mental process in the analytic work, the result of which is a permanent interaction in the *coming-to-be* process.

The pictorial images suggested by the tapestries acted as an incentive to wondering about the passage from an awareness of the facts of external reality to the apprehension of psychic reality. In the first five tapestries, which present significant allegories of the five senses, we can notice that smell and touch are represented by sexual characters since these senses are non-verbal and can be better expressed by means of sexual manifestations. Taste, represented by the oral satisfaction of candy, is also a non-verbal sense and refers to sensual primitive experiences related to breast-feeding. As to hearing, the Lady playing the "organ" is a musical reference corresponding to the assumption that music, song, and the sound of the words have their starting point in the baby's cry. On the panel about sight, there is a pictorial representation of the image reflected in a mirror, corresponding to the sense of sight that is mainly verbal, pictorial, or ideogrammatic. Pretending that I do not understand, I reveal the sources of my inspiration, so that having synthesized the five senses, I can present some of the meaning of the last tapestry, which is suggested in the sentence:

"according to my will". It seems to me that the tapestry reveals that using his free will, the individual can be himself, free of any authority other than "his own will". I use the term "free will" (Alves, 1989) to mean the flow of our most intimate, original, unique, and genuine way of being.

The psychoanalytical session can be a moment in which the analysand and psychoanalyst experience what each one is in this "coming-to-be" venture.

Confronting the first and second movements of this chapter, I suggest that the Kleinian theory of the "interplay" between the paranoid–schizoid and depressive positions is the necessary condition for the establishment of the intuitive process in which the separated and scattered elements acquire meaning through alpha-function. This "interplay" is possible through the apprehension of the selected fact that harmonizes and joins elements that were previously scattered. As suggested by W. R. Bion, I use Colette's story for the narrative of a dream or a myth—that is, like the selected fact that reveals that certain alpha-elements are constantly interrelated so as to express an emotional experience. As the story develops, confrontation between facts of external reality and necessities imposed by the psyche, oscillating from one position to another, becomes understandable.

The evolution of the analytical process is complex; working through of the awareness that the individual is both lonely and dependent is painful. Individuals usually think that the emotional price to be paid is too high. But when it is possible to understand the awareness of solitude, it is liberating because it means contact of the individual with what is genuine in his personality.

In the last two movements I try to represent the consciousness of being alone and what is called common sense.

Frequently, we have to consider that there are sensorial receptive cells, which are located, superficially, in the organism, that receive signals from the outside world; they constitute the exteroceptive system. The interoceptive system is made up of receptive cells located inside the body, which receive signals of changes happening in the body itself.

Common sense seems to be the result of the integration of sensations. It is a term used to express an integrating experience in which we have the feeling of certitude and of confidence that the object that we see, hear, taste, smell, and touch is the same one. Common sense is a term that also expresses the harmony of the senses in the perception of reality, *which is present* even if we do not come to know it. "A feeling of reality or unreality actually follows all the sensations of my senses which would not make sense without it." The understanding of the feeling of reality is experienced as a truthful and harmonious experience.

"Common sense" also means that experiences and objects that have been understood are common to individuals who belong to the same group, even if they have different ways of observation. The members of the group also have in common the same context in which the observation happens.

I think we cannot separate the apprehension of common sense from that of intuition. The perception of reality depends on the particular conditions of each individual, and it can be associated to the working through of elements that, in my opinion, are related: separation, personal authority, awareness of solitude, alpha-function, and curiosity.

These elements of psychoanalytic investigations are elements and configurations that are understood in a fleeting and transitory way and depend on the continuous oscillation of the human being between a schizoid–paranoid and a depressive position and vice-versa.

The process of comparing the above-mentioned movements resulted from an attempt to create a narrative through visual images that could lead the reader to become aware of some experiences that I have made in the psychoanalytic field. I had no intention to lead anyone to conclusions but merely to relate what happens during the psychoanalytic session.

I: Do you think I have passed on an experience?

MYSELF: I don't know yet; possibly not. I think that it is difficult to pass on a "real inner meaning", and maybe it is only
possible to have contact with myself and, even so, only in a
fleeting and imperfect way.

I: Have I tried to be "myself" in this paper?

MYSELF: Curiosity, when preserved, stimulates the search for
what is unknown, but to agree that in a psychoanalysis the

unknown (as in every scientific investigation) is relevant results in an emotional turbulence, since the duality between "public opinion" (or the group's) and free will is always present.

Counterpoints

First counterpoint: comprehension and comprehensibility

I quote Bion from his book, *Cogitations*:

> Drugs are substitutes employed by those who cannot wait.
> The substitute is that which cannot satisfy without destroying the capacity for discrimination of the real from the false.
> Whatever is falsely employed as substitute for the real, is transformed thereby into a poison of the mind. [1992, p. 299]

I consider psychoanalysis as a scientific activity and therefore real, practised by two people who are interested in acquiring further knowledge of the other's psychic reality—the patient's. Consequently, we can postulate that there is a psychoanalytic "field" that has favourable means for making the psychic reality discernible, and it is those means that I would like to consider. The main access to this reality is intuition. The intuitive ability of the psychoanalyst is developed by his personal analysis and becomes a real skill, growing with psychoanalytic work. The patient's intuition can also grow along with the work, but analyst–patient confrontational vicissitudes will fall into this intuitive ability, propitiating conditions for different types of areas of disturbance to emerge, depending on circumstances.

Second counterpoint: comprehension and common sense

The work discipline praised by Bion is well known among psychoanalysts. Comparing the paper "Notes on Memory and Desire" (1967a) and chapter IV from *Attention and Interpretation* (1970), which deal with this discipline in psychoanalytical clinical observation, we notice that in the latter there is, in my opinion, a very important addition: the discipline is expanded to comprehension and sensorial perception. As a result, the causes of opacity in psychoanalytic work are memory, desire, and comprehension. Failure to develop this discipline takes us to a misleading observation of the facts, by compromising the intuitive sharpness that is an essential element for the practice of psychoanalysis. This discipline can be stretched beyond the consulting-room and practised in everyday life, whenever possible, in the observation of psychic phenomena that make up the life of all human beings.

Memory and desire have been the object of more study by psychoanalysts. Now I would like to focus on comprehension and comprehensibility, related to the individual and to his relationships with the group.

I propose to substitute the word comprehension for "drugs" in my previous quotation. Proposing a subject implies that we have some knowledge about this subject, which enables us to propose it. Therefore, I think that it is in the distance between comprehension and incomprehension that we can theorize something that takes us far enough from what we already know.

I will use Shakespeare's tragedy *King Lear*, an action play, to exemplify the relation between narcissism and socialism, as well as its implications in common sense. Lear's initial proposal to his daughters introduces a radical change in the habits of the group and in the way business is run in the kingdom. In order to be favoured with the distribution of the territories, the daughters should expose themselves to the King's discretion, answering a personal and intimate question that compromises the objectivity of the proposal. The new order, on behalf of King Lear's advanced age, seems to be a result of the supremacy of the "pleasure principle": Regan and Goneril, the older daughters, represent greediness, envy, possessiveness; Kent and Cordelia, the youngest, represent common sense. The King's proposal upsets the group order. As a result, Cordelia is excluded from the group, disinherited, and repudiated. The older daughters are controlled by the father's authority, answering the proposed question exactly the way he wants to hear it. The disavowal and suffering of Cordelia and Kent are a result of the failure to submit to the authority established by the social group, which implies sacrificing one's own narcissism.

Common sense seems to be a function of the individual's relationship with his social group. Cordelia and Kent become a threat to the group from the moment they oppose the new social order, creating a threat to the stability of the group. Their free will and well-being become less important to the survival of the group and its ideals. The conflict is more explicit when Cordelia's individuality becomes abominable to the King and his older daughters. The group authoritarianism tries to impose its group values—filial love and fidelity—on Cordelia with promises of wealth, power and benevolence from the group; if controlled by the group, she would be rewarded with taking part in the group communion, in the collective hallucination that manipulates emotions, and, finally, she would share the promise of the leader's protection, as well as of immortality in a future life.

It is noticeable throughout the evolution of the plot that Cordelia feels the group's growing pressure on her. In order to keep her self-esteem and her individuality, feeling distressed, considering that she has to face the fear the group arouses in her, she breaks with the group's authority. The same thing happens to Kent. The King, failing to meet Kent's sensible reflections and unable to wait, extinguishes his ability to discriminate between real and false. Frustrated, blinded by hate, Lear acts. He threatens Kent with death and disinherits Cordelia, handing her over to the candidates for her hand. The King of France thinks over the events and takes sensible action, according to his feelings. Cordelia becomes his wife and Queen of France. Thinking is now a prelude to sensible action.

I conclude that the experience with groups has shown that every free individual position arouses hostility among the group to which the person belongs. Social well-being imposes itself as the goal, and the person is now secondary to the survival of the group.

Bion introduces an important change in the processes of research into thought and its disorders. Now, the focus is given to the development of thoughts and to an "instrument" with which to deal with thoughts. The development of thoughts and of the instrument to think is closely related to the ability to tolerate frustrations. Life's vicissitudes always show that nothing that we experience is exactly as we would like it to be, which creates a constant source of dissatisfaction, until we are able to recognize that frustration is the result of the very apprehension of reality, in the broad sense of the word: internal and external reality.

Omniscience emerges as an alternative to learning through experiencing the emotional experience, in individuals with little tolerance towards frustration. In a clinical observation, the development of omniscience emerges through statements whose meaning is very distant from facts and does not resist the correlation with what belongs to common sense.

In the psychoanalytic relationship, patients try to encourage memory, desire, and comprehension; they also hope for cure, revelations, or possession of knowledge—those are, however, attempts to destroy the link, distorting the vertex of the work: the unknown. Those psychoanalysts who cannot bear frustration are not able to agree that it is the unknown that has relevance for the whole analysis; they escape from the real work, using memory, desire, and comprehensibility of the available material. The harmful aspect of comprehension and comprehensibility originates in the minds of the observers, and the results also enter their minds, particularly affecting their intuitive ability.

Each moment of insight is a unique, singular, peculiar moment that arises only once in a lifetime. It is true to state that every life is a succession of evanescent and transitory moments. Every individual who aims at self-knowledge tries, in his solitude, this succession of transitory emotional experiences that bring within themselves elements of other moments, transformed by mental process. Quoting Hermann Hesse, we can state that "we all have the viscosity and the eggshell of a primitive world". This is comparable to Freud's statement in *Inhibitions, Symptoms and Anxiety*: "There is much more continuity between intra-uterine life and earliest infancy than the impressive caesura of the act of birth would have us believe" (1926d [1925]).

In my opinion we are called by the reality of facts to make decisions. Decisions always stir anxieties. The decision for which we psychoanalysts are responsible is, during research, to keep to the vertex of the unknown. This decision involves the psychoanalytic community, the group, and the individual. If we return to my previous initial suggestion about the tragedy of King Lear, we may think that all intimate decisions arouse a reflection about oneself, about the facts of life, and about the correlation with the group in which we live. The decision process is a function of the maturing process.

I think that in the maturation process we must take into account the working through of hatred of doubt and uncertainty, as manifestations of hostility to reality. I believe that this hatred encourages the desire for comprehension, making it feasible for theories about life to emerge. It is also opposed to that learning which results from emotional experiences, whenever intuitively captured and worked through the mental process. It is possible to suppose that there is a continuous hostility between rationality and the intuitive process, between rational thinking and common sense.

On the other hand, we cannot fail to consider also the hatred felt by the group towards individuality and its consequences for narcissism and common sense. The psychoanalyst must constantly elaborate this conflict, always addressing what is the basis of himself and the tool of his work—that is, his mental process. It is never too much to insist that in every piece of psychoanalytic work the analyst be there as a whole, acting together with the patient's mind, using his own mind.

Third counterpoint: silence, solitude, isolation

> There is an experience that leads to silence in which human beings feel the unity of life.
>
> John Castermane, 1996, p. 33; translated for this edition

I postulate that being alone, aware of one's own solitude, is one aspect of the individual's maturational process. This awareness is linked to the working through of the individual's separation and to the development of his personal authority, which leads to the full exercising of free will and freedom of being. These factors form an inner experience, through which we go in different periods of life.

In the isolation of the consulting-room, by keeping to the work discipline, the analyst goes through the interior experience of solitude and isolation, able to express it as the "silence" in which he perceives being himself, in his genuine way of being, available for work. When it is possible, during the session, the patient may go through similar experiences in which he learns his own psychic skills, coming to terms with what he is. These are fleeting and transitory moments of insight, in which "silence" expresses the consonance with what we are; it is an unutterable experience. Moments of dispersion follow the transitoriness of the experience of insight; we can say that experience is built up and falls apart; however, it is a real and personal experience, different from the usual one. These interior experiences, through the action of the alpha-function, turn themselves into material that can be stored and that is consistent with the setting-up of an unconscious memory, becoming part of the process of mental growth. As a result, the progressive integration of the factors pointed out leads to the accomplishment of a transformation into *being*, where the individual can be himself, deeply experiencing his possibilities and limitations. This is the "silence" of being himself.

Another state of mind, that I have been studying is what I call "prodigality". I try to differentiate it from generosity, because I use the word "prodigality" in a way that implies a certain exaggeration of the condition of being prodigal or generous, an exaggeration parallel to the psychoanalytic experience where studied factors seem enlarged and, sometimes, exaggerated.

Prodigality represents a complement to the helplessness of the psychoanalytic pair confronted with the unknown; it would be the factor that encourages the analyst's trust of feasible alternatives, even when not known; it would permit dealing with the patient's possibilities, without manipulation and interference, making it possible for each patient to be himself. It reveals itself by the willingness to participate actively in the psychoanalytic experience, without expectations of recovery, improvement, and change, just living through the experience of the session. The analyst's "prodigality" involves a real participation, in which his experiences of life, analysis, and culture are available in his work. By this we can assume that psychoanalytic conversation is a real dialogue, enriched by the necessary elements for a broader vision of life and psychic reality to be offered for the patient's consideration. I do not think that an individual who does not have sound culture and knowledge provided by his experience can become an analyst. The psychoanalysis offered must be put to the service of the patient's life. As for patients, prodigality corresponds to being able to use what is offered, contributing their intuition and associative current, and being able to use the opportunities of the psychoanalytic process.

The psychoanalyst can help the patient be aware that his contribution can be enhanced. Elaboration of greediness and envy, providing for the growth of gratitude—especially gratitude for available personal resources—is an important element of the analytic process. The results of greediness and envy can lead the patient to be in a position to deny the possibility of contributing, setting limits to the associative current and his intuition; thus, desire for satisfaction, improvement, possession of knowledge, and so on prevail. If this happens, the psychoanalytic relationship is permeated by the patient's anxieties, his feelings of depression and guilt increased by eager and envious hatred. Failing to perceive the phenomenon appropriately encourages omnipotent and omniscient feelings in the psychoanalyst; a collusion of characteristics that destroy the psychoanalytic process may be established. It is imperative that the psychoanalyst knows and has lived through such experiences in his own psychoanalysis, in order to perceive these vicissitudes in his own patients. The broad perception of the task that is entailed in psychoanalysis enables the psychoanalyst to become a real person.

The psychoanalyst must also dream the material offered by the patient. Whenever the analyst resists against introjecting the patient's material, anxiety and frustration arise. By becoming persistent, these are a factor in leading the analyst to the comprehension of the associations, or to the explanations of the events in the session. If the psychoanalyst does not dream, he does not transform the present emotional experience into alpha-elements that are right for communication.

Finally, I think that Bion's last book, A Memoir of the Future (1991a) has encouraged in me the need to dream my emotional experiences; to be in touch with the text propositions, so suggestive of visual images, has evoked my emotions and life experiences, which have already been worked on and transformed by dream-work-α into dream images available to myself and for my communication.

CHAPTER FOUR

The sick syllogism:
the fear of dying
and the sacrifice of truth

Emanuele Bonasia

"Reason is emotion's slave and exists to rationalise emotional experience", writes Bion (1970).

In this chapter I highlight how, of all the emotions, the fear—or, rather, the terror—of death dominates the scene in the field of human reasoning to varying degrees and in relation to different life experiences and cycles.

It is easy to understand from this introduction that Logic is not the focus of my argument: it is enough for me to say that the theory of syllogism is only one branch of modern Logic, while Aristotle saw it as a general theory of inference. All told, I believe that we can agree that in this specific field we externalize the most sophisticated faculty of thought: deductive reasoning. But how does this latter cope when faced with the ontological condition of the transitoriness of each one of us? I must say that its performance so far cannot be called brilliant.

In previous papers (Bonasia, 1988, 1992), I emphasized how very little space is devoted in the psychoanalytic literature to the theme of our death in contrast to the role this plays in psychopathology, in clinical psychoanalysis, and in the life of every human being. Moreover, alongside its neurotic and psychotic aspects, I maintained that there exists a *real* anxiety (all anxiety is real, but here I use the term to contrast with "neurotic" and "psychotic") about the inevitability of our own end; I also maintained that this state of anxiety has, to a great extent, been denied in psychoanalysis, through the defensive employment of different theories, which include those of castration anxiety and the death instinct. But let us now take a brief look at this denial.

The problem of death in Freud, Melanie Klein, and Bion

In Freud, who was terribly distressed on his own account, according to Jones's (1953) report, the theme appears very often and follows a characteristic two-phased pattern, where this anxiety is acknowledged and yet, on the other hand, denied.

Thus in "Thoughts for the Times on War and Death" (1915b), Freud writes that either man has no wish to acknowledge the reality of death or wants to strip it of its quality of total extinction by giving life to the doctrine of the soul and the belief in immortality, in spirits, and in demons. In "The Uncanny" (1919h) he writes: "Many people experience the feeling in the highest degree in relation to Death and dead bodies. . . . There is scarcely any other matter, however, upon which our thoughts and feelings have changed so little since the very earliest times . . . as our relation to death".

Nevertheless, throughout his entire work Freud interprets the fear of the end as an equivalent of castration anxiety, as a punishment for the fantasized oedipal crime: any associated anxiety is seen as being of a neurotic nature.

The other theory, introduced by Freud in connection with this topic is that of the death instinct (1920g): ignoring the considerations made elsewhere (Bonasia, 1988), I would like to recall only that Freud, by postulating the presence of a "demonic force at work" in the matter (going as far as finding it within the cells), he carried out, in my opinion, a brilliant operation of falsification, through a sort of intracellular animism, rendering *Thanatos*, which is inevitable and necessary, an instinctual goal and therefore, as such, an object of desire. The end becomes an end: the "unfortunately you must die" is now "it's you, in your badness, that wants to die".

This theory came to represent the lay version of the Garden of Eden, where Adam and Eve's mortality is the consequence of their breaking God's laws.

Yet the self-same Freud, in *The Future of an Illusion* (1927c), when pointing out the helplessness and the real impotence of man when faced with certain events in nature, death among them, admirably described the function of animism: ascribing our intentions to the forces of nature is an attempt to control them and sedate "our senseless anxiety".

Melanie Klein (1948) embraces as an axiom the theory of the death instinct, which Freud held as highly speculative. She states that the fear of the end is the primary cause of anxiety and that this fear is set in motion by the death instinct which threatens the organism from the very moment of birth. It comes from two particular sources: from the instinct working within and from that component of the self-same instinct which, projected into external objects, then turns, through the introjection of the same objects, against the self.

In other words, if Freud tries to tame such an anxiety by transforming it into a neurotic one, Klein does much the same thing through its conversion to a psychotic type of anxiety.

It should be noted that Money-Kyrle (1955), the only Kleinian who did not accept the theory of *Eros* and *Thanatos*, emphasized that what we think on the subject is not purely extirpated metapsychology devoid of the practical but that it profoundly influences our working hypotheses and our clinical techniques.

Bion (1959, 1962a, 1962b) accepts as true the Kleinian assumption, connecting, however, within the formulation of the contained–container model, the hypothesis that the infant would feel as though it were about to die with the death instinct and with the function of maternal reverie.

Here we find ourselves faced, as Stern (1985) points out, with a discrepancy between the "clinical infant" of psychoanalysis and the "observed infant" of empirical research. In my opinion, to claim that the inborn baby feels he is about to die and that he projects this into the mother is a construct that finds no empirical support; this assertion seems in truth more like the projection of the fantasy and fear of the adult. We have good (observable) reasons to theorize that it is the mother (or rather the parents) who project their death anxiety into the baby and that the latter is, in the beginning, the unconscious container.

In developmental psychology and in psychoanalysis the biological implications of the parent–child relation have often been underestimated, especially the simple and banal fact that if the mother (or whoever else is in her place) does not take care of the child, it dies.

Now the existence within the mother or the father, whether at a conscious or pre-conscious level, of the real risk of death is what allows them to fulfil the primary *function* of protecting the life of the child.

Hence it is inevitable, even desirable, that the mother transmits to her child the emotions linked with the risk of life, initially through preverbal channels and then by word.

Returning to Bion, he is aware that there is nothing that has any greater effect than always being faced with the probability of death, as he declares (1976d) in his interview with A. G. Banet about his war experiences; nevertheless, except for the account in his autobiography and a few references scattered throughout his works, he allows the theme of death to fall into the shadows where it seems, at times, to be cloaked in the elusiveness and unknowableness of O.

Is it Bion's platonic idealism and his mysticism that prevents the highlighting of the body and its end?

The sick syllogism

Having made these reservations, I nevertheless believe that Bion did develop important conceptual tools for tackling the themes mentioned above—that is, the psychotic part of the personality, transformations, invariance, catastrophic change.

1.   I shall therefore develop the hypothesis that at the base of

psychopathology and of the psychotic features of sanity there is, as an invariance, a suffering of the well-known prototype of the Aristotelian syllogism:

A: All men are mortal

B: Socrates is a man

C: Socrates is mortal

2.   Furthermore, I shall propose that this suffering is determined by a disabling of the thinking apparatus and of reality carried out by the psychotic part of the personality.

3.   I shall examine the type of transformations implemented.

4.   I shall consider the relationship between catastrophic change and the fear of death.

Before going on, I would briefly make clear the way I am going to use some concepts.

According to Bion, the activity of the *psychotic part of the personality* is externalized through attacks on the conscious, on inner and outer reality and the mental apparatus. Conditioned by the theoretical assumptions of inborn envy and avidity operating ever since birth, Bion uses the word "attacks" and overlooks the *denial* identified by Freud (1927e, 1940 [1938]) as a specific mechanism of psychosis, promoted by terror and impotence, without the necessary intervention of hypothetical primary destructiveness.

I shall therefore use the concept of "psychotic part of the personality", integrating it with that of "denial", and I shall employ Bion's distinction between sane and insane psychotics, making use furthermore of the concept of "invariance" to indicate, in a Bionian sense, that which in the transformation process remains unaltered as regards the inchoate situation of O.

At this point we can get back to our syllogism and say without any difficulty that it is humanity's most hated piece of deductive reasoning.

The major premise has so far resisted all Popper's confutation assaults to such an extent that the thought comes to mind that the philosopher lived so long in an attempt to confute it!

Things become really rather complicated from an emotional point of view if we change B and C to get a new formulation:

A: All men are mortal

B: I am a man

C: I am mortal

The formal structure of the syllogism (Barbara) remains un-
changed. What has changed, however, is its emotional structure:
we can accept reluctantly, painfully, or even indifferently that Socrates is mortal, but it is a completely different matter to come to
terms emotionally with the inevitability of our own end, the ultimate and certain truth.

At this point I suggest that the psychotic part of the personality
deploys many of its energies for the very purpose of disabling the
thought apparatus and that it alters the premises of the syllogism
and so sacrifices the truth.

Let me explain what I mean in three short clinical examples.

Case A

The patient tells how, at the age of four, a few days after the
death of an acquaintance, he asked his mother if all men would
inevitably die. When told that such was the case, he burst into
uncontrollable and inconsolable tears: and so his mother told
him that one day they would all rise again, and life would
continue in eternity. He stopped crying, but his alpha function,
despite being weak, could not stop him from asking "Are you
sure, Mummy?" However, he did not have the courage to insist
and ended up by accepting the "lie". He was not all that reas-
sured because, around about that time, he began to think that
when he was big he would become a doctor, so he was able to
see at first hand how things really stood and how they could be
controlled. As an adult his early years in the profession were
rather disastrous: the major premise of the syllogism seemed to
hold firmly, because many of his patients did die and did not
rise again.

He decided to give up treating the body and devote himself to
the psyche (at the time he was still a dualist): and in truth, as
we all know, psychiatrists experience a lower death rate in

their patients than do general practitioners. Nevertheless the deep-rooted restlessness of his "soul" could find no peace: his hopes rose when he read that Freud interpreted the fear of death as an equivalent of the fear of castration and was further consoled when he read that Klein maintained that such a fear was associated with a persecutory return of the death instinct. He found these very interesting concepts and thought that if he went into analysis, while not avoiding extinction, his fear, at least, would disappear.

He also became a psychoanalyst knowing that he would obtain an added advantage in keeping at a safe distance from death: actually, analysts have still fewer patients who die, and they are normally immune to the unhealthy habit, outlawed as scientific curiosity, of carrying out follow-ups.

Case B

The patient was born into an old and noble family. He had led a rather isolated life in his palace until his adolescent years, an age when some episodes took place that were to have a devastating effect on his life.

One day, accompanied by his tutor, he was out when for the first time in his life he met a man with a bent back who walked with difficulty: he was old. Another time he bumped into a man who could hardly breathe: he was ill. And the third episode was even more traumatic, because, on a walk, he found himself in the middle of a crowd of mourners: there was a dead man, of course. On all three occasions, terrified, he asked his tutor whether the same fate would also await him. When he was told that this was also his destiny, he was gripped by an unutterable anxiety and sadness. How could such a fate be prevented? He began to think that by devoting himself to ascetics, he would be able to avoid the painful precariousness of life.

And so a very alarming period began: having left the rich paternal home, he wandered the streets, subjecting his body to all sorts of mortification such as flagellation and refusal of food, to such an extent that he was soon suffering from serious malnutrition; the moment he had the near-certainty of having freed himself of his body, he recovered to some extent, experiencing the sensation that he had been Enlightened.

Instead of near-destruction, he now worried about maintaining his body at a minimum level of survival, believing that an ascetic way of contemplation would free him from the cycle of life and death and would throw open the eternal doors to Nirvana. At this point it is not difficult to understand that the name of the fictitious patient is Buddha.

Case C

A patient tells of her five-year-old son who, since the death of a close family friend, has started to eat very little and with little interest, despite her attempts at feeding him. "Why don't you want to eat?" she asks. "Because I don't want to grow up. Growing up means becoming an adult and adults die."

A feature common to all three examples is the starting point of O: the impotence, the fear, the desperation linked with the condition of mortality; the psychotic defences can be summed up in the falsification of the two premises of the syllogism: "it is not true that all men are mortal" and "it is not true I am a man".

The psychotic part of the personality elaborates, sacrificing truth and reality, *collective and individual* transformations in hallucinosis that present suggestive features of superimposition and whose common component is sometimes the exaltation, but much more often *the mortification* of the body and in extreme cases the total denial of it, as in Cotard's delusion: I have no body, I only have part of a body, or, perversely, the body I have is not mine, I have still to be born, I am still a child or an adolescent, and so on. In these combinations we can recognize the invariables of the changeable signs of psychopathology.

One might almost say that the healthy psychotic employs the *prêt-à-porter* hallucinosis transformations of culture (religions, legends, myths, and pseudo-scientific theories), whereas the mad psychotic, starting at the same point of O, implements transformations that are characterized by a minimal degree of official consensus (private myths, religions, and pseudo-scientific theories): can we say therefore that collective psychosis is the price that the sane psychotic has to pay to avoid becoming insane?

On this subject I would like to quote a passage from Bion (1970) in which I find a fascinating meaningfulness considering the theme I am examining:

> The liars showed courage . . . in their opposition to the scientists who . . . bid fair to strip every shed of self-deception from men leaving them without any of the natural protection necessary for the preservation of *their mental health* against the impact of truth . . . the human race owes its salvation to that small band of gifted liars. . . . Even death was denied and the most ingenious arguments were educed to support obviously ridiculous statements that the dead lived on in bliss. [p. 100]

The transformations of the fear of death

As we know, in Bion the letter O refers to the ultimate reality, the absolute truth, to the thing *in itself* in the Kantian sense, and it is used to refer to that of which the patient is unaware and to that of which the analyst is unaware in the patient.

The inchoate O situation faces various transformations, among them hallucinosis: these comprise a wide range of phenomena not necessarily accompanied by hallucinations and are a function of the psychotic part of the personality.

My hypothesis is that the main distortions of the two premises of the syllogism, and in particular those of religion and of myths, are hallucinosis transformations: I do not think that Bion would have agreed in any way with this statement, yet in developing his argumentation in depth one can hardly arrive at a different conclusion.

A hallucinosis system for Bion finds its base in the *no-thing*—that is, in the absence of the object: the psychotic part of the personality transforms the real situation, "*Now* the object is not *here*", into a fictitious "*Now* the object is *here*". An empty time-space is psychically transformed into an occupied time-space.

In my opinion, in the case of the object's death, a similar trans-formation takes place: the space left empty *forever* by the object is re-formed with *"There"* (or better, "in the *hereafter*"), "it is *forever*".

I would like to emphasize that this very kind of hallucinosis system has a second pole that hinges on the prospect—variable according to the circumstances yet absolutely sure—of the extinc-tion of the subject: the *no-me*, so to say, along with the impotence and terror that accompany it. "*Here* I won't be any more" is trans-formed into "In the *hereafter* I will be *forever*".

This is the operation carried out by the mother of the child in Case A through the wonderful "lie" that, in one fell swoop, re-establishes a space animated with objects and reopens finite time to the dimension of eternity.

Catastrophic change and the fear of death

Bion (1965) takes into consideration a fourth type of transforma-tions, those in O: these are closely bound to mental growth, to change, and to becoming, *to being what we are*.

When hallucinosis transformations become, through analytic work, transformations in O, this means that the patient experi-ences, for example, feelings of being mad, of being a murderer. Bion underlines furthermore how this becoming O is greatly feared and represents a source of notable resistance to psychoanalytic treatment. Moreover, he maintains (1970) that "mental evolution or growth is catastrophic and timeless" (p. 108). And once again in *Attention and Interpretation* (1970) he highlights the hatred for growth and maturity, adding, "It is probably idle to ask why it should be painful" (p. 53).

I think, on the other hand, that precisely because of the clinical and therapeutic reverberations it is very useful, to ask why growth and maturity are so tenaciously opposed.

Since, as I have tried to show, most hallucinosis transforma-tions concern the mortal and anguishing condition of man, there exists their specific becoming in O, which is represented by the emotional awareness of one's own death—*being what one is: first of all, mortal*. I believe this is the number one most feared transformation and this coincides with the main resistance to the analytic treatment.

Talk of growth, maturity, and mental change and considering these as the unique "psychoanalytic objects" favours mind/body splitting, with the body being relegated to a peripheral position.

Change and growth entails, first and foremost, the acceptance of the changes in the growing body (it is not a casual coincidence that many psychological complaints come to the fore in adolescence) as well as those in the waning body (a similar situation occurs at mid-life).

Remember what my patient's child said about not wanting to grow? My way of understanding catastrophic change, which Bion had already linked with evolution and change, is to be placed in relation to the prospect of rupture or the rupture of the hallucinosis category of eternity—to the rupture, that is, of circular time (which is psychotic time) and of the repetition compulsion, which is its offspring. Catastrophic change, when the examination of the reality of our bodies and those of others sets the hands of the clock back onto linear time and its crazy trip, enables us to foresee fearfully and painfully *the ultimate truth*.

To conclude, I would like to recall Montaigne's well-known maxim: "He who would teach men to die, would teach them to live."

"Teaching" how to live is the main purpose of analysis—but "teaching" not in Montaigne's sense, who preached a preventive ascetic detachment from the world and human relationships so as not to suffer their loss too much. On the contrary, it is from the painful emotional "taking on board" of our transitoriness that a passion for life is born.

But could we really do without the "lies"? Perhaps not, and if not, then I must ask the reader to forgive all the lies I have told here.

CHAPTER FIVE

Searching for Bion:
Cogitations, a new "Clinical Diary"?

Franco Borgogno & Silvio Arrigo Merciai

> The analytic situation stimulates very primitive feelings,
> including the feelings of dependence and isolation; they are
> both unpleasant feelings. It is not therefore really surprising if
> one of the pair, and probably both, are aware that the psycho-
> analytic raft to which they cling in the consulting room—
> beautifully disguised of course with comfortable chairs and
> every modern convenience—is nevertheless a very precarious
> raft in a tumultuous sea.
>
> W. R. Bion, *Seminari Italiani* (1985b),
> p. 18; original manuscript

One of the aims of this chapter, which is the result of long hours of study and reflection[1] coupled with the experience of organizing the recent Conference, is to establish,

---

We wish to thank P. Bion Talamo for allowing one of us [S.A.M.] to interview her freely about her father. Citations from the interview are referred to as "personal communication, P. Bion Talamo" and were revised by her.

[1] Begun at the suggestion of P. Bion Talamo with the constitution of a study group on Bion held at CTP and subsequently continued on the basis of

as freely and as honestly as we can, the extent to which Bion's thought may further influence psychoanalysis in the future.

Our central assumption is that a substantial part of the evolution of our discipline has involved and continues to involve combating the use of jargon in representing the psychoanalytic experience. Freud himself showed the way when he posited as the key element of his method the idea of starting with the process of understanding one's own sensations and perceptions exactly as these take shape in the encounter with the other, notwithstanding the fact that they may contain ideas the very thought of which could seem disturbing or even, in Bionian terms, wild.

It is from this perspective that our thesis begins to unfold, considering Bion alongside several other psychoanalysts who have followed similar paths with an equal degree of commitment in an attempt to find their own voice amid the contradictions and limitations that any form of individual expression inevitably involves: first of all, Ferenczi, to whom the title of this work alludes, together with Winnicott and Paula Heimann.

Reading Bion

A play of mirrors that give onto countless, perhaps illusory and false, perspectives—such is the impression with which we were confronted when we undertook the less than easy task of reading Bion and his commentators, an impression heightened by our own responses, which we found increasingly striking and perplexing.

In the first place, there is our irritation at the *fashion* for Bion— the fact that many authors, both in Italy and elsewhere, seem to feel compelled to quote and refer to him as an authority, almost as if being Bionian, or at least quoting certain theories and expressions—which despite representing in the main only an isolated fragment of his *oeuvre* are often elevated to the point of becoming

---

her stating that: "We cannot say that we are Bionians, because being 'Bionian' would mean, above all, being oneself, being mentally free in one's journeys of discovery, always, however, on the basis of iron personal discipline, because liberty and anarchy are not synonyms."

the bearer of its real meaning—were in itself an affirmation of one's psychoanalytic modernity.

Secondly, we must consider the unjust mutilation of his writings and teachings. In the majority of the texts we have looked at, it is made to seem as if Bion had written nothing meaningful after *Attention and Interpretation*,[2] despite the fact that over half his published writings, not to mention more autobiographical texts such as *The Long Weekend*, were produced after this work.

Why has this happened? Perhaps for "fear of a more personal sort of thought, one that has not taken sides", still full of "emotions" and "insufficiently worked out embryonic nuclei", as Parthenope Bion Talamo[3] postulates, a fear no doubt connected with the need—so recurrent a feature in the evolution of psychoanalysis—to institutionalize authors by classifying them among existing well-defined families and schools? Suffice it to recall that at a certain point in his career Bion, tired of this game of pigeonholing which he felt so restricted his freedom to think, decided to leave the United Kingdom. In *Cogitations* (1992), as in several of his published letters, he repeatedly bemoaned the fact that even in the United States he was still considered a "Kleinian"[4], as if the label

---

[2] As evidence of this we have analysed samples from the bibliographies of all the articles published in the *International Journal of Psychoanalysis* during 1996: a simple citation in a bibliography is obviously no guarantee that the work cited is of great relevance to the article as a whole, but we thought it best to leave aside this possible objection. The year in question contained 87 articles (a significant number of which, we might add, referred to the recent IPA convention in San Francisco). Of these, 14 (or 16.09%) cited Bion at least once in their bibliographies. There were 22 citations in all and considered as a whole they break down as follows: *Second Thoughts* (8), *Learning from Experience* (7), *Elements of Psychoanalysis* (3), *Attention and Interpretation* (2), *Transformations* (2), *A Note on Memory and Desire* (1), and *The Grid and the Caesura* (1).

[3] Personal communication, P. Bion Talamo.

[4] It seems to us that the authors of the Kleinian school operate in this manner (Anderson, 1992; Bott Spillius, 1988), dismissing as irrelevant anything that falls too far outside their model. As the Symingtons (1996) point out: "The loyal disciples of Melanie Klein accept Bion's early work but are distrustful of his later work. One senior Kleinian said that he never wrote anything worthwhile after *Elements of Psycho-Analysis*. Others believe that he deteriorated on leaving England and that everything he wrote subsequent to his departure is to be dismissed as the ramblings of a senile man. . . . Therefore Bion's prescription

were sufficient to define and exhaust the extent of his contribution to psychoanalysis.[5]

Finally, there are the idealizing tones in which Bion is spoken of, the way he is exulted to the point of being considered the holy spirit of our Olympus's sacred trinity (the other members being Freud and Klein), which often serves to mask the absence of a profound and critical knowledge of the history of psychoanalysis. But in disregarding the many-faceted and complex background of ideas that have traversed and inspired Bion's thought (a trend that is, unfortunately, so common among us!), and with it the contributions of colleagues who have dealt, in similar ways, with the same problems, do we not run the risk of overlooking the real significance and importance of his innovations, both in method and content, and thus of failing to isolate and specify his own contribution? In short, do we not impoverish the fecundity of his thought, even when it may be neither as polished and coherent, nor as unique, as we would wish?

It must be said that Bion himself has not helped to make things any easier. His mode of discourse is often abstruse and ambiguous, if not enigmatic, and only very rarely does he explicitly acknowledge his debts to other psychoanalysts, the exceptions being Freud and Klein. Furthermore, his frequently terse and seemingly apodictic style is peppered with wonderfully suggestive formulations (e.g. basic assumptions, memory and desire, container/

---

and encouragement towards a personal act of understanding stands as a threat to those anxious to maintain the purity of Melanie Klein's teaching. This attitude is always felt more strongly towards those who have been nurtured within a group's scientific culture" (regarding this point, see also Bion Talamo, 1987; Borgogno, 1990, 1993, 1994). But this is in reality just the tip of the iceberg. Many of these authors are simply trying to appropriate Bion's thought, with the consequence that several different Bions have appeared on the psychoanalytic scene—in addition to the Kleinian and Meltzer's classic versions—independent of their effective compatibility and possibility of integration: the groupists' Bion, the Bion of human relationships, the Bion of the Grid, the Bion proposed by numerous South American authors, and so on.

[5] What irritated Bion was not so much the reference to Kleinian thought as the idea of being rigidly classified as a Kleinian. Indeed, the influence of Klein remains, even in his last writings, irremovably the centre of his reflections.

contained, catastrophic change, etc.) that can have a beguiling effect on the reader, luring him to crystallize them for himself, at the expense of a more balanced appraisal of the complex and profound reasoning behind them.

Yet we must ask ourselves whether transforming Bion into a cumbersome *maître à penser* is really the best way of honouring his work, or if, rather, by doing so we are not simply consigning him to the mausoleum of institutionalization. For, should this happen, we risk losing the foundations of listening, research, and creativity that Bion tirelessly stressed were essential to the analytical and human experience alike.

The above reflections planted in us the seeds of a growing feeling of unease. Though we felt certain elements of Bion's thought to be extremely fertile for the development of the psychoanalytic community, we also had the impression that we were forging our own, more disenchanted and heterodox, path. We too had begun to construct our own Bion, and though not without some misgivings, we became increasingly convinced *that the history of the evolution of Bion's ideas, in all their chiaroscuro splendour, remained in large part to be written, and that it was a task that should be undertaken, in the name of both Bion himself and psychoanalysis in general.*

Meeting Bion

Our encounter with Bion boasted another peculiar feature: unlike so many of his commentators,[6] we have neither met him personally nor as analyst or supervisor. Thus to whom could we compare the image of Bion that had gradually taken shape in our minds, an

<hr>

[6] We find analogous situation in Simon-Daniel Kipman's introductory remarks to the one-day seminar dedicated to Bion by the Association Française de la Psychiatrie on the tenth anniversary of his death. "While it may be said that we have by now a basic grasp of his work, we still lack contact with the man. In all the works you will hear you will notice a considerable difference between the authors who have met Bion and those who have only read him" (Association Française de Psychiatrie, 1991, translated for this edition).

image that seemed to clash with that suggested by the official literature? One possibility might be the portraits of Bion sketched by ex-students and patients (see for example: Eigen, 1997; Green, 1991; Grotstein, 1981; Philips, in Grotstein, 1981; Symington & Symington, 1996; Tustin, 1981). But these, too, were excessively biased, idealized descriptions. Another was Parthenope Bion Talamo, giving her the impossible role of mediator and interpreter of her father's legacy. Indeed, the more "our" Bion differed from the official version, the more we felt the need to find, through his daughter's recollections, some bedrock on which to anchor our impressions. It was not, of course, Bion the person whom we wished to know (though we regard an analyst's human qualities as essential to the analyst–patient relationship) but, rather, his mode of listening, his "emotional attitude", both as a therapist and as a teacher, and his level of empathy and capacity for being "in tune" at the different stages of an analysis.

Yet we sensed that we had to track down Bion for ourselves, both in the resonance of his discourse and in the feelings and thoughts he provoked in us, this of course being the method of reading that Bion himself favoured. But where were the emotions in his "classic" works? As we pored over those pages, so seemingly ponderous and elliptical, we wondered why Bion had removed all trace of affectivity. Where was the Bion who would stress that both human development and the formation of thought itself can only take place in the emotional scenario of a meeting? How were we to reconcile our sensation of being, in a way, his "students"—considering all the reading we had done—with the fact that here we were faced with something so far removed from our daily experience of life and analysis?

Somewhere in close attunement to the position of *attention to the needs and feelings of the other during the meeting*—it was there we expected to find him, but it seemed to us more and more that we were simply trying at all costs to force Bion to comply with our own model of analysis, based on the concept of *"cura"*, in the dual sense this word has in Italian, corresponding to the English terms *treatment* and *concern*. We were unable to accept the idea that Bion was—and wished to be—simply a theorist, interested primarily in observing and knowing, although in this sense it has to be said he was a groundbreaking innovator.

Yet the difficulty of feeling in tune with Bion and his language, and with his expositive style—which seemed to us in many places quite incomprehensible—could not simply be a matter of our ignorance, nor of our mental resistance. It had to be something that Bion himself was in some sense responsible for, a kind of coldness and distance that frustrated all attempts to comprehend him and blocked all possibility of an encounter. In this respect we felt close to Donald Meltzer, Bion's London colleague, in his reflections on Bion's teaching when he speaks of a Bion who boastfully denied any possibility of treatment and relief, and whose typically military tactics instilled in his listeners a sense of inferiority and frustration, if not humiliation and exasperation. On the other hand, to Parthenope Bion Talamo, who stressed that the peculiar feature of Bion's writing was its spareness and emotionally evocative power, we felt like countering that "spare" does not mean incomplete or deliberately obscure, while as to the emotions that Bion's classic texts evoked, these were invariably of a limited though particular tonality, ranging from refusal through irritation and inadequacy to sarcasm.[7]

It was more or less while meditating on all this that *Cogitations* came to our attention. André Green's review of the book (1992) seemed promising, stressing "the exceptional wealth of these private notes" and alluding to "a breath of fresh air from the open sea". Here was a book such that "we literally *follow* him". We

---

[7] We found ourselves more or less in agreement with her later, regarding the *Memoir* (here was a truly evocative work!). "Bion always thought", maintains P. Bion Talamo, "that the problem with psychoanalytical writing is that it is unable to transfer the liveliness of human experience to the written page, so that the theory always seems cut off from emotional reality and to have few connections with it. Bion's evocative way of writing was his answer to this problem" (1997a). ". . . He wanted to be as evocative as possible, so that the reader would find himself face to face with his own emotions, wrenched up, so to speak, from deep within" (1997c). But even here we had to ask ourselves whom to give credence, considering that in the postface, requested by the editor, Bion himself said: "All my life I have been imprisoned, frustrated, dogged by common-sense, reason, memories and—greatest bug-bear of all— understanding and being understood. This is an attempt to express my rebellion, to say 'Good-bye' to all that" (1991a, p. 578). (On this question, see also Borgogno, 1993.)

hoped that these private notes at least would help confirm our thesis and grant us access to Bion's emotional world.

Cogitations, a clinical diary?

Our first impression on reading *Cogitations*, however, threw us back into complete confusion regarding the text's real essence and that of Bion's teachings in general. If what we had expected was a new *Clinical Diary à la Ferenczi*, then we were to be sadly deluded. At first glance *Cogitations* appeared to be the complete opposite, exhibiting what Ferenczi denounced to the analytic community on the opening page of his 1932 clinical diary as inadequate attention to the patient's utterances, which, made with great difficulty, are dense with emotion.

Yet beyond this, if it is true, as Partenope Bion Talamo maintains, that Bion intended to publish his notes, since he kept them with him during all his crossings from the old to the new world and back,[8] it is possible that, like Ferenczi, he secretly wished to lay bare before his colleagues the analyst's mental laziness and insensitivity. These deficiencies Ferenczi had primarily imputed to a Freud who, blinded by passion for his own theory, no longer listened to his patients and misunderstood what they were trying to say. But he was also brave enough and honest enough to recognize such faults in himself, in his hatred and apathy and in his reluctance to feel his entire self called to trial during the analysis.

From such a point of view, *Cogitations* might indeed claim to be a new clinical diary, by the very honesty with which Bion presents

---

[8] "I think that *Cogitations* is a sort of rough-book and that Bion extracted and abstracted the bits and pieces which have now been published from a bigger store. . . . I don't know to what extent *Cogitations* was supposed to be merely private notes, since, for example, he took some of the notes with him to America and back again, I think that he had the idea, somewhere in the back of his mind, that sooner or later he would have published something. So these were rather more formal notes—I have other notes of his, some of which are just one or two words jotted down, which are quite a different matter" (personal communication, P. Bion Talamo).

to the community's gaze the *tragedy* he lived through in those years, when he sought to emerge from the anonymity prescribed by the *chorus* of which he was a part, thus revealing a more intimate and personal side of his mental functioning, whether at work during a session or reflecting and theorizing at his desk. But the Kleinians in particular were at that time extremely hostile to such ideas, treating with great suspicion and heavily censuring any expression of the analyst's subjectivity.[9] Such suspicion and censure at the international level has for decades permitted that Ferenczi's work be continually excluded from the psychoanalytic debate if not made the object of often malicious and gratuitous gossip.

But what is the *tragedy* that emerges in *Cogitations*? Simply that it could let us realize with great lucidity how in the name of some supposed truth an institution may go so far as to kill the individual in all his uniqueness and singularity—yet, despite this awareness, that he remains roped to and duped by the very approach he condemns. At many points in *Cogitations*, Bion, let it be said, unmasks a "social-ism" that in almost delusional fashion asks the individual to sacrifice himself for the sake of the group, while courageously re-evaluating "narciss-ism" as a possible healthy response to murderous group pressures, if not as a potential bid for life and freedom, particularly when the subject is banished, uprooted, and forced into exile.[10]

---

[9] P. Bion Talamo is also of this opinion: "He was always very free, inside himself, but I think that in England there was not then the right sort of climate for expressing this sort of thing, least of all in the Kleinian group, which was very rigid. He was an extremely private sort of person, and on the other hand it is possible that he thought that revealing himself, revealing his emotions might have made him easier prey to his enemies and detractors. Introspection has always been considered with a good deal of suspicion, and it is only now that we are beginning to say officially that it really is important for us to know how we, as analysts, work and communicate this" (personal communication, P. Bion Talamo).

[10] Regarding "narciss-ism" and "social-ism", see the following cogitations: firstly 15 July 1959 (pp. 29–30), but also 16 May 1959 (pp. 23–24); Undated (pp. 103–106); 31 January / 1 February 1960 (p. 122). The theme generally outlined here recurs in fact throughout the book, though not always viewed from this perspective.

Thus during the period covered by *Cogitations* Bion appears as a *tragic hero*, caught up in a struggle for identity that is ultimately doomed to failure because he is still bound to the breast that fed him and first awakened in him the passion for analysis: that of Melanie Klein and her theoretical edifice, to which he looks uncritically and whose theses he bends, with surprising and uncommon ingenuousness, to the shape of truth with a capital T.

It is in this sense, therefore, in Bion's wavering between "knowledge" and "non-knowledge", between listening to the patient's and his own voice and that of the "group", that it seems to us that in *Cogitations* the institution and its dogma finally get the better of him. For he sacrifices or at least dodges the issues of reverie and dream-work-α,[11] which, in theory at least, had suggested mating in the encounter with the *confused and uncertain beast* that lurks in each of us, to emit perhaps a simple grunt, heralding a future individuated voice, one that would no longer be bound by the mortifying chains that assail the subjectivity of any operation of thinking, however humble or inchoate.

The Bionian tragic essence of *Cogitations* thus lies in the *absolute split between theory and clinical attitude.* The theory is moored, as we have just said, to reverie and dream-work-α—the latter a concept that Bion curiously inserts into a *cogitation* entitled "Communication" (Undated, pp. 172–183)—yet all digestion of a calmer, more fluid or dreamlike nature continues to be blocked or barred. It really disturbs the relationship that Bion maintains with the known deductive system to which he constantly refers, which serves practically as a kind of anti-thought and anti-evolution, transgressing the relational context of the *hic et nunc*, from which any signification should derive since this is where the analysis emotionally takes place.

In a famous letter of 7 October 1955, Winnicott (1987) had already suggested to Bion—whom he considered the "the big man of the future" of the British Psychoanalytic Society—that he might do well to amplify his powers of listening by putting himself in touch with other voices who were not strictly upholders of the

---

[11] Concepts present from the beginning in Bion's reflections, initially appearing in the first *cogitation* of 1959.

"Kleinian cause". In this regard he proposed that Bion read the material, precious in terms of its emotional intimacy, of his interactive dialogues between patient and analyst, for example the "I ought to have rung up my mother" of one of his patients (*Second Thoughts*, p. 53), or the patient's restlessness on the couch, or the evident failure of the environment in which he grew up, as attempts, though difficult, to communicate.[12]

But years after Winnicott's frank and warm defence of the patient, who was, in his view, to be approached more democratically as a *baby* and not simply as *crazy*, Bion still could not make this leap, nor did he realize that the patient was really trying to communicate with him during a session, signalling to him the affective geography of their reciprocal moves and positions. In his failure to grasp this fundamental level of analysis, which Ferenczi had insightfully intuited and from the beginning faithfully followed in his own writings and which Freud himself had achieved in the case of Little Hans,[13] it thus seems that Bion renders null and void the patient's desperate appeal.[14] How else to explain his deafness during analysis to a patient's account of "the pullover which is beautifully knitted by his wife but not suited for the baby's cold" or of "trains that did not behave as they should" (7 October 1959, p. 89)? Or to the patient's hallucinated representation a few days later of Bion as his dead wife (16 October 1959, p. 94). Or to dreams such as that of being with a woman "in an old-fashioned bus",

---

[12] Donald Winnicott (1987), moreover, in a subsequent letter to John O. Wisdom of 26 October 1964, laments that Bion's ideas are never discussed in relation to other contemporary authors or connected to his own. And in an earlier letter to Bion of 16 November 1961, he lets it be known that he too is interested in thought processes, though bearing in mind the infant's narcissistic wound and the mother's failure.

[13] In the role of supervisor, Freud was able to give a second opinion on his analytical work, which, he admitted, had sometimes been so unreceptive towards the patient's reasons and attuned unconscious perceptions (Borgogno, 1998).

[14] André Green (1992) also seems to wish to underline Bion's lack of *concern* for the patient: "The same detachment is observed in Bion's position on the therapeutic reaction (both positive *and* negative), in that it is always bound to divert attention from psychoanalysis proper. Such a position is unusual among English-speaking analysts, with their concern for helping the patient."

whose windows proved impossible to open because "a surly kind of man who reminded me of you was very hostile" and prevented him from opening them, thus creating an atmosphere of suffocation (24 February 1960, p. 142)?

In all these passages Bion seems incapable of understanding the material in terms of a dialogue that would involve him as a relevant and influential actor; indeed he never undertakes nor does he facilitate the work of "alpha-beta-ization" required by this particular situation. He always places himself, rather, in the –K position, since his words are the fruit of a single mind and not one that is tuned to that of the patient, the approach he was theorizing at that time.

Thus it is impossible to imagine how the patients in question could overcome their envy at being excluded from a primal scene that Bion insists on interpreting for them without offering any alternative. Indeed throughout this period Bion plays obsessively a single score, the attack on links, a performance that becomes, as Winnicott maintains in the above-mentioned letter, "a plugging of theme songs", destroying any possibility of knowledge. Furthermore, Bion's attitude towards his patients exhibits an *overwhelming interest in and a link with an ideal analysis coupled with a sense of affiliation to his group, an interest far superior to any he might have in the patient's well-being or in his desperate repeated messages.*

Yet it must be said that we would be doing Bion a great injustice by limiting ourselves to these criticisms. For if we read in sequence and in an analytical spirit these *Cogitations* from which we have perhaps over-hastily plucked the above extracts, what begins to emerge is the drama of Bion the man, embarked upon a private exploration whose underlying and unconscious theme might be *who kills whom?*

It is in terms of this question that the torment and anxiety of interrogation experienced by Bion in the texts we have examined begins. For such torment starts with a theory that states (in our view unjustly, since it lacks impartial distributive criteria[15]) that it is the *patient* who always enviously attacks the analyst and his "good interpretation", only to arrive at the idea—unusual in this

---

[15] On this point see also Speziale-Bagliacca, 1997.

group and ideational context—that it may actually be the *analyst* himself who kills the patient by his overly intelligent and brilliant—yet narrow-minded and often unpredictable—perceptions. Yet it is these very perceptions that paralyse the analyst, inducing in him feelings of guilt for his meta-communications that go beyond the immediate context of what is actually said.[16]

These reflections offer a glimmer of freedom and openness that for the moment, however, Bion seems unable to sustain, although he does give them serious consideration to the point of saying that primary envy, which "precludes the possibility of any gratification", is a dubious concept, since it may be "a premature or hallucinatory 'realization'" (Undated, p. 112)[17] of the analyst's credo and not the result of the progressive experience of an encounter within which the disturbed and disturbing vicissitudes of the relationship can be tolerated.

We could very well be accused of being incurable romantics and weak thinkers (such is the way one feels when reading Bion's texts) in identifying with Bion's patients and maintaining that what they probably needed was more of a *"mother figure"* and less of an *"intellectual leader"*[18]. But we feel certain that they might have benefited more from an analyst who generously offered himself to be used and refashioned in various ways by their manifold needs, even at the risk of being momentarily parasitized and of parasitizing them in return—less *morality*, we might even say, and more *play*. In this way the analyst might once again set in motion a poor and blocked thought, thus granting access to a narrative that

---

[16] Regarding this see the work of Paula Heimann (Borgogno, 1992).

[17] Bion is extremely lucid when he defines common sense as the shared beliefs of a particular social or scientific group, underlining that these are not sufficient grounds for evidence: "Such evidence is not proof but is at least not incompatible with the view I am proposing: that certain perceptions of the individual *are not so much qualities under investigation as impositions on the individual's outlook* by common sense (in my terminology) or God's idea (in Berkeley's) or the deception by God and Demon (in Descartes's)" (italics added).

[18] See the cogitation of 24 February 1960 and in particular Bion's reflections (pp. 143–144), which seem to imply that the function of the analyst is precisely that of intellectual leader.

is effectively shared and co-experienced, a narrative that respects the patient's particular idiom and that the analyst knows not to force to his tempo[19].

It is exactly this type of space that Bion lacks in these years, a space that is affective, transitional, and intermediate, one that does not saturate germs of living expressiveness that are blind, un-knowing, as yet psychically unborn, substituting instead an asphyxiating[20] and peremptory theory of symptom formation or "expanding mental universe" (Undated, p. 204) and "trap for light" (Undated, p. 206) constructions (as he himself calls them), which keep him at a safe distance both from the element of the unknown in the sentiments expressed by the present relationship and from the receptive feminine elements of containment.

In short, what is wanting in the Bion of this period is the capac-ity to offer himself to the patient as a container, since he is too busy looking at the session as a chessboard, a space where competition reigns, so as to save himself, to the detriment of his humanity, from the murder that the patient will, alas, inevitably commit. It is sad to think that this Bion does not absolve even the neonate from this inauspicious event, since from the first instant of its life the neonate too will *kill—knowingly*, Bion argues—both the knowledge and the object that nourishes it, for the envy they provoke in him. Here Bion is quite ruthless, convinced as he is that, armed with this supposed "truth", he can initiate a psychoanalytical operation that will promote mental and emotional growth. We, however, see in this, as did Paula Heimann (1989), merely an attempt to suppress and colonize the other, both inside and out, by means of idealiza-tion and highly suggestive primitive fears.

So much for the absence of memory and desire! So much for willingness to exist patiently in conditions of non-differentiation and doubt, or for the capacity for relaxed imaginative reverie, comforting in its dedication to the patient! Bion does not seem to recognize these qualities at all here, and it is probably only by

---

[19] See Borgogno, 1998.

[20] Asphyxiating since it is entirely centred on the description of psycho-pathological mechanisms.

writing about them that he begins to question "reverence and awe" (the title of a 1967 cogitation, pp. 284–292) and "memory and desire" (notes following the aforementioned cogitation) in an attempt to get away from the wastes of jargon (p. 288) and from the idolatrous folly of militant thought, which abhors any form of ignorance, poverty, or pettiness, common features all of the real matings that nourish the mysterious processes of analysis.

But such a road can only be taken if the analyst is willing to merge with the patient, flow, and lose himself momentarily in the analytical field,[21] an undertaking that calls for a long and burdensome working-through process so as to cast off any idea of elitist knowledge accessible only to a chosen handful. This is probably what Bion himself was attempting in the tenacious research and reflection that went into these pages, and in the intense suffering that resulted from them. All this in order to reach the more mature state of being fully subject–object during the session and to achieve a capacity to respond fully to calls for help that would enable the analyst to redirect the act of comprehension towards the specific emotional field of the analyst–patient couple as it exists at that particular moment—in other words, to go from *the application of psychoanalysis to being profoundly a psychoanalyst.*

It was by approaching Bion the analyst's "Odyssey" (the suggestive subtitle of a cogitation that appears well into the book, on p. 218) in this way that we began to feel, even in his hardest moments, a growing sense of attunement towards him. Strangely, we had the impression that it was Bion himself who had permitted us to feel this way, having himself previously elaborated a position whereby experiencing mating as ruthless and dangerous for the establishment (pp. 327–332) distanced and froze both reader and patient alike, thus erecting a barrier between himself and the other.[22]

At this point in the story at the end of the 1960s, when Bion was about to cross the Atlantic, other images of analysis (those we were

---

[21] See Borgogno, 1997.

[22] Bion seems to metacommunicate: "Stay away from me!", "You are different from me, you are not me!"

seeking and that, in our view, constitute the true vitality of his thought and practice!) begin to appear in *Cogitations* and, in a form of crescendo, the space given over to the brilliance of the analyst begins to diminish, consigning to the background the Bion of *dark suits and bowler hats*[23] who wanted to wash his patients' brains without getting his hands dirty:

> the analysis . . . a unique emotional experience recognizably related to an actual human being, and not a conglomerate of psychopathological mechanisms. [p. 288]

> the problem for the analyst is . . . not losing sight of the fact that the personality with whom he is dealing is unique. That is so easily said. . . . but in the reality of a psycho-analytic session it is very easy . . . to give interpretations in terms so near to being statements of basic psycho-analytic theory that they lose meaning for the patient. [p. 290]

> the temptation is always to terminate prematurely the stage of uncertainty and doubt about what the patient is saying. [p. 290]

> I do not think such a patient will ever accept an interpretation, however correct, unless he feels that the analyst has passed through this emotional crisis as a part of the act of giving the interpretation. [p. 291]

> "Unconscious" could sometimes be replaced by "obvious but unobserved". [p. 318]

It is immediately in the wake of such images, in 1976 to be precise, that Bion, now firmly ensconced in the new world, not by chance

---

[23] "Until 1961, more or less, he always went up to town wearing a dark suit and a bowler hat; at a certain point, I don't know what had come over him, he changed his wardrobe completely: he bought two more colourful suits and gave up the bowler, as though he had said to himself: "Oh to hell with it, I can't stand this suit of armour any longer" (personal communication, P. Bion Talamo).

We refer here to an untranslatable pun in Italian between *in gessato* [literally "dressed in a chalk-striped suit"] and *ingessato* [said of someone who is stuffily conventional or old-fashioned], and also between two meanings of *bombetta*: both "bowler hat" and "little bomb"—a fact not without significance, considering Bion's "typically military tactics".

begins to mention Ferenczi (p. 365), while two years later we find him maintaining that the patient requires a "human being" analyst and not "*representations* of a human being" and "artificial interpretations" since the "minimum necessary condition" for getting close to the truth is "sincerity".[24] Thus in the end our intuition of the similarity between Bion's and Ferenczi's path proved correct, though of course such things require time to be digested before they are fully understood.

By this time Bion, less conditioned by theme-songs and more confident in *the genius of his preconscious,* had learned to sing a different tune and was finally able to stretch the horizon of his researches to the I–You of Martin Buber (p. 371) as the next stage in the exploration of the psychoanalytic relationship.

Bion was himself unconsciously aware of this turning point. On 8 August 1978 he quotes Moschus' *Epitaph for Bion,* evoking Shelley's preface to *Adonais*:

> A poison came, Bion, to thy lips, thou sawest the poison.
> How did it run on to thy lips and not be sweetened? And
> what mortal was so savage either to mix the
> poison for thee or to give it thee as thou didst speak?
> He was immune to song.
>
> [p. 369]

---

[24] It is curious that there is no mention of Ferenczi in the analytical index of *Cogitations,* considering that Bion cites him explicitly, even though with a question-mark, when he speaks of "conflict of will" (an old hobby-horse of Ferenczi who sees it in a most original way from the point of view of the group's or parents' imposition on the individual and particularly as a kind of grafting onto the will of others and extraction of one's own). Ferenczi is also implicitly present when Bion goes on to talk about "sincerity" and "non-hypocrisy" (both Ferenczian leitmotifs) and when in the preceding pages he reflects on education and society. In our view undoubted similarities exist between Bion and Ferenczi's respective paths: in their relationship with the group; in their search for recognition and a sense of belonging while at the same time having the courage not to give in to truths that are preconceived and not really felt by the analyst–patient couple; and in their use of imagination as a means of encounter, dialogue, and analytical knowledge.

The Bion of the "turning point"

Closing *Cogitations*, we had thus for the most part overcome our initial bewilderment. We felt that we ourselves had come a long way, like Bion, and that we too had slowly and progressively reached a turning point. We were finally able to look with different eyes on the constants of bitterness, isolation, and detachment that had characterized many of the early cogitations, and we felt emotionally close to him in linking these difficulties to Bion the man, an "emigrant" since early childhood. Thus we could also recoup—as possible ways of sewing up old wounds[25]—the autobiographical works[26], disregarding their scathing and ironical toughness,

---

[25] Referring to his education in England, the Symingtons write: "When he was relating something to grown-ups they would often laugh at him. This made him feel small and put him into a rage against them. This mocking laughter produced what psycho-analysts call a bad internal object. . . . The sense that he retreated into himself while surrounded by uncomprehending adults remained with him through his ten years of schooling, through his traumatic experiences in the army and through the remainder of his life" (Symington & Symington, 1996).

[26] In these works Bion seems to confirm repeatedly the image we have of him being a cold and distant person, afflicted by an oppressive dulling of his own emotional responses. Here the prose is terse, almost telegraphic, as he describes himself as full of self doubts and uncertainty and dominated by the stupid and vapid causality of events, a man who does not feel himself to be the equal of his ideals and behavioural expectations (André Green, 1992, wonders "is this false modesty or an uncommon superego demand?"). Also to be considered is the insistence with which Bion—despite numerous official accolades which, it must be said, he never shied of citing on the cover of his books—depicted himself as a man lacking in courage and daring. Yet as the Symingtons (1996) note: "There is not a shadow of doubt that Bion was a man of outstanding courage. At the age of nineteen he was faced with a crisis of appalling proportions—not just one crisis but an array of crises which strung together make a catastrophe. His courage was indisputable. . . . Bion was conscious of fear, conscious of his own inner states; he was also not identified with Britain and its patriotic purposes. He was always conscious of himself as separate from the group, analysing its nature and questioning its purposes. He was one of the most extreme examples of the outsider. We define the outsider as one who is not identified with the several groups of which he is a member."

much of which was directed against himself, and so approach again those portraits that had in many ways given rise to numerous doubts and perplexities.

It is in Bion's *Seminars*[27] (1980, 1985b, 1987a, 1990, 1994), however, that the changes that *Cogitations* brought about appear in a more permanent and complete form. We see him in more amiable vein working as a supervisor, now that he is able to make himself immediately understood without having to surprise us with his audacious and bizarre remarks. Undoubtedly he is still in many ways obscure and somewhat abstract, but both the ways of taking things out of context that he employs and the inventive byways he forges are now subordinate to the idea of *summoning* thought, rather than paralysing or diverting it. He is of course still making his favourite moves—shaking his listeners with enigmatic silences, or overturning discursive fields to alert and surprise them[28]—but now in his discourse there appears a much more tangible feeling of concern and deeply moved generosity, a new empathic openness and capacity for dialogue.

This changed ground grants him a more authentic maieutic role that also aids his interlocutor, validating and recognizing him as such:

> ... in *theory* we can read what we like in all these great books on analysis; in *practice* we have to have a feeling about what the patient can stand. ... one has to have some concern and make allowances for the patient to whom this is such a frightening experience. I think this is an argument in favour of our behaving in a fairly conventional manner to make it easier for patients, who are under a strain anyway, to say whatever they want to say. [*Clinical Seminars*, Brasilia One, p. 4]

> If you had been practising analysis as long as I have, you wouldn't bother about an inadequate interpretation—I have

---

[27] The seminars all took place between 1973 and 1978 (the year before he died).

[28] Several times during the seminars Bion cites an aphorism of Maurice Blanchot: *La réponse est le malheur de la question* [The answer is the misfortune of the question] made known to him by André Green (personal communication, P. Bion Talamo).

never given any other kind. That is real life—not psycho-analytic fiction. The belief in the existence of an analyst who gives
correct and adequate interpretations is part of the mythology
of psycho-analysis. I certainly would not be inclined to bother
if you felt your interpretation was inadequate. I *would* be
rather bothered if you felt it was adequate. [*Clinical Seminars*,
Brasilia Nine, p. 49]

No longer a guru[29], Bion has come down to earth a more affable
and less *extreme* and provocative figure. What is surprising are no
longer his Pindaric flights and intellectual gymnastics; on the contrary, what we frequently witness now is a disarming directness in
getting to the heart of the matter, along with a new-found patience
and willingness to deal with his own and other people's
stammerings. The wrong-footing tactics that are so much a part of
his former idiosyncrasies appear in the *seminars* in more attenu-
ated form, transformed as they now are into an invitation to
"provide a stamping ground for wild asses"—thoughts—in honour of a conception of analysis which has "to preserve the species"
(*A Memoir of the FutureI*, 1991, p. 5). Here we have a sign and a
communication of Bion's desire for greater *naturalness*, having
done away with the burdens of theory and problems of orthodoxy,
not to mention the unrealistic expectations of his students:

> Will psycho-analysts study the living mind? Or is the author-
> ity of Freud to be used as a deterrent, a barrier to studying
> people? The revolutionary becomes respectable—a barrier
> against revolution. The invasion of the animal by a germ or
> "anticipation" of a means of accurate thinking, is resented by
> the feelings already in possession. That war has not ceased
> yet. [*Making the Best of a Bad Job*, 1979a, p. 331]

In short, the Bion that emerges from the seminars is similar to that
of the final cogitations, more vigilant and able to listen to his own
voice and less moralistic, with fewer scholasticisms, but above all
not omnipotent and omniscient. What we see now is a wish to
work with those who turn to him and a readiness to learn from
their contributions, along with a greater sense of discipline and a

---

[29] Regarding this point, we refer the reader to the work carried out by R.
Speziale Bagliacca (1984).

full awareness that he does not know already—a Bion who responsibly accepts feelings, such as when he says:

> Counter-transference is a technical term, but as often happens the technical term gets worn away and turns into a kind of worn-out coin which has lost its value. . . . You will hear analysts say, "I don't like that patient, but I can make use of my counter-transference". He cannot use his counter-transference. He may be able to make use of the fact that he dislikes the patient, but that is not counter-transference. [*Brazilian Lectures*, Rio de Janeiro, Five, p. 122]

A Bion who, having serenely accepted the limits of experiencing and feeling the inexhaustible palette of people's emotions and more in touch with the terror he speaks of and less phobic (Borgogno, 1993) and alarmed in facing it, declares that the only effective work tools an analyst has at his disposal are his gut, his heart, and his head.[30]

Now that the asepsis of the great schools of logico-mathematical thought has been abandoned and the lack of conceptual and linguistic instruments able to describe the life of the mind verified, now that he is less tied to the duties that come with belonging to a psychoanalytic society[31], perhaps helped by friendlier and more emotionally in touch groups, Bion's legacy can be summed up in two quotations:

> When two personalities meet, an emotional storm is created. If they make sufficient contact to be aware of each other, or even sufficient to be unaware of each other, an emotional state is produced by the conjunction of these two individuals, and the resulting disturbance is hardly likely to be regarded as necessarily an improvement on the state of affairs had they never met at all. But since they *have* met, and since this emotional

---

[30] Personal communication, P. Bion Talamo.

[31] ". . . psycho-analytical training has had an oppressive effect upon Bion. It is perhaps one of the great limitations of this sort of training that the personal analysis takes so long to 'recover from', to use a phrase Bion employed in 1976 in his lecture at the Tavistock Centre. In this regard one should note that all Bion's major publications came after the death of Mrs Klein in 1960" (Meltzer, 1978, p. 19). Green (1992) makes the observation that Bion's most important works were all published outside the more or less official circuits of the IPA.

storm has occurred, the two parties to this storm may decide to "make the best of a bad job". [*Making the Best of a Bad Job*, 1979a, p. 321]

The bad job happens to be me. I cannot get thoroughly analyzed—I don't think there is such a thing. It has to stop some day; after that I have to make the best I can of who I am. [*Bion in New York and São Paulo*, 1980, p. 37]

At the end of his complex and tormented path as an emigrant— both in his life and in his thought—we are left with the peculiar qualities that have endeared him to us and that we believe have made him an important model of inspiration for us all. In the words of Francesca Bion[32]:

His determination not to be moulded into a shape congenial to others, his courage in forging ahead with work he *felt* was on the right track although he could present no evidence to prove his feelings, his refusal to be or do anything untrue to himself. . . [Bion & Bion, 1981, p. 3]

Epilogue

Twenty years ago[33], more precisely on 17 July 1977, the almost 80-year-old Bion was in Rome at *Pollaiolo* to hold the last of his Italian seminars. He remarked:

. . . an activity like psychoanalysis is fashionable, and fashions change. If, therefore, there is any truth in psychoanalysis or any truth in psychiatry, then it would be helpful if any of us could do anything to make that truth explicit. But it does mean cutting through an enormous growth of brambles, thorns, rationalisations. What we cannot afford to lose sight of is the main goal—the truth. Our own mental capacity has to be nourished, but there is nobody to choose for us; we have to be capable of respecting the truth whether that truth is expressed

---

[32] As regards the more personal aspects of Bion the man, we refer the reader to Francesca Bion's published letters (F. Bion, 1985a).

[33] Our paper was read at the Bion Conference in Turin on 17 July 1997, twenty years to the day later.

by our patients, our colleagues, our musicians, painters or religious authorities.

One of the participants started to tell Bion about a patient of his who was dying of acute leukaemia—the illness of which Bion himself was to die two years later—asking him what he as an analyst should do in the face of such an unfavourable prognosis. Among other things, Bion said:

> This particular patient is said to be dying: That again doesn't impress me; we are all dying since we are in fact living. But it does interest me if the life and the space which is left is worth living or not . . . . is there any spark which could be fanned into a flame so that the person could live whatever life, whatever capital he still has in the bank? How much *vital* capital has this person? And could he be assisted to use that capital to good effect? [34]

And he concluded the seminar with the following words:

> —the nearest image I can give to it is this: like a leaf falling off a tree—one never knows which side up it will land. And when I look back on what I know about my life, I would never have been able to guess that I would be here today, at this time, and in such a position.

---

[34] Once again striking here is the closeness of Bion's vision to that of Ferenczi.

CHAPTER SIX

Whom was Bion addressing? "Negative capability" and "listening to listening"

Haydée Faimberg

Listening without memory or desire

Many persons feel that their analysis would make great progress . . . if they could get rid of their analyst. Conversely, some colleagues think they would be great analysts . . . if they managed to get rid of the patient.

You have perhaps recognized Bion in this humorous and deep statement.

I shall refer in this presentation to *one* of the paths I explored to cope with these uncanny temptations. But first let us quote Bion at length once more:

I once had in analysis a charming and co-operative patient. I shall now tell you about a session that was fairly typical of the

---

Part of this article was published in *La Revue Française de Psychanalyse*, 5, 1989, pp. 1453–1460, under the title "Sans mémoire et sans désir: à qui s'adressait Bion?"

way things happened during his first two years of analysis. The patient recounted a dream:

He was on a walk with his girlfriend. She pointed to an object in the sky, which she found quite striking, and was surprised that he could not see it. The patient commented that the young woman was not in fact his girlfriend, but a young lady whose company he was finding increasingly pleasant.

I interpreted that he saw me as a girlfriend, or a sister— although in fact he did not have a sister—and this meant that for him it was important to have a relationship with a kind of analytic sister instead of a direct relationship with me.

The patient said this was quite true.

I had already felt some mistrust about my way of conducting this analysis. And the idea came to my mind that I had not enough material to make such an interpretation. Briefly, I felt like telling him: "All right, but why do you think this is true?"

But it is not easy to put such a question to a patient who has just said that in his opinion the interpretation is correct.

The patient went on to tell me, as if confirming the interpretation, that his mother had told him that he had had a sister who had died before his own birth. And he ended by saying that his mother would be delighted to come and talk to me about it.

I said that I wondered why he thought that his mother could tell me more about himself. The patient completely agreed and felt it was a bad idea that his mother should come to see me.

He told me that the girlfriend in the dream had pointed to some objects too well defined to be clouds and that they were probably flying saucers.

I said that those objects must be highly significant, for him to have included in the dream a sister who had the task of pointing to them. Besides, I underlined that he had been able to have the dream and to recall it: the young woman must then necessarily represent a part of himself.

Once more, he completely agreed, and added that it was not unusual to see a clear day suddenly spoilt by the appearance of heavy clouds. . . .

I felt that he wanted me to interpret something about the objects that attacked him. So I told him that the objects that attacked him during the walk also attacked the relationship with his girlfriend, and would destroy him if he had a real

girlfriend of any kind, including myself in the analytic relationship.

This interpretation was also accepted.

After talking for a good while, Bion said humorously, "You'll be
glad to know that I've finally arrived at the beginning of my lecture". The long preface was aimed at conveying what was missing
in the analysis of that patient. He added that the problem had to be
tackled by following the method Freud described in a letter to Lou
Andreas-Salomé (letter of 25 May 1916):

> . . . in writing I have to blind myself artificially in order to
> focus all the light on one dark spot. . . .
> The fact is that at the beginning of the session the patient
> seems to be saying, "Don't you recognize me? I am the same
> depression and the same anxiety as you met yesterday and the
> day before, and we shall continue to meet in the coming
> years". In this way, analyses become interminable. Only the
> analyst can avoid this trap if he is able in his mind to say to the
> patient: "Go away. Today I have a new patient, and if you
> wish I would be glad to introduce him to you." [I think Bion's
> position is an implicit invitation to think again—from a Freud-
> ian perspective—about the ways of functioning of the mind
> explored after Freud, in particular by Melanie Klein. The ar-
> ticulation of Klein's idea with the works of Marion Milner,
> Winnicott and Fairbairn in the perspective of Bion's sugges-
> tion deserves, in itself, a study].
> Indeed, I shall never be able to rid myself of the slight
> feeling of persecution that I have in a situation that I do not
> understand. But we should concentrate on those situations
> which appear to lack any understandable link or coherence,
> instead of retaining the coherent and understandable ones and
> of thinking that the analysand is the same person as we met
> yesterday. The impatience and persecution we feel when con-
> fronted with the unknown may be so intense that we try at
> once to get over them by devising an interpretation or recall-
> ing a memory. We must resist this temptation, even if we
> know that the situation will not be pleasant for the patient or
> the analyst.

Bion was standing and talked in a calm and ironic voice. The date
was 30 July 1968, and we were at the Argentine Psychoanalytical
Association, attending his first lecture in Buenos Aires. He re-

mained with us for a whole week, giving lectures and many seminars (small groups of six participants) where alternately both candidates and experienced analysts presented clinical material.

Bion's comments belong to that context. The present chapter, partially based on the notes I took during that week, reflects the "oral Bion" I heard at the time and addresses in particular his suggestion that the analyst should listen "without memory or desire". Therefore a distinction should be established between the words actually pronounced by Bion and the recollection I have of them, inasmuch as I am basing myself on my listening to what Bion had to say in such a specific context. I shall not take into account any of Bion's writings, not even the "Notes on Memory and Desire" (1967a), with which I was not acquainted at the time.

In saying this, I am aware of the distance that separates me from Bion's disciples and analysands. I am addressing only one particular aspect of Bion's thinking that I have been able to incorporate into my own way of thinking. This aspect is nonetheless essential and highly representative of the change of perspective that Bion and other authors brought to the psychoanalytical movement.

"Without memory or desire": whom was Bion addressing?

So to whom was Bion talking? In putting forward this clinical material, Bion was addressing himself, in the sense of voicing his suspicion of those cases of his own that went "very well", too well. He mistrusted the patient's systematic confirmation of the analyst's theories. In my view, in his lecture Bion was addressing those analysts who in their work with the patient always remain on the same wavelength, *established by the patient in response to the analyst's desire*. This is my understanding of the word "desire" as employed by Bion.

As I heard him, Bion was addressing those analysts who listen to the patient *from a position of knowing* and therefore can only formulate interpretations that confirm what is already known, by analyst and/or patient. He was addressing analysts who during the session hold on to the memory of what they have discovered and wait for the words that confirm what they expect to hear.

In my view, the analyst's silence does not suffice to go beyond this situation or to prevent the patient from confirming his fantasy that his desire is fulfilled: the analyst's silence also speaks. Neither the analyst's silence nor his words can guarantee exclusively that the analysis is on the right path in its search for psychic truths.

But how should we understand the suppression of the analyst's desire? What is the status of the analyst's desire and of the analyst's memory at the precise moment when the session is in progress? What are we then to do with our memory and desire, we who believe in the constant thrust of unconscious activity? Was Bion suggesting that we abolish our own psychic activity by demanding that we work without memory or desire? These were the questions, raised by his first lecture, that turned in my mind when I attended his first seminar. One analyst was presenting material from a recent session in great detail.

Bion talked about methodology. It was not a question of "that session" which had already taken place and which, in any case, left us without the possibility of knowing what had really occurred. We had to concern ourselves with the session that had not yet taken place.

In his presentation, the analyst said that while listening to the patient he remembered what the patient had told him the previous week, and that that memory helped him to formulate an interpretation.

According to this, we could think that the analyst's recollection of material from a previous session had come to shape the selected fact in the present one. We saw an opportunity to test Bion's ideas and expected him to question the validity of an interpretation, since the analyst himself acknowledged that the interpretation was rooted in a recollection. The interpretation could not be valid according to his precept. Bion seemed to disregard the possibility of commenting on that point. He spoke of unidentified objects.

So we raised our question: how could he consider those objects, as unidentified as they might be, since they derived from a source so perfectly identified as the analyst's memory?

What Bion did not accept was that the analyst should try to remember what had happened in the previous sessions, therefore avoiding nameless anxiety. In this case the interpretation deserved to be taken into account *because the memory had arisen spontaneously while the analyst was listening without memory or desire*. The memory was to be considered an association of the analyst, and as such it belonged to his suspended attention.

At this point, once again, I could identify who it was that Bion was talking to: he was talking to those among us who adopt a reductionistic approach, translating what the patient says into what is already known—in other words, to a potential public at large.

In my view, the formulation that "the analyst should listen without memory or desire" reflects Bion's (implicit) question regarding the analyst's position when listening to the patient. The questioning itself authorizes us to think that, according to Bion, there is no "natural" way of listening.

Bion wishes to define certain conditions that should be satisfied in order to achieve a particular type of psychoanalytic listening.

Though I do not know whether Bion was ever explicit on this point, his line of thinking indicates that he did not believe in a "conflict-free area of the ego" (Hartmann) on which to base a working alliance between patient and analyst. On the contrary, I believe that Bion mistrusted any apparent collaboration on the part of the patient, seeing it as a form of compliance.

The memory of the experience of satisfaction acquired in a previous session might induce both analyst and patient to reproduce consciously or unconsciously the conditions that evoked that satisfaction. (In their own perspective Willy and Madeleine Baranger partly allude to this situation when they coin the concept of "bastion".) The patient cannot but go along with this repetition: it is up to the analyst to create new conditions for hearing the unknown.

The analyst's function of listening and the "negative capability"

I suggested elsewhere that it depends "on the psychic work of the analyst to be able to use negative capability (in the words of

Marion Milner and Bion, both quoting Keats) *to assure the psychic presence of the analyst in a position of not-knowing*" (Faimberg, 1992b, p. 215).

It is particularly interesting to note that the primary example of negative capability cited by Keats is that of Shakespeare:

> ... what quality ... which Shakespeare possessed so enormously—I mean Negative Capability, that is when a man is capable of being in uncertainties, mysteries, doubts, without any irritable reaching after fact and reason. [The letters of John Keats, 1814–1821, I. 193]

Bion has reflected on the necessary conditions for seeking the different versions of psychic truths in a particular analytical situation (and not in a theoretical abstraction far from the experience of the session). Listening without memory or desire means that the analyst must actively develop a new psychic capacity, a negative capability for listening.

In my view, a paradoxical and extremely fruitful situation is produced by this formulation whereby the desire to know the unknown, shared by patient and analyst, can only be satisfied by abolishing in both, and above all in the analyst, the desire for *a particular object*.

I link the negative capability about which Bion speaks to a position of the analyst who sets special store by the dialectic movement in his listening. (I have written on the "countertransference position" of the analyst where this perspective is included.) The negative capability consists in putting in parentheses not only what one does not know, but also the positive representations that might limit one's own listening to the unconscious. This allows one to listen in a new way to the unconscious identifications at stake.

Listening to silence and to interpretations

A patient who has been in analysis for many years tells me that he suddenly felt a great anxiety when approaching the building where I work. At first it seems a nameless anxiety, but then he produces an association. He says that he feels he cannot tell me what occupied his mind during the weekend. A new idea has come to his mind, but he is unable to tell me about it.

I interpret that perhaps he fears that I am unable to transform my mind to listen to his new thoughts. Therefore he feels he is losing me.

From then on and for the rest of the session he speaks in great detail of a decision that, for the first time, he imagines he can take. He speaks of a cherished project that he has for many years been considering with great hope and anxiety.

He says (to my surprise) that he imagines he can give up that project. With deep emotion he explains why he now thinks that he will be able to renounce the project. He loves his wife and children too much to jeopardize his connection with them, considering the time and devotion that would go into the accomplishment of the project. Important changes have happened in his family, and if he wants to acknowledge them, as he does, he must change his projects too.

This is a very surprising discourse: for the first time he says he loves somebody. He has always said that he did not know what love meant. Furthermore, he always tries to find an approval or a criticism that would guide his decisions in my words. At bottom, he would be willing to act only to please my supposed desires about his destiny. For these reasons, I remain silent, trying not to interfere in this unexpected discourse. At that point I think that *the interpretation about my inability to tune in to his changes has been enough*, since in my view his association has confirmed it. (I do not mean that he confirmed the interpretation by saying "yes". I considered his *unconscious* associations as a *confirmation* of my interpretation.)

However, he comes to the next session in an angry mood, saying that at first he had believed I was accompanying him in his new way of seeing things. But then my silence, which left him not knowing what to think of his project, meant to him that all these years I had been silently criticizing his project because I thought that he was not good enough to accomplish it.

I interpret then that at that first moment I could be imagined as someone who changed in order to listen to his new ideas. But afterwards nothing changed: I was there *using his changes to confirm what I had always thought.*

We were now able to recognize *who* was speaking through my silence. We had reconstructed in the course of his analysis "a mother" who always exhibited her son as a phallic part of herself capable of performing wonderful things. This mother was related to "a father" who was excluded and often said "you will see in the future that you are not as you think you are" (as your mother makes you think you are).

By imagining that he could take a decision, this patient was adopting a very different perspective. *But retroactively* my interpretation and my silence were *heard from the repetitive perspective.* Actually, he was afraid of losing *the "kind of parents"* I have just mentioned, and there was a conflict between these unconscious identifications which are part of his psyche and the discovery of his own desire (Faimberg, 1985, p. 71).

"Listening to listening" and Nachträglichkeit

To conceive of the patient as not being always the same—as Bion suggests—means, from my point of view, regarding him as *a non-unified subject, the subject of the unconscious.*

I shall refer here to this non-unified subject by recalling once again a function of the analyst that I called "listening to listening" (Faimberg, 1981). By proposing this function I hope to contribute to creating the appropriate conditions for hearing—as Bion proposed—something unexpected: the speaking of the unconscious and of each of its vicissitudes.

Let us recall what I said of this function (Faimberg, 1981, 1996). An interpretation entails three logical phases of understanding: the first and the third mostly incumbent upon the analyst and the second upon the patient. The analyst *anticipates* a meaning, and he partly actively chooses the formulation and is partly led to it ("I found myself saying" is an expression that conveys what we sometimes recognize retroactively—that it is as if we "were spoken", so to say, as well as speaking). (It is interesting to note that David Liberman, 1970, studied this choice through his concept of "stylistic complementarity of the interpretation", linking psychoanalysis with linguistics and communication theory.) The *patient speaks and listens in accordance with his unconscious identifications*, as a result of which he *reinterprets* the analyst's interpretations. In the third logical phase, by listening to how the patient has listened to the interpretation, the analyst is then able *retroactively* to assign a new meaning to what he said, beyond what he thought he was saying. In other words, the analyst, by comparing both versions, is able to *overcome the dilemma that would arise if we were to ask who is right, the analyst or the patient.*

A new dialectic cycle is opened when the analyst can formulate a reinterpretation that includes the new sense. This may lead both to the retroactive sense of the interpretation and to discovering the unconscious identifications.

I want to recall as well the sense in which I consider that the operation of *Nachträglichkeit* is involved in the function of "listening to listening", giving due credit to Lacan for having drawn attention to the importance of this concept in Freud's work.

> According to the English translation of Laplanche and Pontalis [1973], the fate of *Nachträglichkeit* or "deferred revision" is undergone by "whatever it has been impossible in the first instance to incorporate fully into a meaningful context" [p. 112]. The word "deferred" merely denotes something put off to a later time and does not adequately express the idea of retroactivity and remodelling whereby new values are conferred upon certain psychic contents. [Faimberg, 1996, p. 668]

> I am working on the assumption that our psychical mechanism has come into being by a process of stratification: the material present in the form of memory-traces being subjected from time to time to a *re-arrangement* in accordance with fresh circumstances—to a *re-transcription*. [Freud, 1950a, p. 233]

While in this quotation Freud confines this mechanism to the assignment of new meaning to memory traces, I have proposed to extend the operation of *Nachträglichkeit* to an *"operation of re-attribution of meaning in the analytic relationship that consists of two inseparable phases, one of anticipation and another of retroaction"* (Faimberg, 1996, p. 668).

As we see, the operation of *Nachträglichkeit* participates in the "listening to listening" function:

The analyst anticipates a meaning through his interpretation and assigns a retroactive meaning to this interpretation, listening to how the patient listened to it.

In the case of the patient I mentioned earlier, after a long analysis, he was able to use the "listening to listening" function by himself, and to tell us (him and me) how he had used my interpretation and my silence. This gave us the opportunity to see his decision in a new dialectics. In the following sessions the possibility arose of imagining that he could accomplish the project, once he was able, for the first time, to think of himself as being capable of renouncing it. Perhaps this capacity for accepting loss was the condition for becoming responsible for his own desire.

To conclude

I have attempted to present these notes according to Bion's advice—that is, by setting myself in a space "without memory" with regard to previous ideological discussions in psychoanalysis. Bion, for me, is not the author of just another theory, of some alternative and closed system of thought. I had the uncanny feeling of having "known" him before having met him or read him. One precious piece of Bion's advice I have followed consists in the avoidance of any easy attitude of certainty in our analytic work.

The "Bion" I heard includes in the structure of what he propounds the means of going beyond it. The "Bion" I had listened to had highlighted some essential problems by showing that the fact of "not knowing" during the session does not mean that an analyst is less rigorous in his subsequent conceptualizations. I did not feel the necessity to follow the parameters Bion applied in his research. For instance, even though I understood that the Grid was a useful

element in his thinking, it did not become a part of my conceptualization. I saw it as a particular framework that Bion had chosen
in order to reflect on analytic experience.

The "Bion" I heard is a classic in the sense given by Italo
Calvino: *A classic is a work that in each reading and for each reader
produces a new meaning.*

Recalling Bion's humorous remark that "many persons feel
that their analysis would make great progress if they could get rid
of their analyst; and conversely, some colleagues think they would
be great analysts if they managed to get rid of the patient", I am
willing to say that the function of "listening to listening" could
help both of us, analyst and patient, to resist these uncanny temptations better.

CHAPTER SEVEN

Sexuality as a narrative genre or dialect in the consulting-room: a radical vertex

Antonino Ferro

Stories happen to those who know how to tell them

Henry James

This exists that is its after having been said we know

James Joyce

Introduction

Psychoanalysis has contributed enormously to our knowledge of human sexuality right from Freud's earliest works, and it is to him that we owe the basis of the very concept of psycho-sexuality (Green, 1996).

At the same time, the formulation of theories regarding "sexual states of the mind" have been equally fundamental (Meltzer, 1973).

What psychoanalysis has offered to theories regarding infantile sexual development and its relative phantasies, to sexology and to the psychogenesis of sexual pathologies, is a common and shared patrimony (McDougall, 1995).

This chapter is not a dissertation about sexuality as such, but an attempt at using sexual communications as a means of digging deeper into the functioning of the human mind. I shall therefore focus my attention on the "consulting-room", since in effect it is here that, in almost all cases, we have to deal with stories regarding sexuality—that is, communications about or concerning sexuality. (I shall not take sexual acting during the session into consideration, since on the one hand—the analyst's—this refers back to the analyst's pathology, and on the other—the patient's—it refers back to the vast subject concerning acting in.)

I shall consider the problem of "what the patient and the analyst are talking about"; of whether they can speak about dislocation in time ("the first" of the Freudian theories concerning infant traumas and infant sexuality), about dislocation in space ("the other place" of theories regarding object dynamics—theories that are fundamentally different from those that consider the unconscious as something that forms continually in the actuality of processes of continuing alphabetization; of the transformation of beta-elements into alpha-elements [Bion, 1962b]), or whether, from the point of view that I now intend to privilege (since I think it is the most transformative), the "analyst and patient" also constantly speak of the real patterns in which the mind functions in the field that they form, which is continually supplied with emotional turbulence, transference, and here-and-now phantasies.

The main assumption of this chapter is that the patient goes into analysis because he has "something undigested" (Bion, 1962a) that has to be transformed into alpha-elements. This happens in the best hypothesis because there can also be a deficiency in the "apparatus for thinking thoughts"—PS↔D; ♂↔♀—(Bion, 1962a), or in more serious cases a defect in the alpha-function (Bion, 1962a, 1963a, 1965, 1992).

How these "operations" take place is under constant discussion. In the first case (undigested facts), there is the transformation of these beta-elements (the "betalomi", Barale & Ferro, 1992) into alpha-elements, real emotional pictograms; in the second case (deficiency of the apparatus for thinking thoughts), into the development of ♂↔♀ and PS↔D; and in the third and most serious case (defects of alpha-function), into a progressive introjection of a more adequate alpha-function.

Naturally, the patient chooses his own narrative genre with regard to the "story", which may be a "diary style", or perhaps in the most fortunate of cases a "secret diary", etc., etc.

From the very first meeting, or rather even before it (Baranger & Baranger, 1961–62), there is a deconstruction of history and of the patient's phantasies, such as takes place in the extraordinary tale of W. Allen's *Mr Kugelmass*. This story tells us how an inhabitant of New York, a certain Mr. Kugelmass, has managed with a fantastic machine to project himself back into the pages of *Madame Bovary*. This is how the story of Mr Kugelmass and Madame Bovary starts. However, literary critics who are studying the text are amazed that on a given page they no longer find Madame Bovary, who should, for example, have gone to a ball, because she has gone on a picnic with Mr. Kugelmass, and so on until a new text evolves, which develops with the presence of Mr. Kugelmass and his love "story" with Madame Bovary. But the problems do not stop here, because in the meantime Madame Bovary, after much insistence, manages to be transported, in her turn, to New York into Mr. Kugelmass's world. Mr. Kugelmass is married with children, and he does not really know what to do with Madame Bovary once she has entered his world. There is a direct analogy with what happens to a patient and to the analyst in terms of deconstruction of their previous mental state, already in the first analytic encounter, or even beforehand.

Narrative deconstruction is a function of projective identifications that begin to circulate in the field, of emotional turbulence that is activated in it, of the availability or "mental space" of the analyst, of the capacity of his *reverie*, and of his ability in transforming $\beta \rightarrow \alpha$.

This latter process immediately becomes the fulcrum of the analytic meeting (whatever the dialect chosen by the analyst, be it a reconstructive–historical one, one related to the world and internal objects, or to the actual or field relationship) (Ferro, 1996d).

The quality of the functioning of the $\beta \rightarrow \alpha$ process, as I have mentioned, is constantly pointed out and communicated by the patient in "real time".

From a theoretical point of view, it is not difficult to understand why this is so if you take into consideration what I say further on.

The alpha-element produced, even the one produced by the patient's alpha-function, is not directly recognizable, except in the case of so-called "flashes" (Bezoari & Ferro, 1992a, 1996; Ferro, 1992, 1993a, 1996d; Meltzer, 1982a; 1982b, 1984).

What *are* recognizable are the narrative derivatives of the alpha-element (Ferro, 1996a, 1996b, 1996c), similar to a picture that is covered by a sheet but about which it is possible to get an idea through a verbal communication (Bion Talamo, 1997).

The people in the consulting-room

The patient has at his disposal an almost endless range of possible communications, inasmuch as he can dig into memories, phantasies, dreams, talk about what goes on in his real external life, what is happening to his Self or to others, and so on.

In the consulting-room we take it that what the patient says is not chosen at random but is said, in all cases, in order to communicate "something".

Various theories have focused on this "something" in different ways (Ferro, 1991, 1993b, 1993c, 1996a):

• facts of infancy and family chronicles;
• facts from an internal world;
• facts with relational significance.

I should like to put forward the idea that in the session each mind *also* signals to the other mind present the quality of reciprocal interaction and functioning and the quality of the success of a project that can range from "undigested facts" to "alpha-elements" and approximations to O.

These communications take place through the use of characters such as "my father" ... "my uncle" ... "my cat", which through different reference models have been mostly taken to be:

a.   historical-reference characters that speak "about a before and a then";

b. internal object characters, that speak about the "inside" of the patient, an inside that can sometimes be projected "over" or "into" the analyst;

c. affective hologram characters that indicate function patterns that the field assumes in all its sectors—three-dimensional characters that are the product of the meeting of the analytical couple's "dream thoughts of waking hours", in the endless possible combinations of the characters existing there.

With this in view, we may suppose that "my cat" refers back to a sector or to a relational vector of the field in which "the feline element" reigns supreme.

Every analytical session can be seen from this viewpoint as a constant re-telling of emotional facts of the field (Corrao, 1986). This can take place using various dialects—the one used in the "place of work", for "a love story", for a "travel agenda", and so on.

From this point of view a child who says, after an interpretation saturated with transference: "On television I saw some scientists who were slicing up an egg to see what it was like inside; what a pity they were stopping the chick from being born by doing this" is telling how his alpha-function (or his "apparatus for thinking thoughts") has "visualized" our previous interpretation—that is, his communication is the narrative by-product of a sequence of alpha-elements, unrecognizable in themselves (but which have to do with pictographs of violence and attacks on life).

One might wonder whether to interpret this communication directly, or whether it would be "better" to find a way of transforming our interpretative style into one that is less punishing and will allow the "chick" to be born, while remembering what Bion tells us in *Clinical Seminars* when he says that " . . . you can't launch out into a great explanation of the biology of the alimentary canal to a baby . . ." (Bion, 1987a [1994, p. 12]).

What counts is the "transformation" that we manage to carry out in the field. We might think of the narratives of the field as a Rorschach of the couple, where one needs to pick up the "G" (by the field "G" I mean the "global emotive" of the field itself, as an analogy of Rorschach's G)—that is, the emotion present in that

moment, the quality that according to Bion's (1963a) psychoanalytical interpretation cannot avoid having "an extension into the
field of sense, myth, passion".

One example might be to select the "stupidity of scientists", the
uselessness of their work . . . , or the atrocity committed with regard to the chick . . . , remaining in this way in the C row of the
Grid, but without decoding, without the usual obligatory sterile
interpretation: "You are telling me what I told you. . . ." (perhaps
formulating a saturated interpretative hypothesis to ourselves, if
we really need to) but keeping in the patient's dialect towards O
and unison with him.

Similar considerations can be valid for any communication of
"sexuality" in a session.

Sexuality is therefore a character, or an articulation between
characters, that can be thought of as something that has to do with:

a. a before (infantile sexuality) and an elsewhere (real external
    sexuality);

b. an inside (real internal sexuality/internal object sexuality);

c. a communication *within* and *about* the field in one of the many
    "possible dialects" of the narrative derivatives of the alpha-
    element—that is, a literary genre that is neither more nor less
    meaningful that any other genre.

Bion (1975, p. 46) reminds us clearly: "The mind that is too heavy a
load for the sensuous beast" (that is man) "to carry".

Sexuality, digestion, respiration, and so on are in themselves
considered very stabilizing phylogenetic successes. The big drama
of Homo Sapiens is the weight of the Mind, and the fact that
"thinking" is a new function (the most recent phylogenetically
speaking) for living matter (Bion, 1980).

As analysts, what we are constantly called upon to deal with is
the "mind", or rather the basic and constructive aspect necessary to
its existence—the emotional-affective relationship with the Other
(Faimberg, 1989), and this is what we constantly speak about.

Two minds that feel near to each other speak repeatedly about
themselves and about their interaction, indicating the problems
and the quality of reciprocal functioning, and this they do using

all possible types of speech, all dialects, and all possible literary genres.

Therefore, as an analyst, I consider sexuality in a session as the copulation of two minds, the "quality" and the "modality" of the meeting of a beta-element with an alpha-function, as the organization of thoughts and the communication of them through PS↔D oscillations, the ♂↔♀ interaction, and the *way in which everything is talked about*.

Sexuality is the modality of development of O, which takes place because of the sum of emotions that constitute the weaving of the threads of a net in expansion, of the growth of O that is "a medium in which lie suspended the 'contents'" that protrude from an unknown base, in an atmosphere of tolerance of doubt (Bion, 1962b, p. 92).

I would like to suggest, moreover, that the whole session can be catalogued along the C row of the Grid as a dream that the patient's mind has about the functioning of the analyst's mind and of the field. Other categories are naturally possible, but I believe that they are less useful for allowing transformation in O. In this sense psychoanalysis has a specific interest in "sexuality" as a narrative vertex. My opinion is encouraged by what Bion (1965) says in the final part of his admirable Chapter VI of *Transformations*, in which after affirming the "supremacy of the visible vertex" he confirms that he is convinced that the solution of psychoanalytical communication must be found by passing along row C in the direction of H, and examines the "mental counterpart of the reproductive system", understood not as the awareness of the reproductive activity, but as something that is connected to "anticipation of pleasure and pain", which, if placed in row C of the Grid, immediately refers us back to sexuality as a narrative dialect or that "mental counterpart of the reproductive system" (Bion, 1965).

But let us now see what all this implies clinically.

Martina's phimosis

Martina, a young woman who has been in analysis for a few months, often talks about how she has always liked flying the "flag of independence".

One Monday she starts off her week of analysis by talking about her son's "phimosis" and about the worry it is causing, and about a possible operation that can no longer be put off.

At this point, I feel authorized to underline for her that maybe there is something in the consulting-room, too, that is staying hidden, imprisoned and unspeakable, and that I am wondering what it is.

At the ready, and quickly taking up what I have said, Martina replies: "They are sexual things that I haven't had the courage to speak about", but now she feels that she can't hold back any more. She speaks about how, over the past few days, she has felt excited and got a lot of pleasure when making love to her husband if he ties her up and blindfolds her. Then she tells me about a film by Almodovar *Legami*, whose name she is unsure whether to pronounce with an accent on the "e" or on the "a".[1] It is the story of a man who physically ties a woman to a bed, until the woman ends up loving him deeply and then, without any constriction, they have an affair together.

I respond by saying that what she has told me seems to be at odds with her "flag of independence", and that it seems to be saying that she likes a relationship in which, fundamentally and willingly, she can rely on another person, completely relinquishing any control over the situation, being almost at the whim of her ties, and that she expects that a story started "compulsorily" will become a story, like the one of her analysis, that is important and vital for her.

She replies that in this period she feels her husband to be very near to her and very caring, she feels understood by him, but she recalls the deep uneasiness the first time a fiancé had compelled her to undress, even if it had been nice afterwards.

I do not wish to deny that there was a subtle erotic element present in the whole sequence (which is another side of the story: Martina avoids depressive experiences through excitement that is sometimes erotic, sometimes intellectualized), but

[1] *Légami* means "bind me", and *Legámi* means "bounds".

I should like to underline how the content refers back, in my opinion very clearly, to my questioning her (pseudo) independence and the effective beginning of an ability to relate.

The uncouth countryman and the mother

A patient tells of how she was afraid she had got a flat tyre, and of how afterwards, while she was sitting still in the car, she had felt an earthquake. She then talks about how she had had visions, among others things of shadows, like ghosts, which she really saw, even if she realized they were the fruit of her imagination. Then she remembers a television programme about spiritual seances.

Remembering that she feels direct interpretations to be intrusive, but considering them to be necessary, I say that I am afraid that "her father-in-law will be coming with some of those gifts that disturb her" (in the analytical lexicon her father-in-law appears every time that I actively suggest an interpretation that she agrees with but feels to be intrusive), and I say that the flat tyre and the earthquake make me think of the previous Monday's skipped session, the session with the hole and the changes in our usual set-up.

I add that the ghosts make me think of the previous day's session—memories of childhood situations experienced with her mother, "that were experienced very intensely yesterday, as phantasies yet real".

She replies after a moment that she recalls Guido, an uncouth farm labourer, who when she was little had often tried to get too near to her, trying to kiss her and touch her, and how her mother had never defended her.

I think that "Guido" has taken shape in the field after my direct interpretations, which "touch" her and from which she has not been sufficiently defended by the mother–analyst who has failed to stop the intrusive Guido touching her.

Rather than clear this up in transference, I simply say that it must have been painful to have had a mother who did not defend her in times of difficulty, and that I think that I should hold back more in my interpretations.

The patient, after *my silence* (arising from my previous reflections), says: "I don't feel much like working today."

I say that perhaps she is afraid that if I hold back "Guido", who is getting too near to her and is touching her with interpretations that are too explicit, this is because I don't want to work?

P: "Since I am not used to a mother protecting me, I don't know what it's like."

A: "And you may be afraid that greater respect means coldness and indifference."

P: "But it is true that I am beginning to think about having a mother who can also be a defence lawyer, who can worry about me instead of accusing me."

Let's invert the vertex: a bloodshed

In the month of December a patient tells me about a seriously depressed man, who was being treated in a psychiatric unit, and who, when his landlady had asked for an increase in rent, which was contrary to a unwritten agreement, had immediately got his gun and killed the householder and then himself.

For some time I had been wondering whether it would be possible or opportune to charge a little more for my sessions as of January, and I had decided, for several reasons, not to do so, so I reply:

"Well, it's just as well I didn't decide to ask for an increase in the new year!"

This is followed by a moment of surprised silence, the patient is taken aback, then bursts out laughing.

The patient does not come to the next session; and in the following one he tells me how his eldest daughter has begun to have a lively and playful relationship with him again, giving him a poke in the stomach in the corridor, and yet although he is happy about all this he had not come to his session because during a game of football his younger son had been badly bruised by a hard ball and had had to be kept at home from school for a day.

This account is "back to front" with respect to the preceding examples, an account that has to do with sexuality in the session: his communication, my remark, the effects of this: the joy of finding a good relationship again even if his more infantile parts "bleed" because of my remark.

I think it would be arbitrary to use the patient's communication in analysis to pose questions or to comment on the housing crisis, on the problem of rents, on being social outcasts, or the problem of alternatives to hospitalization: that is to say, to take the consulting-room as a privileged observation point of external-social facts, for which we nowadays have specialized and specific grids and observers.

Theoretical considerations:
alpha-elements and their narrative derivatives

Bion (1962a, 1963a, 1965, 1992) suggests a constant activity of our minds (alpha-function), which synthesizes into a visual element (alpha-element) whatever it gathers, under any form, from the sense organs.

These visual elements are formed constantly and in sequence.

In order to give an example—and to simplify as much as possible—we might use little cards like those used in the game of *Memory* (this is a children's game of cards, which has a different picture on the front of every pair of cards and the same design on the backs; the alpha-element is in reality an emotional pictogram, which is much more complex, but to make my thought clear I have simplified to the maximum, as if it had just one elementary image). A possible sequence might be flower–cherry–mosquito, and this, for example, would form a picture-sequence of a pleasant experience followed by a tasty one, which then becomes a vaguely annoying one, such as one might find in a brief relational exchange between a couple of speakers, of non-speakers, of agents . . . of people in a consulting-room.

As various sense perceptions continue to arrive, more visual photograms are continually being formed. While these elements are being built up, they can remain, as in an imaginary game of Memory, visible, and form the Conscious system, or face downwards and form the Unconscious.

In other words, the Unconscious is not an *a priori*, but an *a posteriori* of the meeting of the beta-element (proper-exteroception) with the alpha-function—it is, that is to say, also made up of facedown alpha-elements, if we wish to continue to use the *Memory* metaphor. However, it can also be inhabited by what Bion defines as "undigested facts", which are accumulations of proto-emotional tensions or perceptive sense that has not been transformed into visual elements and therefore metabolized and rendered thinkable. These undigested facts are not beta-elements; however, we could refer to them as partially digested and metabolized beta-elements or "balpha"-elements.

The alpha-element, or the sequence of alpha-elements flower–cherry–mosquito, is only directly recognizable in two cases:

a.   when the alpha-element, a photogram from the "dream thoughts of waking hours" film (this is what Bion calls a sequence of alpha-elements), escapes from the apparatus that should hold it and is projected and seen from the outside. In this case we could say that the patient sees a flower, a cherry, or a mosquito that syncretizes his mental state in that relational instant;

b.   when we are able to enter into contact and "visualize" this alpha-element directly—that is in the so-called reverie capacity.

In this case a usually well-protected image comes to the surface, and we can see it with the "eyes of the mind". This is the maximum contact that a mind can have with itself.

One characteristic of the alpha-element is that it is pictographic in real time and syncretized in an absolutely unpredictable way— that is, when it is formed, it does not use preordained symbols. Each time it is a unique and unrepeatable poetic-picture work.

Of the former aspect I remember asking for a fee increase from a patient who responded in a very alarmed way: "I can see a chicken being plucked." The alpha-element, the visual photogram, had escaped and was visible.

If we look out for the kinds of phenomena described by Meltzer (1982a, 1982b, 1984), we will find they are much more frequent than we might imagine.

Of the latter aspect I remember how in a session that seemed to me incomprehensibly banal I "saw" a cemetery with graves. It was by finding a way of linking up the content of my reverie with what he was telling me that I entered into contact with the patient's very profound depressive anxieties and was able to find the correct register for contacting his suicidal propositions.

The style of the alpha-element, its quality and pictorial genre, are specific to each human being. They constitute the mind's deepest nucleus of truth, with respect to its emotions and perceptions.

The alpha-element is "private" and can in no way be generalized.

However, we do not usually have patients who project the alpha-element, or analysts capable of *reverie* activity—so is the alpha-element unreachable, except via these two very narrow paths?

Naturally this is not the case: mental life, the root of thought, is made up of such alpha-elements, of which we can get to know the *narrative derivatives* that constantly blossom in consulting-room communications thanks to *the narrative capacity of minds in the waking state* (apparatus for thinking thoughts).

Flower–cherry–mosquito would then lead to a communication by the patient in which the "concentrate", the "meat-cube" (flower–cherry–mosquito), is dissolved in a communication—which, if the actuality of the field is a pleasant experience, becomes tasty and then vaguely annoying, and then all this can be narrated in an *infinite* number of possible genres.

a. a *childhood memory*: when I was small, I was always pleased when my grandparents came to visit bringing sweets, but then I became angry because I always had to wait for lunchtime to eat them;

b. *an apparently external diary style*: today my wife welcomed me warmly at the door, seemingly happy, but then she told me about a telephone call from my sister-in-law that ended up alarming me;

c.   a *sexual genre*: making love to Giulia was very satisfying at the beginning—a pity that her lack of participation irritated me.

We could go on with d, e, f, g, h, i, . . . z. These are all narrative models of the same emotional experience: flower–cherry–mosquito.

From this point of view, the sexual genre is a choice of narrative genre and is to the alpha-element what the plot is to the fabula. (The "fabula" is the fundamental scheme of the tale, the synthesis of the characters; the plot is the story as it is in fact related or as it appears [Eco, 1979].)

I shall not go into the fact that the alpha-element too can form a sexually charged pictogram of an emotional experience. So there are two sexual image locations—the alpha-element itself and the respective narrative genre used.

Where does the alpha-element sequence originate? The answer is immediate—*from the actuality of the emotional field*, of which it becomes an indicator and where transference and phantasies flow together as the propelling matrix of the analysis. Therefore it is the *actuality* of the emotional field that is transformed into α and narrated.

But it is not all so easy.

The creative activity of the two persons in the consulting-room and of any mind is constantly provoked by the arrival of quotas of beta- and balpha-elements.

For this reason a sequence becomes: flower–cherry–mosquito/ beta- or balpha turbulence.

With the turbulence of beta- or balpha (partially digested elements that are regurgitated, elements that can be stored as an "undigested fact" but are different, from both alpha-elements and non-metabolized beta-elements and are, I believe, useful as an idea for introducing the balpha-element as partially digested beta-elements that refer back to a ruminative pre-digestion that has not been finished), we have reached the chapter on the capacity of the minds present to form other alpha-elements that are coherent with the turbulence and that give the latter a sense. Scimitar–lion–lake, for example, signifies a relationship model that recalls something sharp that becomes dangerous and then quietens down.

Things do not always work out so favourably, and in that case the transformation [beta (or balpha) → alpha] and the turbulence remain as they are or are increased and give rise to evacuations.

What has been said up to now belongs to the field and its waking movements. What I have recalled about the alpha-element only in visual terms is in fact more complicated, because the alpha-elements can also be acoustic and kinaesthetic, the basic principles, however, remain essentially the same.

Naturally there is another entrance to the alpha-element—the "royal route" of night dreams and the telling of them. The night dream differs greatly from the alpha-element, inasmuch as it is built up downstream of a selection function, a filter (re-dreaming) of what has been constantly "filmed", alphabetized, and conserved during waking hours. At this point it is as if at the end of the day we have at our disposal myriads of alpha-elements stored up in different ways. Two different paths can be followed from here: either one that arises if there is a lack of meaningful sensorial input, so that one has an alpha-metafunction that this time works on alpha-elements constructing a syncretic narrative mosaic from emotionally salient facts, or hypothesizing that, in the same way as there is an "apparatus for thinking thoughts", which works during waking on thoughts formed through degrees of increasing abstraction relative to the alpha-elements and described by Bion as being formed of $\male \leftrightarrow \female$ PS$\leftrightarrow$D, so there is an "apparatus for dreaming dreams", which works at a sort of second level on the stores of all alpha-elements (and perhaps some balpha-elements) in order to supply a figurative narration that confers meaning on the experiences on the basis of a criterion of urgency. I would call this an "apparatus for dreaming dreams", which necessarily has to dip into the store of alpha-elements, the "narrative capacity of the dreaming mind", a sort of stage-directing function compared to the equally creative work of the cameraman who, moment by moment, forms alpha-elements.

Concluding thoughts

Whatever is communicated in analysis belongs to the "analytical field" and speaks about this and about nothing else, even if the analyst's and the patient's way of interacting can be narrated in an infinite variety of dialects, in the last sequence in an economic-social dialect.

I ask myself why this "analytical vertex" might not be valid if a patient talks about "the dryness of my wife's vagina" or another about the "premature ejaculation" of her husband, which never allows her to feel passion during their love-making, or an adolescent one about the exhibitionist who "shows himself" in front of the school.

I believe that to take it that these or similar communications interest us only when they concern "real sexuality" and not "sexuality in the consulting-room" is to mortify the specific quality of the "analysis laboratory".

By "sexuality in the consulting-room" I mean in the case of "a dry vagina", for example, a possible dryness in the pattern that the field has assumed somewhere within itself, which has caused a painful relationship without adequate lubrication. Premature erection may mean a hasty explanation of meanings that takes away a taste for sharing, the presence in the field of an "incontinent part" that will need to be transformed into one that manages to be continent and is therefore able to experience and live out real passion. The "show-all" is the showing of contents that are too crude and that disorientate. These things I have mentioned as "exercises", because naturally there is no possibility of decoding a communication in the field, but only of generating meanings that articulate and develop progressively (Borgogno, 1995; Corrao, 1981, 1989; Gaburri, 1997; Vallino, 1997).

Taken that this is so, in the consulting-room "*sex alone exists and is constantly taking place*", obviously in the sense that one and the other relate to each other and that this *is sex*, and even if the required rules of abstinence imply that sex be "chaste", yet it is not chaste with regard to the emotions that the couple activate and experience, or even to phantasies in sexual terms of constant copulation *between minds*: the sexuality of $\male \leftrightarrow \female$ and $\beta \rightarrow \alpha$ events.

Of course, analysis is not an end in itself, but it serves to transform deeply the people who turn to it. In the case of the woman with a husband who suffered from precocious ejaculation, it might, for example, serve to "transform" the woman's incontinent part, which obliges her to marry a man with precocious ejaculation in order to find a way of coping with her own problem of incontinence (and then talk about it), or, once capable of continence, she may not make love to her husband in such a way as to favour the symptom, and there are infinite other possible paths. However, the "husband's" premature ejaculation can be treated, in the same way as a symptom relative to "not knowing how to keep business papers in order" might be treated, in the consulting-room.

Having resolved the problem of the room and carried out transformation operations within it, it is obvious that external effects that are outside our realm as analysts do exist but which we can accede to as can anyone else.

The analyst, in order to be such, must be alive, and have a living patient and a working setting; outside this context he/she is a person with the right to speak about anything, but not in the specific role of analyst.

This does not mean denying our common and shared history, as I mentioned at the beginning, or our gratitude for those theories and models that are our greatest common factors, and upon which we should never tire of reflecting. On the contrary, it implies being able to use what we know to see—from a position using the title of an interesting book by Speziale-Bagliacca, *On the Shoulders of Freud*, but, I would add, also on Klein's and Bion's and on all of our Masters'—something that today is more specific compared to the field that psychoanalysis is constantly exploring and enlarging (Bion), the field within which in any and all cases the vertices, organizational possibilities, models, and theories of others co-exist.

CHAPTER EIGHT

The primordial mind and the work of the negative

André Green

When I was invited by Parthenope Bion Talamo and Francesca Bion to give the opening lecture of the Conference on which this chapter is based, I felt not only honoured, I was also moved. I have had the privilege of meeting Bion personally, of having long conversations and exchanging letters with him. I keep a vivid and strong memory of our relationship. In her invitation, Parthenope Bion Talamo told me that her father had a sort of "fellow feeling" for me—a remark that struck me, as on my part I had a sort of filial respect for him. Another reason I was moved was that, as every one knows, I am neither a "Bionian" nor even a Kleinian. Replying with this objection, I was told that not being a disciple of Bion was in fact one of the reasons why I was invited. It seemed that, while knowing Bion's ideas, I could "use" them and remain true to my own thinking. Bion, who was probably the best example of independent thought in psychoanalysis, encouraged those who went to him to act in the same way. During my oral or written exchanges with

Bion he never tried to "convert" me to his ideas or to Klein's. We both agreed that our greatest debt was towards Freud.

As for the fact that I did not even belong to the Kleinian herd, Bion himself wrote that sometimes he felt closer to people who were not Kleinian than to his Kleinian mates. At the beginning of October 1955, Bion received a letter stating "I think of you as the big man of the future in the British Psycho-Analytical Society". It was signed D. W. Winnicott (1987, p. 89). On 16 November 1961 Winnicott reaffirmed his valuation of Bion's work on thinking: "Like a lot of other people, I find it difficult but extremely important"(1987, p. 133). I can say the same. I first met Bion while I was writing, in collaboration with Jean-Luc Donnet, on blank psychosis, in which a theory of thinking was developed. His ideas had been of great help to me at the time.

* * *

Bion's work can be divided into two categories: the first represents his attempts to build a new psychoanalytic theory, which would be not only an extension of Freud's work or even of Klein's, but a contemporary new formulation of psychoanalysis starting from an entirely different point of view. The ground for conceptualization would not be the neurotic patient but the psychotic. Psychoanalytic theory has proven inadequate for understanding and analysing psychotics. Freud's main writing on psychosis was Schreber's "Memoirs", and everyone knows that he had no inclination to treat psychotic patients. Melanie Klein had started to explore this new field, but, if I may say so, she did not have the right conceptual tools to make significant discoveries: she lacked a theory of thinking. Bion's ideas were synthesized with the Grid, which represents his achievement in formalization. This goes on up to *Attention and Interpretation*. The second category, which is more limited in quantitative terms, is the result of an opposite inspiration. *A Memoir of the Future* and particularly the third volume, *The Dawn of Oblivion*, tells us about it. In these books Bion appears as an author of fiction, perhaps as a representative of "psychoanalytic science fiction". This other side of Bion's work has puzzled many, as he started it when he went to the United States. The *Memoir* begins with the sentence, "I am tired". Perhaps the tiredness is not only physical but has to do with his efforts in building a scientific theory. As one of the notes of our meeting recalls, he wrote: "Psychoanalysis itself is just a stripe on the coat of the tiger. Ultimately it may meet the tiger. The thing itself, O." Bion had to take seriously into account the fact that the thing-in-itself is unknowable. We can only approximate its derivatives. Here the reference is not only Kant as he quotes him, but Freud too. And if the result seems too far from what we suppose to look like truth, then perhaps another method can be tried. To interpret dreams is one thing, to construct a discourse on the model of an artificial dream is another, especially when one has had a nightmare. In the copy of his *Memoir* that Bion gave me, he wrote: "No nightmares please" after having signed it. He may have wanted to protect me from what he had experienced. To sum up: formalization is an evidence of the power of the mind, but also of its limitations; it may be limited to its wakefulness. Fiction is its opposite—that is what we experience with dreams (the subtitle of the first volume of the book). But it could be a better method for coming closer to the unknowable, the void, the formless infinite. Not that it can say anything about it, but it gets rid of the risk of rationalization and tries to explore the layers of the mind beyond the visible, or the thinkable.

One hundred years ago, Wilfred Ruprecht Bion experienced the caesura between his mother's womb and himself. About this experience he wrote the following: "In his mother's womb man knows the universe and forgets it at birth" (Bion, 1977b). In the course of his lifetime, Bion made enormous efforts to try to gain anew some of the lost knowledge. A similar statement can be found in the Talmud—perhaps an unidentified reminiscence.

Using his capacity for identification, Bion has been able, through the analysis of his patients and his own self-analysis, to conceptualize the roots of psychic activity, the point from which we are supposed to start, or if not, at least in the fiction we build about ourselves and others. He called it the primordial mind. I will try to shed light on some of Bion's ideas about it, keeping in mind that many of you have an even better knowledge of his conceptions, and I will present some of my own ideas related to it. On my way, I shall more than once meet Freud's work, which is an essential link between Bion and myself.

* * *

The expression "primordial mind" is not so obvious at first sight. Its consistency rests on its opposition with the "civilized, individual, educated, and articulate" parts of the human being. Bion sees it as a survival of our ancestry, the way the branchial cleft is a sign of the anatomy of a kind of fish. It is interesting here to note that Bion relates to some sort of imaginary embryology of the mind. He shares a common hypothesis with Freud that there is something primitive in the mind, which is not entirely explained by the early stages of object relationships in the development of the baby. The traces left by phylogenesis and ontogenesis in the structure of the mind should play a significant role in later stages of development. This speculation is linked with his hypothesis of beta-elements. The most primitive elements of psyche are for him the beta-elements linked with sensuous experience. In *Cogitations*, Bion will say that the beta-element may correspond to the phenomena under the dominance of the pleasure–unpleasure principle. The important thing is that beta-elements—just as what he has called beta-space—are unthinkable because this is a domain of thoughts that have no thinker (Bion, 1992, p. 313). This idea of thoughts for which there is no thinker brings us to the paradox of thoughts, which cannot be thought by someone because at that stage he is lacking the apparatus to treat them, and so they cannot be communicated. If thoughts need a thinker, it could be that the thinker is not to be confused with the organism that has thoughts that need to be projected into an object who is a thinker. As the object has an apparatus for thoughts, he can transform the primitive thoughts and send them back to the infant in order to enable him to reintroject them and to become himself a thinker who will have to deal with his thoughts all by himself. This conception is one of the rarest examples showing the articulation of an intrapsychic perspective with an intersubjective one. It is also a remarkable conception that shows the transition from concrete thinking (thoughts without a thinker) to abstract thinking (thoughts produced by a thinker). The primordial mind is made of thoughts that, because of their raw and crude nature, are not workable as such. So they have to be expelled from the psyche. The destiny of thoughts produced by a thinker is their ability to be kept in the mind and continue to be transformed into mental abstractions. One question remains: how can a thought, without a thinker, be expelled out of the mind, considering that the discharge process sends them out of the mind and does not carry with it the whole of the primitive mental activity? The probable answer is that it is impossible to get rid entirely of the beta-elements that stay blocked in the mind and will poison other mental processes if they gain the upper hand again.

During my conversations with Bion, I was struck by his great interest in Descartes. He thought that Descartes' aim to arrive at "clear and distinct ideas" could also be applied to psychoanalysis. This, at least, was a task that should be achieved in theory. Descartes' project was, in dealing with the mind, to reach the same degree of certainty that one experiences with mathematical demonstrations. Bion and Lacan, though starting from very different premises, were both on the same track, pursuing the same ultimate goal. But, as I said earlier, this ideal at the beginning of Bion's work led in the end to a disillusionment. What was the reason for this disillusionment, if it was not because of the ineffaceable influence of the primordial mind represented in the Grid by the beta-elements? In the row of the beta-element, Columns 3, 4, 5 are empty, which means that nothing stands between ψ and action. It is important to notice that evacuation through action is the most radical attempt at a denial.

Thinking is often confused with psychic activity. Freud, like Bion, was interested in that difference—for instance, when he said that the drives were rooted in the somatic, though they are already a primitive psychic activity "in a form unknown to us". Can we say "unthinkable"? There surely is a difference compared with what we would have to say about thinking. The conclusion is that we have to distinguish between *psychic events*, which have to be understood as rooted in the body, *thoughts without a thinker*, which are very close to this primitive psychic activity, and *thinking, which has to be thought by a thinker* and therefore can be communicated to another thinker. Bion's hypothesis that emotional experience is the matrix of the mind is related to the closeness of the thoughts without a thinker to the models drawn from bodily activity. Thinking is a digestion of the mind.

Frances Tustin, who was analysed by Bion and has worked with autistic patients, has convincingly shown this, reporting a session. The price that must be paid for thinking is that the thinker is almost necessarily a liar. Bion applied this conclusion to himself. The thinker who had constructed this sophisticated theory inevitably falsified the experience. I suppose that we can say that the primordial mind is made of a psychic activity rooted in the body, which is already a form of thought but without a thinker. To understand what is a thought without a thinker would probably mean equating the psychic element with the drive and the thought that can only be expressed through action, which in Bion's system corresponds to evacuation. To some extent, Bion agrees with Descartes about the relationship of thought to a thinker: "I think therefore I am." But he adds to this: "Descartes himself in his concept of philosophical doubt failed to doubt the necessity of a thinker" (Bion, 1977b, p. 12). Bion thinks that a psychoanalyst should consider the belief of a personality without thought, just as he wished Descartes to accept the idea of thoughts without a thinker. These highly speculative assertions are based on clinical experience. Bion was alluding to patients who would say that they have no thoughts, or they would say they are "thinking of nothing".

Bion recalls Keats's *negative capability*, of which these patients are incapable, rushing to action. This does not necessarily mean explicit acting out; it is more the *model* of action than the *fact* of action that enlightens all their psychic processes of any kind. Therefore we can assume that thoughts without a thinker can never be recognized as having been thought and attributed to the personality who had them. This may be an important difference between the psychotic part and the neurotic part of the personality. The neurotic, after the interpretation has been given by the analyst, has the capacity to recognize the truth lying behind it even if resistance opposes this insight. The psychotic will not recognize it, as if it were somebody else's possession, which means that he does not recognize himself in a state of alien-action. Would he do so, he would have to become aware of an image of himself that will terrorize him. This gives us an indication about the fact that the radical denial of the primordial mind is caused by a terror raising the risk of mental death. Denial and excessive projective identification can be one and the same process. Denial and excessive projective identification may mean that after their happening, the mind is empty.

If projective identification is not possible because it may itself cause a threat of annihilation through the emptying of the mind, another mechanism is still at hand: a process of erasure, an activity of effacing or deletion that has nothing to do with repression as a censorship but, rather, with a radical suppression of what happens in the mind. This is what happens, I believe, in blank psychosis or to a lesser degree in states of blankness. The result is a " blank hole " in the mind, which not only acts as an inner void but also has a power of attracting all mental contents or thoughts that are linked with the main topic in the centre of the blank hole. An extremely powerful –K activity, a sort of negative linking, is here in action. Freud had some idea of it when he wrote on Schreber first and on the Wolf Man, to a lesser degree, later on. He substituted "abolition" for "repression" in his text describing the process of refusal of the President. Lacan proposed the concept of foreclosure (for the abolition: *Verwerfung*), making a distinction between the two notions as to their consequences. In abolition the symbolization processes are impaired. There is an agreement among those who have made similar observations: the symbolic function has been damaged indeed, which explains the use of the expression "concrete thinking".

* * *

Is it possible to construct a psychoanalytic theory of thinking while ignoring the writings of philosophy? Probably not. Each psychoanalyst has his own choice of philosophers with whom he finds himself, if not in total agreement, at least in consonance. In any case, quoting from philosophers forces us, as psychoanalysts, to interpret their ideas to match them with our clinical experience. That is to accept the idea that deformation of what they said cannot be avoided. Kant was an important reference for Bion. But contemporary philosophers will probably complain of Bion's misunderstandings, interpreting Kant's conceptions for his own use.

Bion made an important distinction between the "nothing" and the "no thing". This couple is understandable only through the category of the negative. He was the first psychoanalyst to express their differences clearly. For years, psychoanalysts have not been aware of the implicit presence of the negative in psychoanalytic theory, which can be associated with the work of Hegel, among others. The hypothesis of the *un*conscious was adopted by all those who were convinced of the existence of a psychic activity beyond conscious thinking. And because all of Freud's work consisted in the attempt to unveil what was repressed and to give it a positive meaning—that is, an unconscious one becoming conscious by interpretation—all the attention was drawn to the content that was emerging from the unconscious after being interpreted rather than on its specificity as *being* unconscious. The unconscious could only be thought of in its positive form—that is, in the form by which we could perceive its content as a positive thought, wish, desire, fantasy, and so on. But what about its nature while unconscious? Apart from Freud, there were very few people who dared to ask questions about the nature of the unconscious as unconscious. In a circular statement we can say that the possibility to interpret what is unconscious by making it conscious was due to the capacity of the unconscious to be potentially interpretable. Therefore the question is how the interpretability or analysability of the unconscious material is acquired. This was one of Bion's major concerns.

When in 1923 Freud changed his first topographical model into the second, the unconscious was abandoned as a system and replaced by the Id. The main difference between Id and unconscious is that in Freud's thinking there were no representations in the Id. The Id was made of impulses—a concept very close to Bion's beta-elements. He was aware of that. The main difference between Bion and Freud could be that for Freud the drives always had their source in the most inner part of the body, whereas for Bion beta-elements may arise from external stimuli in the primordial mind as well. What is sensuous in them is more their relationship to the primitive body that lacks a thinker than the source of the element. On the whole we can say that the presence of a thinker could be related less to the experience of the "I" as such than to the possibility of representing. In *Cogitations*, Bion tries to enlighten the alpha-function. The alpha-function, as we all know, transforms the raw products of the mind to make them suitable and sensible to interpretation. This is the essential step that is decisive for the condition of analysability. It requires an apparatus to think the thoughts.

What is the main step for this transformation? In order to develop, the mind has to be able to introject and to keep what it has introjected, whether good or bad. Bion is here very close to Freud. I am thinking in particular of Freud's paper on *Negation*. According to him, what is supposed to happen at the beginning of life is the equation between what is bad, what is alien, and what is external. It is only the constitution of the primitive pleasure ego that allows further working through when the objects that provided satisfaction are lost. This is the way Freud explains the passage from the predominance of the judgement of attribution based on the pleasure–unpleasure principle to the judgement of existence— having to decide whether or not something exists, independently of its quality as good or bad. In Bion's model, though he recognizes the inevitability of primitive projective identification, he emphasizes the importance of keeping what has been introjected in order to transform it by elaboration. Otherwise the condition of the beta-elements becomes predominant, and evacuation seems to be the only way. Needless to say, a part of beta-elements, which can only be expelled, remains in fact permanently in the mind but is in a state of exclusion. Knowledge is the combination of alpha- and beta-elements referring to what we know and what we do not know. To keep what has been introjected inside the mind—that is, to be contained in the psychic space as a content for transformation—is our only chance to think and therefore to know, and therefore to know how much we do not know. This important process corresponds to what Freud calls representation. "Thinking possesses the capacity to bring before the mind once more something that has once been perceived, by reproducing it as a presentation without the external object having still to be there." This is not Bion but Freud, in his paper on Negation (1925h, 237). It is obvious that, in order to be able to reproduce internally what has been once perceived from the outside in order to form a presentation, the contents or the perception or its traces in the mind must have been preserved. If this has been accomplished, it is because what has been preserved had to be of some value, or interest, or usefulness to prevent evacuation. For Freud, the first move of the primordial mind was to split between what is good and what is bad and is to be thrown out. Freud opposes here introjection and *ejection* (not projection). If we refer to another couple, incorporation would be opposed to *excorporation* (Green). With this last wording the use of the pattern related to the digestive function is common to Freud and to Bion.

I have proposed a model to conceptualize these processes. If we draw a vertical line between the inside and the outside, we schematize the process of evacuation from within to without and the basis for the differentiation between what is internal and what is external. If we then draw a horizontal line in the middle of inner space, we separate the conscious from the unconscious. We have constructed a model of *the double limit* (between inside and outside, and between conscious and unconscious). With neurotic patients the psychic representations move from the unconscious through the preconscious to the conscious in the first move and are then expressed through verbalization; they are communicated to the other in the outside world. With the psychotic patient it is as if the messages were directly evacuated from the unconscious and projected to the object outside, bypassing the working through that transforms them through the preconscious before their verbalization. In this last case either the language is poor, or it is filled with delusions projected onto the analyst. We can think here of Bion's conception of the bizarre object. In both cases the lack of elaboration corresponds to the failure to think the thoughts because of the thinker's breakdown.

* * *

The concept of representation in Freud is a very complex one. It is usually schematized in the single pair of thing presentation and word presentation. In fact, this abbreviated theory ignores other additional references, which are of importance. Freud's concept of the drive has also to be understood in the frame of a general theory of representation. He (Freud, 1915c, p. 122) defines the drive as "the psychical representative of the stimuli originating from within the organism and reaching the mind" . But after this definition, he adds that the drive is a "measure of the demand made upon the mind for work in consequence of its connection with the body". So we can see that in this "basic assumption" of Freud, or this "definitory hypothesis", there is a dual process: the first is the transformation of the stimuli born in the body and reaching the mind, changing themselves from somatic excitations to psychic representatives; the second is the work imposed on the mind in aiming to change the situation of frustration. We know that the first attempt will result in the hypothesis of hallucinatory wish-fulfilment, which can be related to a thing-presentation of the breast—in fact, a re-presentation. I think that this can be considered as the first achievement of an alpha-function. Further on, the working through will shift from the thing presentation to the word presentation in the adult. In the speechless infant, the cry stands for language. Its status is ambiguous. If it is only a means of evacuating the anxiety raised in the anger of frustration, it is related to beta-elements, but if it is used as a means of communication, helping to establish a relationship with the mother through a message, it can be noted as a tool to notice a constant conjunction arousing the mother's help, which can be the root of an alpha-function. In that last case, the maternal psyche—that is, her capacity for reverie—will be of importance.

But another category is still missing, one that is usually not included in the exposition of Freud's theory of representation. I am speaking here of what Freud calls "representations of reality" (Freud, 1924e). He describes them as "thoughts and judgements which represent reality in the Ego" (Freud, 1924e, p. 185). You will notice here the direct reference to thinking. *We can now conclude that Freud's theory of representation is a spectrum that includes the drive, the psychic representative of the drive, the thing presentation or ideational representative or object presentation, the word presentation, and the representation of reality through thinking.* If we consider the elements that take part in all these processes, the more we progress towards thinking, the less we refer directly to the object or to the senses, and the more we have to achieve a work of abstraction. As Bion suggests, emotional experience—another expression for drive activation—is at the beginning. Emotional experience is the first step towards a thought. At the end of the road, we find thinking. To eliminate emotional experience and to replace it by abstract thinking is usually the work of science and especially mathematics, but in psychoanalysis we have to keep the emotional experience in the mind and to reflect on it, to transform it without evacuating it, to be aware of it, without either being overwhelmed by it or murdering it. So thought cannot be dissociated from pain, suffering, pleasure, ecstasy. Painful affects are difficult to tolerate, just as extremely enjoyable ones are. The French *jouissance* has no equivalent in English, as we know; it may sometimes have a disorganizing quality. Psychoanalysts should be able, as far as possible, to continue to analyse—that is, to think under these circumstances.

When we have dealt with the aspects of representation, we have been confronted with another aspect of negativity. Here the mind is not empty. The patient has something to say, but he finds it difficult to do so. He has thoughts and representations. And if he stays silent, neither he nor the analyst will think that the patient's mind is blank. The analyst knows that the patient represses something, and he can tell the difference between what the patient is experiencing in the session, what the analyst will call resistance, and the other situation, where the patient is in fact experiencing nothingness. So, we are now aware of the necessity of a clearer distinction between these two forms of negativity, which makes all the difference between the "nothing" and the "no thing", between a hole in the mind and an evanescent dream as something embarrassing to tell, which can easily be forgotten. It is not available any longer to the thinker, but it is producing a "penumbra of associations". A psychoanalytical theory of thinking cannot take its point of departure in abstraction or ideas, as is the case in many philosophical systems. The psychoanalytical theory will reach the end in the domain of abstraction, but it has to start from some more raw material. Therefore, Bion starts from beta-elements or sensuous experience. The main problem becomes how to explain the transition from this primordial mind to the mind of the thinker? . . . the acquisition of the apparatus for thinking the thoughts?

The difference between Freud and Bion could be seen in their basic assumptions. Freud's model takes for granted that the child will always be able to build a conception of the breast in hallucinatory wish-fulfilment. The alien, the external, the bad have been expelled, and the purified pleasure ego has achieved its fantasy of a nourishing breast, which is a creation of the mind. It will prove inappropriate, the child having to find other ways of obtaining satisfaction and finally getting what he wants when the mother interprets these signals of unpleasure. Bion starts from a different point of view, wanting to explain the psychotic failure. For him, it is not taken for granted that the hallucinatory wish-fulfilment will take place. It may not happen because of the experience of the threat of annihilation or the baby's fear of dying. The baby cannot get rid so easily of what is bad, which continues to persecute him notwithstanding projective identification. How to get rid of an anxiety that lies in the deepest layers of the primordial mind? Projection is followed by the return of the projected. Therefore the fate of the early experiences and their transformations needs to be explained in a new way. Bion excludes the spontaneous transformation from beta-elements to alpha-elements without the help of the object. It is here that the capacity for reverie of the mother represents the intervention of an adult, mature mind that can be introjected by the child in order to transform his inner destructive experience.

* * *

Bion's conception of the object is quite personal. It is not Freud's, and it is also different from Klein's. Though it may sound abstract, it is in fact more plausible than many others are. For Bion the direct feeding relationship, which relates to the breast, cannot explain the richness of the experience. The mother feeds the infant not only with her milk or her breast; she nourishes him, she daydreams on the child's feelings and "mental" states. And so she enables the child to reintroject his own projections, which are now changed through her. The Furies, the bloodthirsty goddesses who persecute Orestes, after the murder of his mother, are changed, thanks to Athena's persuasion, into the Eumenides, the benevolent goddesses who will protect the city. The mother's capacity for reverie is commanded by empathy and is the essential factor of transformation of the beta-elements to alpha-function. The role of the object in promoting alpha-function is to enable the infant to establish links leading to the awareness of constant conjunctions. I would like to emphasize something that may seem obvious but should be openly stated. The linking function is two-sided. On the one side, it is an intersubjective link—that is, a link between the infant and the mother; but seen from another angle it is an internal link or, more precisely, an intrapsychic one, connecting different elements in order to build a system of signs that can be used by the mind. It is an illusion to imagine that the capacity to think is extended over all the mind: one can be a great mathematician and be still fixated in perverse fantasies, or perverse acting-out to one's mother's breasts, not so much as feeding organs than as erotic ones. I am speaking here from clinical experience. One of the first achievements of the alpha-function is to allow attention and notation, which are supposed to conserve the contents of the emotional experience and to register them. This is the first step towards further transformations. It is clear that this achievement is possible through the mother's care. She pays attention to the baby and notes what happens to him; she feels compassion and understanding, which she expresses to him through her voice and her attitude when the baby is distressed.

Where is the model from which Bion draws his theory? It is not child observation, but clinical experience with regressed adults. What Bion describes is a translation of a good session with an analysable patient. He refers to his own capacity for reverie on the patient during the session leading to an interpretation, which proves effective. He then observes the effect of his interpretation in the modification of the patient's communication and his ability to interpret all by himself what he experiences in the session. Bion's constant concern for the facts is a priority before any attempt at speculation. The first registration is pictographic (an embryonic thing presentation). If this fails, the beta-elements in the form of sensuous experiences are not transformed into visual images (primitive representations), but are felt as "things in themselves".

The thing-in-itself is a concept that Bion borrows from Kant, but its meaning is quite different in this psychoanalytic context. For Bion, the thing in itself refers to "undigested facts", non-symbolized experiences, a little less than psychic events; they are raw-material stuff, improper for psychic elaboration. In my penumbra of association I remembered King Lear. When Lear meets Edgar disguised as a mad-man escaped from Bedlam on the heath, a strange conversation begins between the debased king, the fool, and poor Tom. Poor Tom seems, like Lear, to have lost everything; he stands nude on the heath. Lear says to him: " Thou art the thing itself " (King Lear, 3, 4, 106). This was long before Kant dreamt of these words.

In my review of *Attention and Interpretation* (Green, 1973), I noticed the parallel between Bion's conception of the unknowable object and Freud's ideas about the object as stated in the *Project*. It is not only the object that is unknowable but also the mental space "as a thing of itself unknowable, but that can be represented by thoughts" (Bion, 1970, p. 111). This original state of the unknowable thing in itself meets a final state, the one of the symbol O. Bion writes: " I shall use the sign O to denote that which is the ultimate reality represented by terms such as ultimate reality, absolute truth, the formless, the infinite, the thing in itself" (Bion, 1970, p. 26). All that we know stands in-between these two extremes: the unknowable beginning and end. Speaking of the aim of analysis, Bion will not claim to reach anything beyond approximation. To some extent all knowledge is a loss of absolute truth compared to the formless infinite.

Hence Keats's negative capability: another figure of negativity. Bion advocates an attitude where "a man is capable of being in uncertainties, mysteries, doubts without irritable reaching after fact and reason" (Keats, 1817). Observation shows us that some patients (as well as many analysts) do not tolerate the state of uncertainty, mystery, or doubt. Patients take refuge in evacuation or omniscience; analysts have ready-made answers. I remember how struck Bion was when I quoted Maurice Blanchot's sentence, *"La réponse est le malheur de la question"* [The answer is the misfortune of the question]. He used that phrase many times.

* * *

Among many innovations in Bion's theory, one is of great consequence: the symbol K for Knowledge. Contrary to Freud and to Melanie Klein, Bion decided to defend the existence of knowledge as an independent category, which could not be reduced to the interplay of the two others: love and hate. It was impossible to explain the scientific conquest of the mind with the single development of love and hate as expression of the drives. But it was also impossible to defend the capacity to know independently from them.

Bion's attempt is more interesting than just adding a new axis dealing with knowledge. K symbolizes knowledge, and –K is its opposite. It symbolizes not only ignorance, but also a trend to remain actively in ignorance with the adoption of an attitude in which there is an advantage of avoiding awareness or a disadvantage to approximating to the truth. Again, I find myself meeting Bion's thinking when I have been trying to conceptualize "*The Work of the Negative*".

Evacuation is surely one way of getting rid of noxious excitations. We have already raised the question: how can the mind, the primordial mind, get rid of the state created by frustration? Projection is, of course, a possibility. The object becomes bad and is attacked and thrown away. But the feeling of persecution is felt "inside"—the anxiety, the threat of annihilation are internal. Like Freud, I believe that only a part of it can be projected outside. I also believe that, in the beginning, the object is not separated from the self of the baby, so the persecution is felt as an *internal* persecutor mixed up with the self, because I suppose there is no separation between a persecutory object and a persecuted subject. A French expression says "*persécuté—persécuteur*": that is, "persecuted—persecutor". This leads me to propose an alternative to evacuation. I suggest that the thoughts—because we cannot yet talk of a thinker—the thoughts and their most primitive expression, "pictographs", are destroyed. It maybe that the notion of the pictograph is not adequate. I am here close to some of Winnicott's ideas. I assume that there is some form of presentation, as primitive as can be, that is close to a pictorial image. Instead of having, as a result, an image torn into pieces—the image of the breast, for instance— we have a destruction of the image, a blotting out of it or a fading, which creates a wound in the mind, produces a haemorrhage of the representation, a pain with no image of the wound—just a blank state, as I said, or a hole. Bion mentioned the role of the black holes of the mind, attracting and destroying the thoughts. This could complete the theory of beta-elements as re-enacting the destruction of the capacity to represent. Therefore the preliminary draft of the apparatus to think the thoughts is impaired. The total picture of the situation is either blotted out or leaves remains of fragmented pieces (which will later become bizarre objects), with no bonds to unite them. As Bion says, the psychotic patient has sequences but ignores consequences. Constant conjunctions are lost.

Is there a mechanism by which we can figure out the psychic *action* undertaken? Negative hallucination could be the answer. If we remember that Freud said that "any attempt to explain hallucination would have to start out from *negative* [rather] than positive hallucinations" (Freud, 1917d [1915], p. 232 n. 3), we could have a clue here.

Negative hallucination is not applicable only to perceptions of sensory data. It also applies to the perception of thoughts. Thoughts are perceived when speech activates the memory traces of words. Negative hallucinations can also apply to representations. In these cases representations are not only repressed, they are suppressed—that is, not available any longer for representation in a way different from repression or splitting. Repression keeps the representation as far as possible from consciousness. It is conserved in the mind though out of reach, impossible to awaken to memory but still there. In the case of negative hallucination, the thoughts, some capital thoughts, are lost, because they have been erased; there is no trace of them as ever having existed or of their "underground" performances. Sometimes somatic diseases appear instead of mental symptoms. Could we say that the model of evasion still holds here? We will have to consider two fates of evasion: one is banishment. This corresponds to Bion's model based on an analogy with the digestive tract: elimination outside, evacuation. The other would be burying with no remains, no traces of a corpse. From time to time, the analyst as the archaeologist finds one tooth, one mandible, and reconstructs a whole personality most hypothetically. Our psychoanalytic constructions are myths. It would be of no use to rely on realistic methods. In our age of science we are overwhelmed with oversimplifications.

> The discoveries of psychoanalysis make it no longer possible to be satisfied with the methodology of scientists or philosophers of science even in the refinements of method they have produced to counter their own dissatisfaction. The psychoanalyst is in the curious position of studying a subject that illuminates the most ineradicable source of unscientific enquiry, namely the human mind, using that same mind as his scientific instrument, and having to do so without the comfort of thinking his observations are made by an inanimate machine, that by virtue of being dead, must be objective. But

clearly an inability to be satisfied that the methods of scientists of other disciplines are scientific decreases rather than increases the psychoanalyst's hope to be successful. [Bion, 1992, p. 244]

* * *

We began by opposing two categories in Bion's work: the first one, which led to the building of a scientific deductive system, and the second, closer to science fiction, in the last part of his work. But if we consider the whole of Bion's work as a process of growth, and if we apply to his thinking his own model, what can we learn from the experience of reading him? We are inclined to have a developmental view of his writings, which will help us to grasp the thinking of the author. We can, for instance, label the scattered papers of *Second Thoughts* as representing thoughts without a thinker. I do not mean of course that Bion as a thinker was not already present in these papers. That would be outrageously wrong. During this phase, Bion had written some of his most significant papers, as, for example, "Differentiation of the Psychotic from the Non-Psychotic Personalities", "Attacks on Linking", and, in the end, his paper, "A Theory of Thinking", which is an announcement of what will follow. What I am trying to say is that until *Learning from Experience*, where the aim of constructing a theoretical system is clearly stated, such an enterprise is only possible with the assumption that there is a thinker, a theoretician, an author articulating the different aspects of his findings. This needs a dual movement: prospective, looking at the future in order to achieve the project, and retrospective, trying to link together the scattered explorations of the mind. The following phase then shows a very significant evolution. It can be divided in two subphases. In the first, represented by *Learning from Experience* and *Elements of Psychoanalysis*, Bion's capacity for thinking and linking is at its most admirable. He reaches a degree of clarity that will remain unsurpassed. I suppose that most of the knowledge that we have acquired from thinking was made available through these two books. The second sub-phase is represented in *Transformations* and *Attention and Interpretation*. It is as if, being afraid of falling into the sin of arrogance himself, Bion's self-criticism is the first to raise objections against his findings or to show their limited value.

It is indisputable that his previous work showed the presence of a thinker, and this work says that the thinker was almost necessarily a liar. Of course, Bion did not deliberately falsify his findings, but he became aware that to "publicize" his analytic experience was inevitably to give a false picture of its nature. Usually psychoanalysts content themselves with having succeeded in contributing a small piece of knowledge to an immense continent of ignorance. But Bion was obsessed by the enormous amount of darkness compared to the flash of light of an ephemeral illumination. What he did was to some extent comparable to what Freud did before him when he was confronted with the enigma of the repetition compulsion. In *Beyond the Pleasure Principle* he turned to the biology of micro-organisms. Of course, we understand now that it was because he was unable to find the answers to the questions raised by psychoanalytic practice. In his own way Bion, puzzled by the same kinds of problems, turns to painting, music, poetry, philosophy, theology, and, most of all, geometry. In *Attention and Interpretation* there is a mixture of the old trend to develop the attempt to reach the achievement of a scientific deductive system and the new one, with his references to astronomy, sociology, and the study of mystics. We can see that the further Bion goes in order to approximate the truth, the more he realizes that one model cannot encompass the totality of psychic experience.

So, we can see that there was a long preparatory phase to the *Memoir*. It was less a mutation than an evolution. What can we say about this significant change? Freud discovered psychoanalysis after his early experiences with neurotic patients. He was then no longer satisfied with his early findings, even if his insight was far-seeing. He had the intuition of the unconscious but was too bothered by his preconceived ideas, which came from his consciousness. So he decided to put himself in the place of his patients and to shut himself every night into the world of dreams. When he awoke, he tried to remember his dreams, to note them down, to associate on their contents, and to build a theory in order to *explain* the dream—that is, to translate what came from the unconscious into the language of consciousness. What Freud wanted to do was to master the drives and their unconscious expressions. Bion made a different choice. Having achieved a great deal in order to reach a scientific system of the mind, he considered that it was in fact impossible to tame an inner world in which dinosaurs were still alive. Did not Freud write, on 12 July 1938, a few months before dying: "With neurotics it is as though we were in a prehistoric landscape—for instance in the Jurassic. The great saurians are still running about" (Freud, 1941f [1938])? So, instead of "explaining" the dream thoughts with the language of consciousness, it seems that Bion decided to use the dream to construct artificially the kind of knowledge that only the dream is capable of conveying—hence his idea that no psychoanalytic theory could contain what psychoanalytic experience can teach us. Did the contained make the container explode? If that had happened, we would not be here commenting on his work, but I think we are aware that, as far as our thoughts will travel, it may be assumed that the thinker may not be able to think all the thoughts Bion had.

So, applying Bion's ideas and developing them in a direction that he did not explicitly state, we can come to the conclusion that perhaps no psychoanalytic theory will succeed in building a full and true theory of the mind. The primordial mind may have more than one direction in which to develop. In this, we are discovering the idea of the vertices dear to Bion. After all, what makes the world habitable is its diversity. It is beyond my reach to give a picture of the various possible vicissitudes of the primordial. As far as Bion is concerned, if my hypothesis of two main trends in his work is right, I shall label them differently. The first belongs most probably to science, or perhaps to a philosophy of science; the second, the fiction or even the science fiction, is a form of literature and belongs to art. While visiting China, I was attracted immediately by a very fascinating ideograph. Of course, I was sensitive to its aesthetic impact and was not able to decipher anything about what it said. One could consider it as a work of art, independently of its meaning as a sentence. When I asked what the ideograph meant, I was told that it said something like "It is useless to get angry about unimportant matters". Those who know me know also that this happens frequently to me. Was there a link between my attraction for this calligraphy and its secret meaning for me? I will not dare to suggest it. This brings us to the symbol used by Bion on the most primitive form of representation, the pictograph.

* * *

In Bion's work, one very important point is the result of the work-ing through of the alpha-elements. According to his conception, the "matter of the mind" undergoes a decisive transformation in order to create the stuff of dreams—dreams and myths. Such is the relationship between the Oedipus myth with the emotional infan-tile experience of the Oedipal experience. I would like to end by offering to Bion's memory two myths borrowed from the Vedas. According to the first, the Supreme Genitor is so fond of his daugh-ter, the Goddess Speech, that the gods decide to make a creature in order to prevent incest. They create Rudra, which means the "yeller" or the "howler". This creature is a monster made up of the collection of all the horrible parts belonging to different animals. So only the fear of the monster will be able to stop the Supreme Genitor from an incestuous realization. Here, Freud's expression, the horror of incest, finds its illustration. I shall not let myself go on to interpret this myth but instead will present another one, which also deals with the Goddess Speech, who is so appropriate to our work. This Goddess Speech is a very feminine creature, very at-tractive, who can only be captured if she is sexually possessed. As she is part of the Vedic word, she has an affinity for sacrifice—that is, for its mythological representation in the Veda. This attraction ends with a copulation between Speech and Sacrifice. Were a being to result from this possible conception, this god would be so om-nipotent that he would threaten all the other gods, making their existence useless and superfluous. So they call Indra, the god of war and fighting. He becomes their herald and has the mission of preventing the birth of the eventual new-born. Indra changes him-self into an embryo and insinuates himself in the sexual relationship between the two partners, Speech and Sacrifice. He enters the womb of Speech and takes the place of the eventual child to be conceived. At the birth of the substitute child, Indra, changed into a foetus, will be evacuated, tearing off his mother's womb, and so the unmatchable product of the conception of Speech and Sacrifice will never come to life. The contained has ripped off the container. Could this union of Speech and Sacrifice be the absolute truth that we can never reach? I will leave the question open to avoid the misfortune of an answer.

CHAPTER NINE

Bion's "transformations in 'O'" and the concept of the "transcendent position"

James Grotstein

In the title of this chapter, I suggest that Bion's concept of O transcends Klein's concept of the paranoid–schizoid and depressive positions as well as preceding and succeeding them. I could also have said that it goes beyond not only Freud's pleasure principle but also his and Klein's notions of the death instinct, each of which my thesis renders as signifying mediators of O, thereby making O the ultimate, though unknowable, signified. From another perspective one can think of O as analogous to the "dark matter", that amorphous mass that is hidden in our universe, which thoroughly perfuses it (Tucker & Tucker, 1988). It also summons concepts of pure ontology for psychoanalysis, especially the idea of Ananke[1] (Greek: "Necessity" or "Fate"; Ricoeur, 1970), Lacan's (1966) concept of the Register of the Real, and Peirce's (1931) concept of "brute reality". I believe that the concept of O transforms all existing psychoanalytic theories (e.g. the pleasure principle, the death instinct, and the paranoid–schizoid and de-

---

[1] I am indebted to O. H. D. Blomfield (personal communication, 1995) for this idea and its source in Ricoeur (1970).

pressive positions) into veritable psychoanalytic manic defences against the unknown, unknowable, ineffable, inscrutable, ontological experience of ultimate being, what Bion terms "Absolute Truth, Ultimate Reality". It is beyond words, beyond contemplation, beyond knowing, and it always remains "beyond" in dimensions forever unreachable by man.

Furthermore, I believe that Bion's O interfaces with Heidegger's (1931, 1968) concept of "Being".[2] Although Bion never referred to the works of Lacan, Sartre, or Heidegger, I believe that he was attempting to re-position psychoanalytic thinking away from its ontic (deterministic, scientific) roots and recast it in an ontological perspective. While I shall endeavour to explicate the concept of transcendence to encompass Bion's endeavour, this very term may be misleading if one does not glean that the intrinsic aim of psychoanalysis is to help the analysand transcend the veils of illusion that obtrude between him and the other and between him and his Being-in-itself—his *"Dasein"* as well as his desires. Thus, the seeming "beyondness" of transcendence signifies one's being just beyond the veil of defensiveness on one's way to the unknown that is immediately near, both inside and out. In other words, what we commonly call reality itself is an illusion that disguises the Real (O).

Bion's endeavour

The Bion enterprise constitutes an endeavour to understand how we learn from experience—that is, how we develop a mind that is able to accept, encode, symbolize, "digest", experience, store, remember, and act upon the raw sensory and emotional data of impacting event-stimuli. His approach to this problem was first to impart an epistemological dimension to psychoanalytic inquiry. In so doing he realized that the human individual from infancy on-

---

[2] Heidegger (1968) states: "Every philosophical—that is, thoughtful—doctrine of man's essential nature is *in itself alone* a doctrine of the Being of beings [i.e. what it means for a being to be]. Every doctrine of Being is *in itself alone* a doctrine of man's essential nature" (p. 79).

ward learns bimodally, that is, by the verdict of its sensory organization (empiricism) and by the verdict of *a priori* attributes (rationalism), which Kant called (transcendental) categories and Bion
called inherent preconceptions—and noumena (beta-elements). It
is the quality of rationalism that has always distinguished psychoanalysis from other empirically based phenomenological psychol-
ogies, but the rationalism that inhered in psychoanalysis had always been confined to its positivistic *Zeitgeist* with regard to the
instinctual drives. The question that Bion confronted was *how do
we format the events we confront in order to render (transduce) them into
personal and then objective experiences.* Bion became dissatisfied, I
believe, with the positivistic limitations of Freud's theory of drives
and even of Klein's extension of them as unconscious phantasies.
He was aware that the rationalistic enterprise required *transcendental*[3] (*a priori*) considerations beyond the drives that could account for the uniqueness of how we format our experiences—that
is, prepare a suitable *container* that can anticipate its future contents. In considering these *a priori* categories, he borrowed the
concept of the Ideal Forms from Plato and termed them "inherent
preconceptions", which along with the sensory apparatus (as
"common sense"), container/contained, L, H, and K linkages, and
intuition, became the instruments of apprehending the "psychoanalytic object" and resonating with O (Ultimate Truth, Absolute
Reality).

In his epistemological pilgrimage Bion retraced the philosophical contributions of leading thinkers of the past, including Plato,
Aristotle, Meister Eckart, Hume, and Kant in particular. He also
consulted mathematicians like Poincaré and Georg Cantor. The
point of resorting to mathematics was to arrive at tools for understanding that were unsaturated with preconceived meanings. His
endeavour was to find out what inheres within us that allows us to
grasp, process, and internalize our experiences so that we can
grow from them. Ultimately, he was to come upon "O" and *intuition*, the former being, in the Kantian sense, a *transcendent* entity
and the latter a *transcendental* (a priori) entity which allows us to

---

[3] In a later section I cite the distinction that Kant (1783) proffers in his
Prolegomena about the distinction he makes between *transcendental* and *transcendent*.

divine the beyond from the beyond within us (Bion, 1965, 1970, 1992).

These achievements are hard to overestimate. They constitute an epistemic and ontological metapsychological metatheory that elegantly extends and graces Klein's enterprise and transcends that of Freud. This metatheory, especially with the Truth[4] of emotional experience as its centrepiece, Faith as its all-hovering guardian and presence[5], and O as its realization, introduces not only epistemic and ontological theory into psychoanalysis but also teleology and especially transcendence, as I hope to demonstrate. The focus of my contribution is on the capacity to experience[6] O, the Subject of subjects that, like the conception of God, can never be the object of the senses or of contemplation. The capacity to experience O is the privilege of the ineffable subject of psychoanalysis (Grotstein, in press), the "Man of Achievement". It is my belief that the ineffable subject of psychoanalysis, the unconscious aspect of ourselves that experiences *being* "O", is presented to the patient as what Bion (1963a) terms the "psychoanalytic object", as symptoms, dreams, and free associations, especially in regard to its being the locale of significant *"constant conjunctions"* of elements that, when united together, signify unique meaning.

Through self-abnegation (abandonment of ego), we *become* O[7], according to Bion. In so doing, I shall also propose that "becoming 'O'" represents the achievement, albeit transitory, of what I propose is the *"transcendent position"*, a gradually developing capacity in the individual from infancy (or perhaps even fetaldom) onward

---

[4] I am indebted to Elizabeth de Bianchedi (1993, 1997) for her deep understanding of Bion's ideas on truth, lies, and falsities.

[5] By "presence" I have in mind my concept of the background presence of primary identification (Grotstein, 1978).

[6] At the point where "K" is transformed into O, the verb "experience" transmutes from a transitive verb into a linking verb. My reading of Bion's conception of O is that it is the consummate Subject and never the object.

[7] Though it seems that I have earlier introduced a contradiction when I said that Bion hints that O is the Subject and now I cite him as stating that O is the psychoanalytic "object", I must, with the greatest humility, disagree with Bion on this point. To me, O is never an object. It eludes all verbs except for the linking verb, *"becoming"*.

to be able eventually to tolerate (suffer) and therefore to resonate with 'O', the ultimate realness of anything and everything. This capacity therefore exists before, during, and after and hovers over, surrounds, embraces, is beyond (in every dimension and perspective) the paranoid–schizoid and depressive positions, both of which I believe constitute an emotional and epistemic "ozone layer" or protective lens or filter against the blinding illumination of the Absolute[8], O's *nom de plume*. As mentioned earlier, O is but another name for "Being-in-itself" [*Dasein*]—without disguise and what *Being* purely and meaningfully experiences. It is *aletheia* ["without concealment"] (Heidegger, 1931) as well as impersonal reality.

Caveats

Some caveats are in order before I proceed. First, I use the term "transcendent" or "transcending" as a way of approximating Bion's quintessential episteme, and while it may *seem* to have religious/spiritual/ "mystical" overtones as well as a parallel usage in analytical psychology (Jung, 1916), my usage is confined to the psychoanalytic and epistemological vertices even when applied to mysticism itself. The concept of a transcendent position does not constitute a whimsical journey into lofty, ethereal abandon, nor does it necessarily validate religion, spirituality, or the belief in God, except as the need by humans whereby they attempt to close the maw of the ineffable with an all-encompassing name. It is not in the oeuvre of W. Somerset Maugham's Larry Darrell, who sought "enlightenment" atop the Himalayas in *The Razor's Edge*. In other words, it is not a blissful "autistic enclave". O is one's reality without pretence or distortion. This reality can be a symptom, the pain of viewing beautiful autumn leaves, gazing upon the mystique of the Mona Lisa de la Gioconda, contemplating the horror of Ypres (for Bion), trying to remember Hiroshima, Nagasaki,

---

[8] Here, again, the idea of the Absolute must be "traded in" for something like "*Absoluting*", but this gerund is awkward.

Auschwitz, or Vietnam, or resting comfortably beside one's mate, trying to contemplate the exquisiteness and ineffability of the moment.

Transcendence is the mute "Other" that lies "just beyond, within, and around" where we are. It is the core of our very Being-in-itself. As I shall hypothesize, the mystic or genius is that aspect of us which is potentially able to be at one with transcendence as O—but only after we have "cleared" with P↔S and D. *The mystic, according to Bion, is one who sees things as they really are—through the deception or camouflage of words and symbols.* It is fascinating how the term "mysticism" has acquired such prejudice. The generally feared connotation of "mysticism" has occurred through the projective identification of "mystique" onto it by those who, according to Bion, are afraid of truth and so mystify its clarity.

A reconsideration of Klein's positions in light of the transcendent position

The paranoid–schizoid position, according to this formulation, constitutes a primitive digitalizing mode that reduces the chaotic, infinite, non-linear complexity of O to linear, Manichean good and bad mythic objects, phantasmal chimeras with which we can live in our ever so limited wave-band of perceptual and apperceptual tolerance, until we are ready for the depressive position, in which mode we can further process these elements of thought into *realizations* within the waveband of objectivity. The Kleinian concept of the depressive position has been moored to its provenance in the death instinct, and both P↔S and D remain constitutive of Klein's theory of the *infantile neurosis* (actually, as "psychotic" positions because of the *omnipotence* that characterizes their operations and worldview). With O as the centrepiece of this new metapsychology, P↔S and D can be understood as adaptive (normal) manic and/or depressive defences against the inexorable emergence of O. Furthermore, atavistic prey–predator anxiety becomes sexualized and aggressivized and therefore personalized as categories of autochthonous (springing from the self) subjectivity and agency.

The long and the short of the above reassessment of the positions is as follows: With O as a new consideration, we can now distinguish between *terror* (*dread*) and *persecution* and *guilt*—In other words, between *infantile catastrophe* and the *infantile neurosis* (*psychosis*). P↔S mediates O by primary subjectivization (personalization) whereby nameless O becomes "baptized" with a subjective stamp of "persecutor" and is no longer dread namelessly adrift. The hope that unconsciously subtends both P↔S and D is that chaos (O) *is* organized by a "selected fact" ("strange attractor") that gives it a coherence unto itself before our own alpha function can bestow personal and objective meaning on it. As I have already adumbrated, I believe, and I believe that Bion hinted, the paranoid–schizoid position is not primary; rather, it has been set up as the first operational filter to contain and process the chaos, infinity, randomness, Ananke, brute reality of O, which may also be associated with Fate. The second filter is the depressive position. This concept of "filter" requires more development, and I shall take up that idea later. Theoretical questions and clinical experience tell me that even though mourning, the quintessential capacity that is achieved in the depressive position, is thought never to end, in fact it does and should, notwithstanding the probability that reparations and restorative attempts may normally continue throughout one's lifetime. Wounds heal, and the need to continue mourning past its proper time becomes pathological, as the *Talmud* advises us. In other words, while the *capacity* for mourning becomes the legacy, as a *personality trait*, of having *achieved* the depressive position, the continuation of "mourning" as a *clinical state* would be an indication of the *presence* and *continuation* of as yet unresolved *clinical depressive illness* (melancholia).

This contribution concerns a transcendence that exists before, beyond, during, and following both the paranoid–schizoid *and* the depressive positions. I am merely suggesting that there is a *"beyond" the depressive position*. The same principle applies to the *paranoid–schizoid position*. A position—or shall I say a "positioning"?—of non-linearity hovers over the microcosm of our limited linear *Weltanschauung*. Furthermore, in consideration of P↔S, is it not true that the very name explicates two major defensive functions, "paranoid" (projective identification) and "schizoid" (splitting), which together help the infant re-establish the "puri-fied pleasure ego" (Freud, 1911b, p. 222)? By using the concept of transcendent(-*ing*) position, one is able to interpose a positioning that exists with, before, during, and after the other positions, one that interpenetrates them and conveys the supraordinate theme of transcending: transcending O to get to P↔S, transcending P↔S to get to D, transcending D to get to "O". In other words, it is as if we human individuals must, from the very beginning and with the benignly collusive help of our objects, establish an ongoing and ever varying covenant with Absolute Truth or Ultimate Reality— so as gradually to come to peace with it finally as "O". Its primal name is "emotional turbulence" (Bion, 1962a, 1963a).

Towards the concept of the transcendent position: transcendences

With regard to transcendence, Bion states:

> My object is to show that certain elements in the development of psycho-analysis are not new or peculiar to analysis, but have in fact a history that suggests that they *transcend* barriers of race, time, and discipline, and are inherent in the relation-ship of the mystic to the group. [Bion, 1970, p. 75]

And:

> One result of separation [from the Establishment] is no direct access of the individual to the god with whom he used for-merly to be on familiar terms [as in the Homeric concept of man's relationship to his gods]. But the god has undergone a change as a part of the process of discrimination. The god with whom he was familiar was finite; the god from whom he is now separated is *transcendent* and infinite. [Bion, 1970, pp. 75–76]

As mentioned above, I understand Bion to employ both *transcend-ence* and *transcendentalism* (*a priori*) in his episteme. The former includes his concept of O, whereas the latter includes his concepts of intuition, L, H, and K linkages, container/contained, and inherent preconceptions. His theory of transformations in and from "K" and O represent the epitome of the phenomenon of *transcendence*— perhaps what I might now also call "transcend*ingness*".

Kant's theory of transcendence and transcendentalism

My re-reading of Kant's *Critique of Pure Reason* (1787) suggests to me that Kant's concept of *"a priori"*, including the categories of reasoning, along with the *noumenon* and the thing-in-itself, constituted what he meant by "transcendental" and thus constitute the *deep structures* of the mind. These are the preformed entities that help to format incoming data with categorical anticipations, so the organism should not be surprised. To them I would extend O (the "Real"). Thus, the fundamental nature of the psychoanalytic concept of psychic reality is basically *"transcendental"* insofar as it depends on *a priori* assumptions.[9] By contrast, however, infantile developmental progression, say, from orality to anality, or from the paranoid–schizoid position to the depressive position can be considered *"transcendent"* (my view as well as Jung's [1916]). Kant himself differentiated between *"transcendental"* and *"transcendent"* by arrogating the notion of a priori to the former and speculative expansion beyond reason to the latter—that is, speculations that are as yet unwarranted by logical reasoning. It is at this juncture that my own views (and, by association, Bion's) differ somewhat from Kant's. In his *Prolegomena* (Kant, 1783) he archly responded to a critic of the first edition of his *Critique of Pure Reason* (Kant, 1781).

---

[9] In this regard Freud (1915e) states: "Just as Kant warned us not to overlook the fact that our perceptions are subjectively conditioned and must not be regarded as identical with what is perceived though unknowable, so psychoanalysis warns us not to equate perceptions by means of consciousness with the unconscious mental processes which are their object. Like the physical, the psychical is not necessarily in reality what it appears to us to be" (p. 171). In other words, the internal world is *transcendental*, if not also *transcendent*.

After first quoting an unnamed critic's evaluation of his work, "This work [Kant's][10] is a system of transcendent (or, as he translates it, of higher) Idealism", Kant then states in a footnote:

> By no means *"higher"*. High towers, and metaphysically great men resembling them, round both of which there is commonly much wind, are not for me. My place is the fruitful *bathos*, the bottom-land of experience; and the word transcendental, the meaning of which is so often explained by me but not once grasped by my reviewer . . . does not signify something passing beyond all experience, but something that indeed precedes it *a priori*, but that is intended simply to make cognition of experience possible. If these conceptions overstep experience, their employment is termed transcendent, a word which must be distinguished from transcendental, the later being limited to immanent use, that is, experience. [p. 150–151]

My reconciliation between my views as well as those I assume to be Bion's and Kant's with regard to "transcendent" as "something passing beyond all experience" is that O is not "experienced" per se—that is, as an *object* of experience. O, like the God of Moses in *Exodus* ("I am that I am") is the *subject*, something with which one can only subjectively resonate.

In *Cogitations* Bion entitled a chapter "Reverence and Awe". As soon as I read it, I could not help wondering whether he had me in mind when he discussed the patient who experienced the propensity of reverence towards and awe for an object that could not be apprehended. I believe that reverence, awe, and the aesthetic vertex are yet other manifestations of O. In that regard it should be mentioned that Neil Maizels, an Australian analyst, has, simultaneously with me, found inadequacies with the Kleinian formulation of the depressive position (the issue between "attaining" and "transcending") and independently conceived of the *"spiritual position."* Because of our common interest in the theme, we have decided to embark on a reassessment of the conception of the depressive position.

---

[10] The brackets are mine.

"'O' is a dark spot that must be illuminated by blindness"

Whereas Bion's conception of container/contained represented a needed extension of Kleinian theory into external reality, his conception of O was a sortie into the surreal. Bion broke the procrustean confines that characterized the time-warped logical positivism of Freud and Klein and thrust psychoanalysis into the "deep and formless infinite", O. To his erstwhile flatlander colleagues he had gone over the edge of the known world. What I believe that he in fact had done was to transcend the strictures of our known psychoanalytic *Weltanschauung*, transcend the limitations of the pleasure principle, thrust past the limitations of the death instinct, realizing all the while that they were merely stepping stones, markers, signifiers to, or hieroglyphs of, an ineffable signified, O. The task of each analytic session, if I read Bion correctly, is for the analyst to so discipline him/herself with the suspension of memory, desire, preconceptions, and understanding (suspension of ego) that (s)he becomes all the more intuitively responsive to his/her inner sense receptor that is sensitive to his/her "waveband" of O, which then resonates with the analysand's *psychoanalytic object*,[11] his/her own O, which is characterized by his/her Ultimate Reality, his/her Absolute[12] Truth. Thus, the analyst's O becomes resonant on that ineffable "waveband" with the O of the analysand, which the former must then transduce or transform to him/her in "K" as symbols in the form of interpretation and, if accepted, it becomes re-transformed back into their "O."

---

[11] I am aware that when I stated earlier that "O", like the concept of the deity, is the Subject of subjects and can never be the object and yet cite Bion as equating O with the "psychoanalytic object", I stand in contradiction. My resolution of the dilemma is that Bion here is inconsistent with his own theory of O, the ultimate Subject of Being.

[12] Paradoxically, Bion himself got caught up in his own conceptual trap. By daring to *name* Truth "Absolute" and Reality "Ultimate", he reduced them to name-confinable entities, to verbal conventions that now limit them. I shall say more about this contradiction when I refer to the "apophatic language of unsaying" of the mystics.

O is either Sodom and Gomorrah or harmony and serenity, depending on our ontological disposition. There is a pendulum that inexorably swings between Beauty and Horror. The pendulum's fulcrum is O. With O in place, we realize along with Heidegger that the tongue is the listener to an inner ineffable voice. Words depict but do not encompass Truth. They are a transient reward for the achievement of the depressive position but, like Derrida's erasures, must be barred and erased once we use them so that we can keep our rendezvous with the ineffable, inscrutable, unknowable—that domain where words and their quotidian meanings end and O begins. O—or should I say O-ing?—is paradoxically ineffable but is also immanent and seeks revelation as the psychoanalytic object or, as I should like to put it, as the phenomenal or immanent subject of psychoanalysis, which I associate with Ogden's (1994) "analytic third".

"O", symmetry, and the death instinct

Thanks to Matte Blanco's (1975, 1981, 1988) radical mathematics-based revision of our conception of the unconscious, which is isomorphic to O, we are now able to comprehend a graded, stratified layering to "O." In other words, by his reasoning there is a lack of uniformity in the unconscious, which, along with its quality of infinity and properties of infinite sets, presents itself as chaos or, paradoxically, as "asymmetrical symmetry" or infinity. Matte Blanco postulates that the unconscious is characterized by an infinite number of graded layerings or stratifications of varying descending and ascending "bi-logic structures", which consist of differing proportions of symmetrical logic (infinity) and asymmetrical logic. Side by side with this binary oppositional structure there exists "bivalent logic" (classical or Aristotelian). The mind, according to Matte Blanco, is ultimately dominated by the dialectical interaction of two principal modes, the *homogeneous* (infinity, infinite sets, symmetrical logic) and the *heterogeneous* (divisible, classically logical). The results of this thinking would consequently attribute a picture of O (the unconscious, the psychoanalytic object) as being infinite with varying degrees of asymmetrization of that infinite symmetry, which would characterize an infinite number of sets of infinity itself, and thus *chaos* and/or complexity.

It is conceivable by Matte Blanco's "psycho-mathematical" theorems, consequently, to postulate that the inchoate infant's proto-experience of O is one of Absolute Chaos. When the infant "experiences"—that is, takes in the impact of this first confrontation with Prime, Absolute Otherness (other than the breast)—its very experiencing of it conveys a sense of *agency* and *personal subjectivity* to it. I suggest that primal transformation causes the infant to believe that it has been attacked by its own death instinct,[13] a tropism that it now assesses as belonging to itself. Subjectivity and agency have then begun (Grotstein, 1996, 1997, 1998).

The background of my own thoughts on Bion

What I have just stated represents the barest of bones of Bion's emotional epistemology, as I understand it. The provenance of this contribution rests in part on a series of remarks, stated as interpretations, that Bion often made to me during my analysis with him, including his almost rude dismissal of the idea of "understanding". Once when I used it, he quipped, "Why didn't you say, 'overstand' or 'circumstand'?" The following is reconstructed but representative of my experience with him: "Although your associations point to where the pain seems to be located and allow me access to interpret, both your associations and my interpretations

---

[13] It is now my belief that the death instinct does exist but is not primary. Rather, it is an adaptive attribute of the organism that punitively comes to its rescue when it, the death instinct organization, believes that the organism is in danger. It either sponsors attack against the relationship to objects, which are considered the source of the difficulty, and/or towards the self, suicidally, in order to end one's misery. This probably was the case with the hospitalized children René Spitz discussed in his observations on foundling children in French West Africa. The function of the death instinct can readily be observed in the example of airplane passengers who know they are going to die shortly. Evidence has accumulated that they die emotionally—that is, they go numb—before they die physically.

can do no better than approximate the truth of the pain. That is something that we can never know. It is not to be known, only approached, and then only from a distance." I recall conjuring at the time the image of Marlowe's Samarkand in his *Tamburlaine*, "the always distant, ever receding city on the horizon; one destined never to be reached".

On another occasion I happened to mention Mary, Queen of Scots, upon which Bion made the following comment: "The trouble with Mary, you see, was that she actually thought she *was* the queen rather than trying to *become* one." This point, Platonic in origin, was Bion's signature. "That which is is always becoming", he so frequently reminded me. Thus, "understanding" in "K" was transitory, but a stepping stone for the moment to O, not unlike Derrida's erasures. Bion always emphasized the *transitory* nature of analysis and of life.[14] He was aware of Heraclitus' sage comment that we can never swim in the same river twice. Even terms such as "Ultimate Reality" and "Absolute Truth" are casualties, as I alluded earlier. The apophatic language of the "saying/unsaying" of the mystics has been the only way thus far of addressing this issue (Webb & Sells, 1997). O, however, so constructed by Bion as to represent infinite nothingness—always becoming more and more nothing—seems to qualify as the quintessential container.

At other times I received glimpses of ideas that reminded me later of the *dialogics* of Bahktin. I was reminded of this when I read Bion's trilogy, *A Memoir of the Future* (1991), in which different conversations were conducted by seemingly separate personalities within a single self. What was so unique about this phenomenon was that, in my own case as well as in Bion's in his trilogy, the different "personalities" were readily identifiable as me rather than being encoded in terms of somewhat alien internal objects.

There is yet another memory of my analysis that has a bearing on the topic of this presentation, that of the thing-in-itself or

---

[14] Dr. José Américo Junqueira de Mattos (1997) has kindly given me a preview of his Conference presentation, "Transference and Counter-Transference as Transience", the theme of which seems to *me* to support my thesis on transcendence and O as well as proffering the concept of teleology, with which I am also in agreement.

noumenon, each of which Bion seemed to have equated with the other and with his concept of beta-elements, to the distress of some Kantian scholars. I recall an analytic session when I remembered an episode from my medical internship. An ex-girl-friend suddenly contacted me unexpectedly and told me that she was flying to San Francisco but would be making a brief stopover at Chicago airport (I was interning in Chicago at the time). We saw each other briefly. I recall being very unemotional about the encounter. Later, when I saw her plane take off towards the west, I experienced a series of uncanny visualizations. First, the image of the aeroplane seemed to darken into a shadowy form. Then it was transformed into the image of a huge raven, and I even imagined that I saw the wings flapping. Next, it became even more eerie, perhaps mechanical, but unlike an aeroplane. Every time I subsequently read Kant or authors who cited Kant, the memory of that uncanny episode returned to me.[15] Finally, when I introduced this into analysis with Bion, he helped me to understand it as a return of the memory of a very early significant loss that had occurred in the first few months of my life, but he employed such terms as "thing-in-itself", "beta-element", and "noumenon" in his analysis of my experience. Thus, if I err in my Kantian scholarship, I feel that I am in very good company indeed.

An "imaginative conjecture" on Bion's personal relationship to "O"

Bion, the intrepid explorer of "the deep and formless infinite", seems to have navigated by consulting the "stars of darkness". He arrived at this new concept of transformation *and* evolution in O,

---

[15] I was also aware of the potentially psychotic nature of the episode and was reminded of it when I read Freud (1911b) on the subject of decathexis in the Schreber case. In that case decathexis of objects resulted in a decathexis of *word* presentations and a resulting hypercathexis of *thing* presentations. For me in that very brief moment the plane had become a personified "thing".

first by intuiting the existence (presence) of the absent breast, the "no-thing", in the clinical situation. He may also have arrived at it from having experienced the terrors and traumas of his own life, according to Meg Harris Williams (1985).[16] When we read in his autobiography that he " . . . died on the Amiens–Roye Road on August 8, 1917", we get a haunting piece of subjective archive that informs us with graphic certainty that he had been baptised into, and thus had become, an "orphan of O" of "the Real", and had been certified in the experience of "nameless dread" (Bion, 1982). Who could be more qualified to be our guide in that indescribable domain, the very existence of which most of us are privileged never even to have suspected. With regard to those experiences, one wonders whether in his few but trenchant critiques of Klein, his analyst, in his autobiography he was not suggesting that Klein effectively analysed the envy, greed, and omnipotence of the puta-tively surviving Bion (i.e. she helped him to evolve from P↔S to D), but she may have neglected the "dead" one, the one who was amberized on the holocaustal side of O. Bion, who had been nomi-nated in the field for the Victoria Cross and had received the DSO, always maintained that he was a "coward". This paradox is under-standable if we think of him as having suffered from what we now prosaically term a "post-traumatic stress disorder", in which he may have believed that he had surrendered to the darkness of dread. His autobiography and metapsychology may constitute desperate "radio signals" from an "undead"/"dead" self who is struggling to be heard—from the other side. When he spoke of "making the best of a bad job", we perhaps begin to realize that, in his attempted rehabilitation from that ultimate trauma, he was trying to put his agony, surrender, and reconciliation to optimum use—to experience hope under the foreboding shadow of intimi-dating dread and demonstrate how to use our sublimated agony as an analytic instrument.

---

[16] See also Meltzer (1978, 1980, 1985) and the Symingtons (1996) for their readings of Bion's *Memoir of the Future* (1975, 1977b, 1979b).

CHAPTER TEN

Thinking aloud about technique

Isabel Luzuriaga

T he title of this chapter is "Thinking aloud about technique". Its contents try to be exactly what it says. When I learned that this conference was going to take place, I just sat down and wrote what came into my mind, as if indeed thinking aloud. I did not consult any bibliography; I did not try to cite quotations; I did not try to learn better what I already knew about Bion's work; and I did not use the words he uses when describing his concepts, but, rather, my "everyday" way of expressing them. I just wrote. And only later did I realize that my intention had been not only to pay tribute to his memory, but also to satisfy a private need of my own to communicate with him in personal homage. You can then, perhaps, understand my enormous surprise and fright when, months later, I was told that this private dialogue of mine had been chosen to be read in public. Then, perhaps in order to become a bit more relaxed, I tried to think that perhaps the working method I had used might somehow have been the one he would have wanted me to use, by just describing the *emotional experience* of this dialogue taking place between me and the *Dr. Bion I have in my inner self*, as a private inner object of my own personality. Had I then perhaps, even in a modest way, approached that enormous effort he expects us to make in our analytical technique, when he asks us to work "without memory and desire"?

I was not, of course, completely comfortable with this optimistic thought. But I *did* make use of all my courage and just went on writing, realizing, as I did, that mostly I kept on asking questions but did not offer answers. For me, this was perhaps the best thing to do because, again with Bion in mind, I do not believe that psychoanalytical technique can be discussed by way of definitions or generalizations, as nothing that happens in one session is ever repeated in any other. The only statement I could now make, in fact, would be that, after Bion, technique has become much more difficult than it was before he came into existence as the psychoanalytical genius he was. We *should* add, of course, that psychoanalytical practice has also become much richer, more thrilling, and perhaps more useful to our patients, which is what really counts. So I thought that the best thing to do would be to limit myself to making a list of a few of the technical problems that seem to me the most difficult and that are due to the advances Bion has made in understanding human beings, both "normal" and in their most pathological states:

1. How should we define, after Bion, what, as Kleinians, we first called a "good object" and a "bad object"?

2. The primitive definition of the "good object" is the one who loves, while the "bad" one is the one who hates or is absent (taking into account, of course, all distortions made on them by the projective mechanisms that Klein herself so richly described). But, is this enough to explain *completely* what could really be called today a "good" or a "bad" object?

3. Perhaps this concept has become a more complex one now, on account of Bion's investigations being carried on in greater depth than before and with more severely ill patients. To this we could add having in mind the concept that *could* be considered one of its most important functions: that of acting as the *container of a content.*

4. If this is so, does this function the patient requires of us affect *our own capacity to know and to think*?

5. In what mental and emotional state of mind are we left after having used this enriched knowledge in our daily practice—for instance, when we also take into account Bion's view that, even in the worst kind of massive evacuation of the patient's mental contents there may exist not only a wish to destroy all kinds of self-knowledge, but also, and in total opposition to this, some degree of the desire to know, which can only find this very primitive and pathological way of expression?

6. Can we really be the containers of such a dreadful mixture of violence, despair, and hope without it destroying our capacity to think clearly?

7. What technical weapons do we have to make use of, in order to be able to discover and to retain even the *smallest* sign of the patient's wish to live, and to hold on to it before he manages to get rid of it in his indiscriminate evacuation?

8. If we make use of our countertransference to help us, and by doing so move away from what Klein advised us to do, do we stop being "Kleinians"?

9. Also, if we make use of this difficult method of investigation, how can we discriminate not only *how*, but also *when* and *what* to try to reintroject into the patient of what we *feel* he has projected into us before? And also, can we do this without running the risk of making a serious mistake by confusing our own emotions with his?

10. Should we then, perhaps, come back again to Klein for help by re-reading the sessions she described when working with very small children? This would give us the opportunity to have before our eyes, ears, and the rest of our *sensorial perceptive apparatus* some knowledge that we may *add* to our psychic empathy and countertransference feelings. Could this reassure us about the way we are working by getting us nearer to the more concrete and primitive form of expression children use in their symbolic play with toys?

In Point 4, there is a passing remark about the possibility of Bion's findings affecting or altering not only the technique used externally for the formulation of interpretations, but also the internal

"technique" with which we *usually think or feel ourselves.* In many of
us, a certain modification has certainly taken place, sometimes to
the extent of altering our mental systems at a structural level. As
far as I myself am concerned, I know that since knowing Bion, both
through his work and personally, I have not been the same person
I was before, either as an analyst or as an individual. I believe that
many of us have this feeling. He has, for instance, made us *more
aware* of the constant relativity of all knowledge, including, in the
first place, psychoanalytical knowledge, as well as of having to
bear the certainty that we will fail many times in our task, while, at
the same time, having to be able to keep alive the desire to go on
investigating. And also, although both he and Melanie Klein agree
on the notion that both life and death instincts affect us constantly,
I think only Bion has managed to make us have the *emotional
experience of them* and of their effect on us when they are acting on
us. Klein's enormous contribution to psychoanalysis when she discovered the intricate way in which the projective mechanisms
work when used as defences against self-knowledge holds a very
important place in today's investigations, and Bion's theories are
to a great extent based on them. But, as I said, I believe only he has
asked us to *live them emotionally* by using them in a technique that
is based to a great extent on his theory of *"container and contained"*.

He tells us how important it is to allow oneself to be *penetrated*
by what has been projected into us, taking well into account, however disturbing this may be, that keeping these emotions inside us
without "theoretical memory" may allow the patient later on to
make contact with them himself. He tries to make us understand
how, *during that period of time in which we act as containers,* we have
the *unique* opportunity to live, *along with the patient,* the *attack* he is
making on the contact he may previously have made with himself
and with us *and,* at the same time, the *defence* that even the smallest
part of his identity may be making in favour of such a contact,
because he also wants to live. The level on which the patient is
moving then may be very primitive, and perhaps also very pathological; but this modality of behaviour is still alive and functioning
inside him. It may even represent the most harmful quality of his
identity and his illness, not only because of the distortion *he* can
then make of the perception of both his internal and external
worlds, but also because of the distorted view he also produces *of*

himself (about his own self) in *others*. This can lead us perhaps to make a wrong evaluation of the state he is in, or of elements of his identity that we may not be able to recognize, but which may be of extreme value both to him and to our task.

This is because, as Bion says, even in states of confusional and massive expulsion of parts of the patient and of his inner objects, with some luck there *may* be one part of him, however small, that does not feel so utterly desperate. This may permit him to hope, even if it is only for a very short period of time, that these contents, that *he himself* can only expel, may be picked up by some kind of container (which we ourselves would call an analyst) that *is* able and *willing* to take them into himself and to hold them there for him for as long as necessary, until he himself feels able to take over. We could remember here, as an example of technique, the extraordinary capacity of Bion's when, in treating psychotic patients, he was able to remember, assemble, and give meaning to bits of material from sessions that had taken place years before *but came alive in the present*. These were composed of small bits of whole objects or of the identity of his patient, that had been mutilated, split, and spread apart in time as well as in space, or, conversely, condensed into a single word, and that now he could put back *together* or *spread out*, as the case might be. (But *can* anyone but he do this again, I wonder?)

All of which brings us to the next problem: *for how long can we,* or *should we,* perform this function of container in a treatment?

Going back to Points 1 and 2 of our initial list: the "good" and the "bad" object, taken in relation with what we are dealing with now, could perhaps be called the *"adequate"* or *"inadequate"* objects. This stresses the importance of the analyst's being capable or not of playing an adequate role for the patient, *with* him or *instead* of him, as the case might be. Adequate would then consist not only of loving him and the task he is performing with him (analysing him), but also becoming the mother–analyst who can bear to be *seen* and *treated* as *bad* and, by so doing, allowing the child–patient to put into her, for as long as he may need, whatever part he himself cannot bear, and which could also be his capacity to love, because love is what makes him suffer, so that the "good *loving* object" may have become for him a *"bad"* one, and he cannot take it in.

This, of course, does not mean that the analyst should act out the role appointed to him. But from an emotional point of view, the *apparently passive part* the analyst is asked to play may cost him an enormous emotional effort because of the *quality* of the contents he has to hold. Being a good *analyst* would then entail being able to *think clearly* while bearing the commotion caused in him by the impact of the contents he is receiving, which could be producing in him a pain as difficult to endure as that from which the patient may be trying to escape.

The defences erected against such difficult countertransference feelings can sometimes be recognized consciously. But at times it is difficult not to fall into making an appeasing interpretation or using an analytical theory in a hurry in order to cancel the emotions stirred both in the analyst and in the "atmosphere" of the consulting-room. If the analyst did this, he would perhaps burden the patient with his own anxiety. The "inadequate" analyst would then become yet another edition of the first historical object of the patient's life, thus becoming a *real* bad object.

Another defence against holding countertransference feelings can also be hiding behind a silence not adequate to the situation, and rationalizing perhaps this acting-out with the argument that the catharsis of the emotions thrown into him is the only thing that *can* be done, or is the only thing the patient needs.

Which leads us now, as I said before, to the problem of deciding for *how long* we should function *only* as containers. *When* and *how* should we "give up" being the "*passive good object*" he wants us to be and become the "*real good professional*" whose task is mainly to interpret and thus re-introject the material projected into him before? As I said, this, for me at least, constitutes one of the more difficult problems to solve. If the patient is not yet able to become aware of some part of his own identity, he may feel that we have suddenly become someone or something quite different from what we were before, and who now, instead of understanding him, criticizes, rejects, or persecutes him. If, on the other hand, we take too long in centring the contents of the interpretations on the patient himself instead of on what he *experiences* us to be when we act only as containers, we may, with a greater or lesser consciousness of it, become accomplices to the more regressive or ill parts of himself, keeping up a "pseudo-analysis" in which nothing is really happening, and also leaving aside his healthier part. We would then free him from the suffering that is inevitably produced in the growing-up process and from which he originally ran away, turning instead into some kind of a pathological defence. But we would also be abandoning his healthier part, which is the one that came to us for help. For if it *is* true that he came asking for a place into which he could expel what he could not tolerate, if he is still coming to his sessions, he is also asking for these contents and parts of himself to be placed *within his reach*. Something in him may have changed and allows him to know, as Dr. John Steiner would perhaps say, that the price he is paying for being caught in what he calls a "pathological defensive organization" is too high, costs him now more pain than he was aware of before, and is narrowing or destroying more and more of his psychic abilities.

Being then a real "good object", *even to him*, might then consist, at a given point, of knowing *when* to increase or modify the *number* and *quality* of the interpretations, in order to help the patient endure the confusion that re-introjection also produces, which is the same as making him more able to come closer to the depressive position. We would then make interpretations more centred on him than on ourselves, who, up to now, have mostly been used as a provisional place of storage.

As Bion has shown us, psychical change and growth can become something experienced as catastrophic for the patient, and re-introjecting too soon can increase this feeling. But even when this error does not produce the exaggerated results it has in psychotics, even *small modifications* of our interpretative technique may produce some kind of shock that may have unfavourable effects on the analytical process.

I am not talking, of course, about making drastic technical changes arbitrarily. Some modifications have been taking place all the time from the very beginning of each analysis, caused by the experience of each session and a growing knowledge of our patient. We also know that it is always he who opens the door to the kind of interpretations we may use each day, although he may want to close it immediately afterwards. But if it may be true that the *rhythm* and *quality* of our interpretative work may have changed, perhaps because the total transference neurosis may be beginning to set in within our reach, it must also be because we may think that the patient has also changed sufficiently for us to make more contact with him, so that he may not need to evacuate or project so much.

However, it is sometimes impressive to see the way some patients experience this new line of interpretation for the first time, even though we may have been working with an adequate dose of intuition and empathy before. At times not even *we* may be able to realize soon enough that we are getting in touch with them more deeply, or in some other way differently from the way we did before. Theoretically, we know that sometimes we may feel that we should "let pass" interpretations of contents we think we recognize, but that the patient may not yet be able to deal with. On other occasions we *do dare* to make them, taking well into account, of course, the reaction to them. But in some analyses it is at times striking to see the way a patient realizes this "change", as if it were something that had happened suddenly. This he may experience with relief and gratitude because the "modification", although it may cause him some kind of displeasure, also conveys the "good news" that he is moving forward. Simultaneously, it may also cause him fear and the wish to "run away from it all" because the modifications taking place both in him and in the analyst spoil for him the "advantages" offered by his illness.

Regarding Points 4 and 5: in discussions with colleagues I have sometimes found that "being a Kleinian" is a difficult task, and that declaring oneself to be a follower of Bion's ideas is even more so. Some of the comments I have heard were loaded with an emotional content so out of proportion to the arguments used, that they led me to think that we were not involved in a scientific discussion but facing an emotional problem. But perhaps it would be *fair play* and helpful to think seriously of the risks we really *do* run if we become "too Kleinian" or "too Bionian". To be sure, being "*too much*" of anything means having turned ideas into dogma that leaves no door open to further investigation, and it was Bion himself who, after a lecture, advised us to forget all the hypotheses he had just made. Only thus could we, he said, have access to a scientific way of thinking that—I may now add—is as difficult to maintain as it is to place ourselves in the depressive position all the time. The temptation to fall into dogma is always there, and we run the risk, like our patients, of not being able to bear seeing the very many points of view of a single situation (vertices) that Bion asks us to bear in mind. The result is that we may be tempted to come back to a single one, falling again into the paranoid–schizoid position. Again following Bion's ideas, we also have to try to tolerate being aware of the constant influence that the death instinct has on us by attacking, for instance, our ability to learn from experience. But we must also bear in mind that at times, in wanting to discover in our patients these hostile forces that could become of extreme violence if not dealt with soon enough, we ourselves may fall into a defence of a paranoid "texture" (that we may want to call being on the "lookout" for the negative transference), by thinking that *all* negative reaction, which may really be our own, is due to feelings the patient has *induced* in us. *This* could be "too much", and by doing it we could be, unconsciously, trying not to admit that we ourselves, like the patient, can be cruel, destructive, and vengeful to a degree that may frighten us.

On the other hand, we could also fall into a state of mind resembling that of a melancholic patient by saying that *all* that goes wrong with the session is *only* due to our bad method of working, and thus denying the seriousness and the intelligence with which the patient may *really* be attacking us, the treatment, and the state of mind we need to be in in order to work.

It is also difficult to know how to handle technically the knowledge that the patient is always functioning on several levels of evolution, or with two psychic qualities, a neurotic and a psychotic one, as Bion tells us. Being "too Bionian" in this case could perhaps lead us to pay too much attention to the attacks the patient may be directing against his own perceptive system and thus not giving enough importance to the more *neurotic* part of himself, which has aims other than to destroy *all* possibility of knowledge, as the schizophrenic tries to do. What can we do then with this infinite variety of possibilities in order to work well? The theoretical answer may be to make use of our countertransference feelings. But even though Bion himself has repeatedly told us that this is a risky path to take, he has nevertheless by taking it himself invited us also to take it. Perhaps, by taking so much into account, he is asking too much of our identities as psychoanalysts. But I also believe that, by being encouraged to take these risky paths of investigation and to make more use of our capacities to think and feel, we may, with some luck, be more able to see and understand both details and whole patterns of mental behaviour. It may also enable us to be more understanding, compassionate, and tolerant at times when we can do no more than wait for things to happen in order to learn about them.

And so on.

So, thank you for your efforts, Dr Bion.

CHAPTER ELEVEN

A dreamlike vision

Alberto Meotti

Is it possible to use dreamlike visual images in order to imagine in the present the interpretation of past events (real or imaginary) that a future historian will give in years to come? Recently, some historians have looked back and given an interpretation of the psychoanalytic controversies of 1943 between Anna Freud and Melanie Klein. Instead, what Bion proposes in the Trilogy is a sort of dream full of images, a kind of manifest content that could be the anticipation of a latent controversy that might involve in the future the collapse of a substantial part of the present knowledge and the development of new psychoanalytic theories.

Bion's Trilogy, entitled *A Memoir of the Future* (1991), was written in California in the 1970s. In terms of structure, it is modelled on the three cantos of Dante and Milton (Bléandonu, 1990), while its literary style is inspired by the example of James Joyce and Ezra Pound. It is a rich fresco containing the most varied assortment of scenes, events, relationships, discourses, dialogues, and thoughts, all expressed in a form deliberately lacking in order, as if Bion were trying to represent the dream or the mind of a researcher absorbed in the earliest stage of one of science's revolutionary phases.

As a dream interwoven with images, the Trilogy is open to an infinite number of interpretations and may even be seen as the description of the hard work of an individual or of a group involved in a transition that brings advancement of knowledge with it, and therefore greater opportunities to operate and intervene in areas hitherto inaccessible to human activity.

Bion seems to want the most innovative elements of the group to be equated with the servants of Hegel's *Phenomenology of Spirit*, who labour obscurely in the attempt to humanize, to make accessible to human intervention, those aspects of nature and matter still ruled by the mechanistic processes with all their violence and brutality, and return them to the sphere of the teleology of human activity. Thus, for example, the mechanistic nature of illness can be overcome by the advancement of knowledge and of therapeutic techniques.

The first volume of the Trilogy can be seen as a description anticipating a revolutionary period, which brings about the inversion of the master–servant relationship in psychoanalysis. Going beyond this metaphor, Bion is perhaps trying to represent a period in which the old theories are being replaced by new ones. The premonitory power of the dream (or quasi-dream) corresponds to a long-established idea of Bion's: when a transformation takes place, a person may not necessarily be conscious of it, but it may be anticipated in a dream in the form of visual images. This may happen in a waking state too, if the mind is sufficiently free of intentions or memories.

If, as Bion proposes, psychoanalysis is before all else the exercise of compassion towards the human mind, and not only a theory, then the advancement of knowledge, though it may have catastrophic consequences for the present, can still provide us with opportunities to further alleviate the pain caused by mental suffering. The ultimate aim of a revolutionary movement like the one represented by Freud's theories is to free more of those parts of the human mind enslaved by illness, while illness reigns supreme where the advancement of knowledge is delayed and the old theories manage to impede the progress of more efficient new theories.

The contrast between old and new theories can be represented very appropriately in terms of the clash between masters (the old theories) and the servants (the quest of new theories with its usual chaos).

Perhaps *A Memoir of the Future* indicates as well that without contrasts and subsequent readjustments that can produce a more far-reaching theory than Freud's and Bion's (Meotti, 1981), psychoanalysis is bound to go into a decline. This decline will be of the same nature as that affecting philosophical thinking when it degenerates into empty repetition.

According to *A Memoir of the Future*, discussing and working on existing theories in a revolutionary way leads to boredom coming from what is well known and to thinking of something new. Sleeping, dreaming, swerving attention, interruptions, all this is the stuff of research. *A Memoir of the Future* is full of yawns, indifference, or distrust with regard to culture, learning, and the holy shrines of acquired knowledge. Whoever turns their attention towards change may have to get bored, may simply not know or remember, or feel sleepy, just as Rosemary, the protagonist of *A Memoir of the Future*, often feels sleepy or yawns or goes to bed; she is the daughter of a prostitute and has never read Tolstoy because her mother has told her it is a waste of time.

Freud too described himself on occasions as poor, shabby, and not belonging to the establishment. Think of his beginnings in research, of his relationship with Vienna's academic establishment. Think of the elegant contempt of De Ruggiero and Flora, of the criticisms of Benedetto Croce, of the hostility of the medical establishment. Freud was considered the servant–intruder who dealt with drugs, sex, faeces, urine, castration, patricide, incest, and so on. And Bion too feels himself to be a disturbing factor: he is dealing with unrecognizable fragments of thought that emerge from a mind that cannot contain them and bury themselves in material things, making them strange and persecutory.

So what is the new material to be introduced into psychoanalysis? Who is making (or has already made) the effort to introduce a new realm of the mind into psychoanalysis with the aim of making the mind itself more tractable? An example of new subjects might be the concrete traces of individuals and generations belonging to a distant past who are present in the mind of the analysand now facing his analyst and expecting to be helped to free himself from repetitions and destinies not his own.

A Memoir of the Future depicts a more complicated situation than that of the servant threatening to kill his master or of the mystic terrified by the lack of followers. There is a whole series of intermediary figures and roles, which contribute to expanding and renewing a discipline, like psychoanalysis. As we know, research moves along the lines and columns of the Grid and the anti-Grid. Dream, attention, inquiry, research, change may move in both directions: progression and regression lead to change or to its opposite, repetitive stiffness. Maturation and evolution are opposed to crisis, decadence, and decline; "male" and "female" elements, "servile" and "aristocratic" ones combine to create new situations that are either fragments of new theories or repetitions indicating interruptions of vital movements.

We can use *A Memoir of the Future* in order to see that the preparation of new theories requires occupations, invasions, appropriations, betrayals, brutality, and the spilling of blood both aristocratic and plebeian. "The 'future' was in fact at hand this very night, as Rosemary played sensuously with Roland in Alice's bed" (Bion, 1975, p. 25). Roland and Alice are two members of the land-owning aristocracy, while Rosemary and Tom are their servants. The aristocracy is on the verge of decline, and the old system of master–servant relationships begins to break down, one might almost say naturally, under the strain.

So new blood will be brought in, and there will be oppression and turbulence. Only later will dialogue slowly begin to prevail over violent action, and research begin to move tentatively towards new theoretical configurations.

What could be added in the form of new material to widen the sphere of intervention and renew a praxis, which is perhaps old and inadequate? In Bion's view, the new material has to be outrageous: even the Bible can be considered as a book of dirty stories (Bion & Bion, 1981, p. 14). The alternative is the "salon" where you take delight in received theories mistakenly seen as being eternal, accompanied by the anxious wait for the longed-for confirmation inevitably found in the clinical material. Outside, the rabble is already stirring in a kind of dark *Untergang des Abendlandes*.

Bion says that the rabble and the aliens will seize power in psychoanalysis. The question is whether they will stay the same or become the new aristocracy by appropriate intermingling with what is left of the old aristocracy. Consciously or not, Bion is going back to the story of the founder of psychoanalysis himself. Like Freud, "Man" is the *invader*, a marauding barbarian, and at the same time a dark being who opens up to what is new. He will ask Rosemary to marry him: both will give themselves over to violence and murder, but they are also smart dialecticians, who seem actually to guide at times both the priest and the psychoanalyst. Then there is another invasion of impersonal aggressive parts (psychotic fragments), bullets that frighten, subdue, depersonalize, and humiliate. The violence of the new rule imposed by the invaders recalls the violence of the old regime.

Towards the end of the first book of the Trilogy, after the more tumultuous, chaotic phase of simple collection of data, Bion seems to enter the more serene phase of attention and inquiry, in which the past begins to resurface and be transfigured. The second and third books contain classic dialogues on religion, philosophy, theology, psychoanalysis, society, and history. A series of characters continues to appear in the text, representing the complexity of the new group structure in the individual mind.

ALICE   Surely it should be possible to discuss reasonably.

BION   It is also possible—as we have reason to know—to resort to arms. The disastrous meeting I have been imagining as taking place between a potentially gifted foetal mind and its divorced but equally gifted post-natal self, also occurs when two or more groups of individuals meet. The history of the relationship between French and English, German and British, and now Black and White races looks likely to end in mutual annihilation, not mutual beneficent stimulation.

ROLAND   What is the ground for disagreement—colour? sex? prosperity?

ROBIN   Father and son? Guardian and ward? Exploiter and exploitee? Mother and daughter?

P.A.   The possibilities are endless. ... Detailed psychoanalytic scrutiny reveals movements, up and down, of the individual particles composing a group; . . . [Bion, 1979b, p. 116]

In the third book, the conflict can actually exist also between the premature and post-mature parts present in the same body. Thus the usual discussions about god, religion, and so on, are not only related to the incessant *bellum omnium contra omnes*, but also involve the individual's war against himself. God and religion are an expression of that necessary repentance for the unlimited exercise of cruelty, and a turning towards the exercise of compassion towards oneself and towards others, others who are felt to be compassionate in turn towards themselves and others (Bion, 1992, p. 125).

However, by a process of projection that would seem Feuerbachian in nature, the capacity to protect oneself and others (together with the belief that others are shepherds too in just the same way) can be lost because of projections and be shifted outside man onto god: lost in god. In a similar way, all-consuming cruelty is shifted onto god as well (Bion, 1979b, p. 87).

Perhaps for this reason, the second and third books are also devoted to replacing this capacity for love and protection in man and groups. This recovery is strongly needed after the ferocity of the previous revolutionary movement, the cruelty of which may be temporarily mitigated through psychoanalysis.

A clear sign of the compassion that, according to Bion, is characteristic of psychoanalysis is to be found in the following passage (Bion, 1979b, p. 97): "Mental pain is regarded, even today, as a fuss about nothing. *Theories* are discussed—rarely the pain the sufferer inflicts or embodies." There follows a description of the suffering of a German prisoner-of-war and of the contempt for the soldier's suffering expressed by a German naval officer, who uses words instead of guns as weapons against the English too. Something similar happens when language is used to express hatred for psychoanalysis and a desire to attack it.

> I think it is erroneous to assume that because there is a past that seems to bear a certain resemblance to the present, the present therefore bears a resemblance to the future, which can be described in terms of the past. I can perfectly well see that

there may be a crisis of development in which the human being is absolutely terrified by the fact that the future is unknown, cannot be known by himself at the present time, and may only be known to certain people, described in terms of "genius" or "mystic", who have a peculiar relationship with reality. It is possible that the human being is indeed doomed to extinction because he is incapable of further development; some quite different species may be required to go on from the point that has been reached so far by the human animal, in the way that saurians were replaced by the mammalians. However feeble embryonic mammals may have been, they were nevertheless superior to the saurians. [Bion, 1992, p. 373]

Here Bion seems to be rejecting the principle of induction and the inductive postulate of the regularity of the universe (Meotti, 1978): after a series of expansions and contractions of love and hatred, the evolutionary cycle of the human race might come to an end, and it could be replaced by something else or simply disappear. Psychoanalysis could be a religious or an ecological phenomenon, one of the manifestations of the attempts to prolong the existence of the human species by limiting the exercise of cruelty. Psychoanalysis is on a similar level to art and poetry, which reinforce the cohesion of the human being by representing its underlying structure.

But Bion hints that psychoanalysis might be a more temporary phenomenon than either art or poetry: in other words, as has happened to other products of the human intellect, it might disappear without anyone ever mentioning it or remembering it. Indeed, Hume remarked centuries ago that mathematics and geometry are expressions of the human intellect, which seem destined to last longer than others do.

What might the general meaning of *A Memoir of the Future* be? One of the meanings closest to Bion's thinking might be that there are areas of intense suffering in the most enslaved, subjected part of the human mind (as well as of the human race), and that these areas, so threatening to the survival of the species, have still not been reached by the instruments of psychoanalysis. These areas of unbearable pain and suffering are capable of triggering destructive processes on a very large scale, and some of these may be those same destructive processes that can be witnessed every day.

In a similar way to Freud and Einstein in *Why War?* (Freud, 1933b [1932]), Bion might be trying to gain a clearer understanding of the relationship between psychoanalysis and aggressiveness giving a positive meaning to violence when (like after the barbarian invasions) it can be blended with dialogue, compassion, and the retrieval of those aspects of the previous civilization destroyed by the invader.

So on the one hand, the officer is lashing out against the suffering soldier being sent to his death and against Bion the psychoanalyst, who would like to treat him, and he uses language to attack, but he would prefer to use arms. On the other hand, Bion seems to be implying that the explosive use of language that tends to degenerate into the use of arms can be opposed by the therapeutic use of language, as in psychoanalysis, which is primarily the use of compassionate language towards others, preceded by the sharing of pain through empathy and identification.

According to Bion, then, the only analyst who can hope to survive is the one who kills himself off as an aristocrat and abandons his "received" theories and noble habits and accepts radical renewal, which involves mixing with the invader, the alien—even if this means becoming a barbarian himself if necessary. In Bion's view, the psychoanalyst has to know how to use the experience of war as well.

Another passage in Bion refers to the experiences the analyst has with analysands during analysis, experiences that mean that the analysands actually contribute to the advancement of knowledge. The analyst's experiences with his analysands can therefore be crucial in bringing about radical steps forward: "I may be able to fall back on the analysand's capacity for cooperation to make good deficiencies which I cannot [make up] by resorting to any of the disciplines and theories and formulations known to me" (Bion, 1975, p. 214).

We might say, then, that the analysand who most successfully makes good the analyst's deficiencies from the point of view of going beyond knowledge and renewing it is the analysand who manages to invade and subvert those commonplaces most dear to the analyst (not all of them though, since something has to be saved for future new mixing), without hesitating to resort to any kind of instrument in order to subject the psychoanalyst to the new order.

Both psychoanalysis and psychoanalysts, then, need wild, alien analysands if psychoanalysis is to remain alive and thrive. Whereas the analysands who, so to say, belong to the established system or ask to be inserted into it may rush psychoanalysis to its end because they pose no challenge to the aristocratic theories underlying the analyst's dangerous calm—dangerous because it is inhabited by images and visions no longer fresh, but worn out by being used by the multitudes.

The analyst without memory or desire has already provided the precursor to the figure of the psychoanalyst who, so as not to disappear, has to learn how to communicate with the parts of the mind most inaccessible to psychoanalysis. Today, for example, instead of thinking of war, as in Freud and Einstein's day, we might think of certain economic processes as an expression both of constructive forces and of a complex and still largely uninvestigated malaise of the human mind, and we might begin to look around for the most suitable instruments to eliminate the most threatening aspects of contemporary economic processes.

In conclusion, what Bion seems to be saying is that the psychoanalyst who will contribute the most to the survival of life (and psychoanalysis) is the one able to mingle with what is today farthest removed from psychoanalysis.

CHAPTER TWELVE

The theoretical and clinical significance of the concept of "common sense" in Bion's work

Gianni Nebbiosi & Romolo Petrini

In this chapter we would like to examine in greater depth the meaning of one of Bion's concepts—that of *common sense,* which to us seems to be fundamental. This concept, which has little coverage in the literature regarding Bion's thinking, appears to be essential in the examination of some theoretical aspects—the relationship between narcissism and social-ism, or the meaning of public-ation—and some theoretical–clinical aspects—opacity of memory and desire.

First of all, it must be stated that Bion attributes to the concept of common sense (CS) two meanings that can be joined together.

1. The two meanings of common sense in Bion's thinking

1.1 In terms of the more focused meaning and in his perceptive experience on the subject, Bion defines CS as a sense that is common in more than one sense and in more than one sensory perception:

As a criterion for what constitutes a sensible experience I propose common sense in the meaning that I have given it elsewhere, namely *some sense that is common to more than one sense*. I shall consider an object to be sensible to psycho-analytic scrutiny if, and only if, it fulfils conditions analogous to the conditions that are fulfilled *when a physical object's presence is confirmed by the evidence of two or more senses*. . . . The correlation thus established entitles one to claim the term common sense to characterize one's view that the given object is a stone: and that the view that it is a stone is common to one's senses and therefore a common sense view, the term common sense being used with more than conversational precision. [Bion, 1963a, pp. 10–11, italics added]

This concept was already proposed by Bion in his work, "A Theory of Thinking" which was presented at the Edinburgh Congress in 1961 and republished in *Second Thoughts*:

The failure to bring about this conjunction of sense-data, *and therefore of a commonsense view*, induces a mental state of debility in the patient as if starvation of truth was somehow analogous to alimentary starvation. [Bion, 1967b, p. 119, italics added]

An effective *negative* example of the first meaning of CS is to be found at the beginning of *Transformations*. According to Bion, the example clarifies that in the absence of a correlation between senses, it is impossible to speak about CS:

Suppose now that we view a stretch of railway line that is straight as far as the eye can see. The two lines of the track will be seen to converge. We know that if we were to test the convergence by walking up the line this convergence would not be confirmed; but, if we were to walk far enough and to look back the way we had come, the convergence would appear to lie behind us and to be confirmed by our sense of sight; the two parallel lines meet in a point. Where then is this point? One theory would explain the apparent meeting as an optical illusion. I propose not to accept this explanation, for *in a domain in which the sense of sight only is employed correlations based on common sense are not available*. . . . [Bion, 1965, pp. 1–2, italics added]

1.2 We have chosen to relate a report of great importance, which was instituted by Bion alongside this first meaning. It suggests that *emotions carry out a function in the psyche which is similar to that of perceptions in relationship to objects that are placed in space and time* and that the counterpart of CS, from the point of view of emotions, is a common way of considering emotions:

> The emotions fulfil a similar function for the psyche to that of the senses in relation to objects in space and time. That is to say the counterpart of the *commonsense view* in private knowledge is the *common emotional view*; a sense of truth is experienced if the view of an object which is hated can be conjoined to a view of the same object when it is loved and the conjunction confirms that the object experienced by different emotions is the same object. A correlation is established. [Bion, 1967b, p. 119, italics added]

We will reconsider this point further on; however, for the moment we will reiterate the following: (a) in the first meaning, CS indicates that the sensation of community of the senses—sight, sound, touch, and so on—tell us the same thing; (b) that one has the counterpart of CS in the emotive world when an object is tested by means of different emotions—for example, the fact of loving and hating the same person helps us to experience the truth regarding our relationship with that person and therefore get to know both the person and ourselves better.

1.3 In *Cogitations* we are able to find a definition of CS that joins the meaning that we have just proposed to a *second meaning* that institutes the relationship between the individual and the group:

> ... the nature of the common sense to which I appeal and to which, in conformity with the views of a powerful school of philosophers to which I adhere, I accord an extremely important role. For the time being I shall leave this thought ... merely contenting myself with a partial limitation of the term to cover *that aspect of the personality which is a compact of a component of the senses, common to two or more of the senses, and which in my belief has a social component analogous to that which Freud supposed might be the case with the sexual impulses, and*

which appears to me to be true of all emotional drives. [Bion, 1992, pp. 16–17, italics added]

Slightly further on in the same text, Bion better defines this meaning of CS, which, as he says, also "has a social component:"

. . . common sense, that is to say a group or socially orientated sense whose purposes go beyond the individual. I, as individual, need to consider what the group will accept as reality testing before I can feel that my view has the sanction of my common sense. [Bion, 1992, p. 20]

An accurate reading of this passage underlines a primary social component that for Bion exists in the individual, and how CS *is the sense of this primary relationship with the group.* In order to clarify further our reading of this meaning of CS, we will quote another passage, which seems to be even clearer:

If for some reason the patient lacks these, or some similar series of capacities for attaining subordination to the group, he has to defend himself against his fear of the group . . . *by destroying his common sense or sense of group pressures on himself as an individual,* as the only method by which he can preserve his narcissism. In the extreme form of defence in the psychotic the result of these destructive attacks appears as a superabundance of primary narcissism. *But this is an appearance—the supposedly primary narcissism must be recognized as secondary to a fear of socialism.* [Bion, 1992, p. 30, italics added]

In conclusion, CS is that which allows us to maintain contact with other people. When such contact terrorizes us or is disturbed, we tend to attack or destroy CS and therefore experience megalomania, indolence, or psychosis. If, however, such contact is tolerable, we are able to communicate with the group and therefore with a shared knowledge:

Megalomania. A matter of having to *be* as well as have everything. Common sense produces, from this point of view, a restrictive state of mind; it conflicts with megalomanic narcissism. Without common sense, phantasy can be felt as fact. Indolence can be the need to remain free to indulge phantasy: again, common sense is the obstructing force. [Bion, 1992, p. 24]

It would now be opportune to introduce the concept of *public-ation* and clarify its meaning as regards CS:

> Public-ation is an essential of scientific method, and this means that common sense plays a vital part. If it is inoperative for any reason, the individual in whom it is inoperative cannot publish, and unpublished work is unscientific work. [Bion, 1992, p. 24]

We would like to avoid the possibility of a misunderstanding at this point by underlining that in Bion's mind CS is a profound personality component and therefore far removed from having "common sense" in a conformist way. This position of Bion's is well clarified when, for example, we consider the relationship that he sees between dreams and CS:

> Then why is it that dreams we report, or have reported to us, are so often in terms of visual images? Is it not a modification of the stimuli reaching us? And could this be something to do with the dream-work as an attempt to achieve common sense as part of the synthesizing function of the dream? [Bion, 1992, p. 49]

In conclusion, then, according to the second meaning of CS, Bion views this as the sense of shared reality, of linkage to the group.

From the point of view of both meanings, this sense has a fundamental function in as much as that it gives the individual: (1) the capacity to synthesize his own sensory perceptions, which produces a sense of coherence and harmony in the sensory, subjective experience; (2) the capacity of being able to share his own examination of reality and therefore the capacity of learning from his own experience in a communicative way with the group—"public-ation"—this means communicative within the community of the others. In this case, there is also a sense of coherence regarding a certain harmony, or at least a compatibility between the person's own personality and the group, between his own personality and the social world.

The way in which these two meanings join together was expressed in an exemplary way by Bion, when in *Cogitations* he speaks about interpretation and publication of private knowledge.

> When is the private fact made public? In the individual, when it has become a matter of common sense; that is, all his senses

combine to give the same information. But amongst these elements of personality, in which I include the sense perceptions, I wish to include also that aspect of the senses which is held in common with the group. Private knowledge becomes public knowledge when the common sense of analyst and analysand agree that the perceptions of both indicate that some idea corresponds to an external fact independent of both observers. . . . When the psycho-analyst gives an interpretation that is a public-ation of private knowledge, he is translating thought into action, word into deed, just as much as the physicist conducting a laboratory experiment. [Bion, 1992, p. 197]

2.   *Common sense and clinical experience*

In the following paragraph we examine the importance that Bion gave to CS in his clinical experience. In *Cogitations*, which in most parts and from most aspects makes up Bion's clinical diary, there are numerous clinical sequences and thoughts about these which consider the utilization of this concept. One is then able to understand how Bion regarded the monitoring of CS in patients, in the analyst, and in the communication between them. This then constituted a very good example of the way Bion's clinical practice was filled with a sense of the group, going well beyond the theorization that was examined in *Experiences in Groups* (1961). One must not forget that the latter was his first work.

In the following quote we can see quite clearly the dramatic relationship that Bion saw growing in serious, violent patients between group CS, society, and the patient's internal CS:

That is to say that one should never forget that the patient is both murderous and irresponsible, and that common sense, i.e. the common sense of the society, dictates a particular diagnosis and a particular attitude of individual members of the society to the patient. Resistance to this dictation carries the penalties which the group always threatens to exact from those who resist its dictates. The common sense of the patient, however invisible and undetectable it may seem to be, tells him this, for he *has* common sense though he makes uncommon use of it. [Bion, 1992, p. 103]

Bion managed to draw some precious consequences for the management of a correct analytical position from these complex character considerations.

> Although the analyst must never cease to be a member of his group ... neither must he ever permit the socialism of his orientation to obscure the immediate vivid reality that confronts him in the consulting room. ... The analyst is thus forced to experience the split which the patient himself suffers between his narcissism and his socialism. [Bion, 1992, pp. 103–104]

A little further on, Bion further clarifies the clinical relationship between narcissism and socialism and CS:

> ... the patient resents the analyst's awareness of social pressures and obligations, but he ... resents the pressures that originate in the exactions of his narcissism and does so by exploiting the interest the analyst shows in his welfare as a failure on the part of the analyst to show the common sense which everyone, except the analyst, might be supposed to possess. [Bion, 1992, p. 104]

These affirmations present us with the possibility of reflecting on contemporary clinical practice with more difficult patients. In certain serious pathologies—the borderline pathology constitutes a very good example—one may rightly consider using an analytical attitude of constant empathic immersion towards the subjective experience of the patient. As we strongly adhere to this attitude, we deem it the right moment to state how useful it is to consider Bion's clinical position on CS. In other words, a sustained empathic immersion in the subjectivity of the patient should not generate the sensation, either in the patient or in the analyst, that the analyst is losing his relationship with (a) the CS of the patient and above all with the terrorizing or violent emotions that it induces; (b) the CS of the analyst himself; and therefore with (c) the CS of the group. From this point of view, the analytical positions that lead to the analyst's forgetting or, worse still, not wanting to consider that the patient "*has* common sense though he makes uncommon use of it", are to be emphatically considered as being incorrect.

It must be stated that this analytical attitude, for which the analytical pair should never forget their deep relationship with the group, in our opinion constitutes the core of the theoretical/clinical position of Bion, which is profoundly *relational* (Greenberg & Mitchell, 1983).

Let us now examine the clinical value that Bion assigns to CS by citing his position as regards the relationship between CS and interpretation.

> . . . no interpretation is of value unless at the moment at which it is given it involves, partly through the element of contrast which is inseparable from the juxtaposition, the illumination of the disorder of scattered, familiar, and apparently unrelated elements, and the order, cohesion, and relatedness of those same elements. Furthermore, this interpretation is not psychoanalytically effective unless, when given, it is common sense. [Bion, 1992, p. 104]

One should not be shocked by Bion's bringing together of order and disorder—a cohesive and relationship structure of elements that are "scattered and apparently unrelated"—with a theme of CS, even in an argument as sensitive as that of the technique of interpretation. We are reminded of two definitions of CS that Bion examined in his work. Is CS not perhaps that sense which institutes a relationship structure and cohesion between the sensory perceptions, which are potentially diffused throughout an individual? Is it not really thanks to CS, which co-ordinates the sight of a table to the touch of a table, that we have CS that the table exists in so much as we perceive it in different ways? On the other hand, are subjectivities (Corrao, 1998) as spread throughout a group not rendered cohesive and relational by the CS, which permits us to secure ourselves to them, both in the external and internal world? From this point of view, the necessity of the interpretative act that "is common sense" appears stronger. This is underlined by Bion:

> No cure can be permanent . . . unless it is based on what reason and common sense alike tell both analyst and analysand is the truth about the personality and mental mechanisms of the analysand. . . . The truth about the personality and mental mechanisms of the analysand, as demonstrable by the analyst to the analysand, leads to a permanent cure—as that would be understood by analyst and analysand taking a common-sense view of the results of such a demonstration. [Bion, 1992, pp. 117–118]

3. The counterpart of common sense in emotions: communication and correlation

Let us return to the citation as quoted in 1.2 (Bion, 1967b, p. 182) in order to reconsider the relationship between common sense and emotions. As a premise we can say that one of Bion's important concepts (Symington & Symington, 1996, p. 175) is that which institutes incompatibility between perception of senses and perception of psychic reality and therefore emotions; seen in these terms, CS would not find any space in the argument concerning the emotive world. However, this is not the case, for two reasons.

The first is made up of the fact that the analyst finds himself having to relate to his experiences in common sense as soon as he comes into contact with the patient's emotions. It is sufficient to remember Bion's recommendations regarding the act of interpreting and its relationship with CS in order to have a full awareness of the essential as presented by CS in Bion's theory concerning *communication of affects*.

The relationship between communication and CS—the identity of the linguistic roots of "communication" and "common" underlines the depth of Bion's intuition—was a *Leitmotiv* in the last years of his life. We know that just before his death, he was collecting an anthology of poetic writings for psychoanalysts (F. Bion, 1981). We also know how much this theme is central in the three volumes of *A Memoir of the Future*.

From this point of view, we wish to underline how the responsibility of utilization of CS is, for Bion, a qualifying element of the analyst's attitude.

The second reason is that for which Bion institutes an analogy between sensory correlations of CS (common sense view) and affective correlations of a "sense" of affects, which has the characteristic of instituting the correlation between different emotions (common emotional view).

The things that join the "common sense view"—the point of view of CS—to the "common emotional view"—the point of view of emotions—is the possibility of correlating, and the possibility that these correlations converge into defining an experience. For correct perception, I need the sense of touch to tell me that I am touching a table whilst the sense of sight tells me that I am seeing a table; similarly, for correct emotive perception, I need to be able to correlate my emotions towards one same object in my experience: my love for you, my hate for you, my envy for you, and my admiration for you. If they are all correlated in my relationship with you, they allow, according to Bion, an experience of truth. We can say more precisely that the possibility of correlation between various experiences—either perceptive or emotive—is one of the characteristics of becoming O. We believe that this is the deepest sense that Bion attributed to the term "common" when he spoke about perceptions, emotions, and relationship with the group.

4.   Common sense and selected fact

The theme of correlation brings the concept of CS and the concept of selected fact together. It would be worth while here to underline the marked difference between the two concepts.

The "selected fact" allows an individual to correlate and thus give sense to a series of elements that were seemingly lacking in any relationship: a fact is chosen based upon the way in which many other facts take on a meaning. In the final analysis, an element from external reality suggests a correlation to the personality, which, in turn, the personality is ready to pick up.

CS does not need any external induction. It is a "sense", an innate endowment (even though in its content it is strongly influenced by the environment), that establishes correlations between sensory perception and between the individual and the group, without any more or less selected fact activating it. The difference between CS and selected fact is fundamentally the difference between an innate correlated function and learned capacity: for example, learning to tolerate frustration and to have a "negative capacity" to seize from external reality an element that is able to order others.

Besides, the selected fact can be only a part of the consciousness; in fact it is tied to the phenomenon of establishment. When personality suddenly orders a series of events that seem to be lacking in any relationship through a selected fact, it notes a presence of a new meaning and therefore a new consciousness.

Instead, CS is a sense that may be conscious but more often than not is unconscious. Besides, it may belong to both a dynamic unconscious (for example when the individual feels unconscious conflict with the group and thus unconsciously attacks his own CS), as well as a procedural one. For example, when CS is applied to the co-ordination of sensory perception, this phenomenon does not play a part in the consciousness—not because there is some conflictual reason that prohibits it, but because it may be part of all procedures that are outside consciousness as much as they are automatic, such as riding a bicycle, driving a car, or walking. In psychology they are defined as belonging to procedural memory. It is worth noting that this arrangement, which is in part in the procedural unconscious and in part in the dynamic unconscious, brings together the concept of CS and the concept of the internal operative model as examined by theorists of this line of thought (Bowlby, Ainsworth, Main).

5.   "Vox populi, vox dei": narcissism/social-ism and common sense

Bion's theories on drive are significantly different from those of either Freud or Klein, who are his two real and only psychoanalytical referents. Today they take on a role of great interest compared to that which seems to be the most important epistemological argument in contemporary psychoanalytical thought: to opt for a drive or a relational paradigm.

We would like to clarify that the two paradigms arose not so much because the drive paradigm did not consider the relationships—or, conversely, because the relational paradigm did not consider psychic biological and drive-derived elements—but rather because a paradigm sees the drives as being superordinate to the relationships, and the other sees the relationships superordinate to the drives. In neither case do we speak of minimizing or eliminating certain phenomenologies or concepts, but of explaining them in terms of different theoretical co-ordinates.

The particular meaning of Bion's theory is that of having suggested, rather precociously, a drive-and-relationship-coordinated view. The theoretical concepts in terms of which Bion considered these themes are those of narcissism, socialism, and their combined relationship:

> By these two terms I wish to indicate the two poles of all instincts. This bi-polarity of the instincts refers to their operation as elements in the fulfilment of the individual's life as an individual, and as elements in his life as a social or, as Aristotle would describe it, as a political animal. The exclusive mention of sexuality ignores the striking fact that the individual has an even more dangerous problem to solve in the operation of his aggressive impulses. . . . There need be no conflict, but experience shows that in fact there is such a conflict—not between sexuality and ego instincts, but rather between his narcissism and his socialism, and this conflict may manifest itself no matter what the instincts are that are dominant at the time. [Bion, 1992, pp. 105–106]

In another passage Bion says that:

> These two terms might be employed to describe tendencies, one ego-centric, the other socio-centric, which may at any moment be seen to inform groups of impulsive drives in the personality. They are equal in amount and opposite in sign. Thus, if the love impulses are narcissistic at any time, then the hate impulses are social-istic, i.e. directed towards the group, and, vice versa: if the hate is directed against an individual as a part of narcissistic tendency, then the group will be loved socialistically. [Bion, 1992, p. 122]

Taking the Bion citation in 1.3 (Bion, 1992, p. 30) as an illustration, we can see how CS fills a key position in the oscillation between narcissism and socialism—drives towards the individual and drives towards the group. We can see how conflict shows itself in a dramatic way as regards the personality. Bion has hinted at this in previous writings. That which is attacked is the link between narcissism and socialism—that is, CS. It would be a good idea to highlight this linking function of CS because from the clinical point of view the attacks on CS by the patient have a both singular and dramatic effect in light of the Bion model. Desperately protecting his own narcissism, separating himself from the group that feels hostile and attacking to the CS, means that the correlation between the other group members and within the group itself has the result of attacking the person's own capacity of correlation between sensory perceptions.

This point in Bion's thinking seems to be quite original and in our opinion, genial—meaning that the same thing that for an individual establishes a direct connection between his relationship with the group establishes the correlation between his own senses. This has not received sufficient attention from Bion scholars. Bion's position on this takes him nearer that part of contemporary psychoanalysis which refers to theories of development in which the perceptive/affective/cognitive outlines of a person evolve directly inside the relationship with the mother and with those who take care of the infant (Emde, 1989; Klein, 1976; Lachmann & Beebe, 1996; Lichtenberg, 1983; Sander, 1962; Stern, 1995). Today it appears increasingly more evident that what is part of the genetic constitution of a child—the capacity of reading one's own perceptions and correlating them—is expressly dependent on the quality of the relationship with the mother and caretakers. Winnicott's fundamental intuitions in this field have been rightly noted, but in our opinion Bion's are even more precious.

We can conclude by noting once again the importance that Bion himself allotted to CS in the overall complexity of its meanings. In this case, Bion underlines the value and the danger of CS, the function of revelation, and simultaneously the possible function of a trick. He tries to lead us to the heart of dialectic ability between CS as a positive function and CS as a coercive function. The value of this dialectic ability is not that of an option of one or the other, but the continuous capacity of knowing and recognizing the function that both carry out. In a cogitation that Bion himself called "common sense and group polarity of instincts", he says:

> Berkeley says the stimulus may be God; so does Descartes. I shall maintain there is truth in this and that amongst all the objects that any given hypothesis at any given moment asserts to be constantly conjoined there is always the element that is that aspect which "God" presents. Thus if I say I see a table, I am stating that this is an empirical experience in which my hypothesis that certain elements are constantly conjoined— those elements in fact whose constant conjunction I have decided to call, a "table"—are again conjoined; furthermore,

that amongst these elements, hardness, shape, etc., is an element that is "God's" contribution, a presenting in me the awareness of certain sensations. . . . What is this God or Demon? In my view it is none other than the social component, "*Vox populi, vox dei*", of the instinctual equipment. . . . Such evidence . . . is at least not incompatible with the view I am proposing: that certain perceptions of the individual are not so much qualities under investigation as impositions on the individual's outlook by common sense (in my terminology) or God's idea (in Berkeley's) or the deceptions by God and Demon (in Descartes'). [Bion, 1992, p. 189]

Conclusions:
myths as common non-sense

In concluding our chapter we will underline how Bion was able to keep the element linked to the correlation of perceptions and group dimensions of the individual in mind in moments when the individual seemed to be more free to express his deepest creativity: in the alpha-function and in myth-making. The idea that even dreams and myths must account for themselves to CS makes Bion's vision of human reality exquisitely psychoanalytical—a vision that seeks to characterize the most intimate creative capacities of a human being, not in his capacity to escape from a bond (perceptive or group type) but to know how to use it in a creative way:

To what extent is myth-making an essential function of α? It may be that the sense impression has to be transformed to make it suitable material for dream-thought, but that it is the function of dream-thought to use the material put at its disposal by α, the units of dream-thoughts so to speak, in order to produce myths. Myths must be defined; they must be communicable and have some of the qualities of common sense—one might call them common non-sense. [Bion, 1992, p. 186]

CHAPTER THIRTEEN

The fundamental role of the Grid in Bion's work

Rosa Beatriz Pontes Miranda de Ferreira

Introduction

The Grid has become an essential part of psychoanalysis, and its role has to be examined in the light of Bion's encouragement of individual contributions to its application. In essence, this "instrument" created by Bion is a notation—a type of symbolic representation. Symbolic representations such as the alphabet, numerical notations, Euclid's elements, and the symbols for measuring space, time and temperature have, throughout history, contributed to the development of science. Of great importance, is Mendeleev's classification of the chemical elements. In psychoanalysis, the person who perhaps contributed most to the development of notations was Dr. Herman Rorschach, who elaborated the well-known Rorschach Test (1921) to help in the identification of the structure of an individual's personality. This test was further developed by a Brazilian psychoanalyst, Dr. Alcyon Bahia, who, in 1949, designed a graphic representation of the test. Working with the Grid, individually or in a group, with no memory and desire, helps to achieve a mental stability and scientific scrutiny.

The structure and uses of the Grid

Since *Learning from Experience* (1962a), Bion had already been sketching a notation system: "The Kleinian theory of projective identification would be referred to by initials and a page and paragraph reference. Similarly, Freud's view of 'attention' would be replaced by a reference. This can in fact be done, though clumsily, by reference to page and line of a standard edition even now."

In *The Grid* (1963b), Bion introduces a method useful in thinking about problems that arise in the course of psychoanalytical practice (Figure 13.1):

> The Grid is intended to aid the analyst in categorization of statements. It is not a theory, though psychoanalytical theories have been used to construct it, but has the status of an instrument ... By statement I mean anything from an inarticulate grunt to quite elaborate constructions ... A single word is a statement, a gesture or grimace is a statement; in short, it is

	Defini-tory Hypo-theses 1	Ψ 2	Nota-tion 3	Atten-tion 4	Oedipus 5	Action 6	...n
A β-elements	A1	A2				A6	...An
B α-elements	B1	B2	B3	B4	B5	B6	...Bn
C Dream Thoughts, Myth Dream, Model	C1	C2	C3	C4	C5	C6	...Cn
D Pre - Conception	D1	D2	D3	D4	D5	D6	...Dn
E Conception	E1	E2	E3	E4	E5	E6	...En
F Concept	F1	F2	F3	F4	F5	F6	...Fn
G Scientific Deductive System	G1	G2	G3	G4			
H Algebraic Calculus		H2					

FIGURE 13.1

any event that is part of communication between analyst and analysand, or any personality and itself. [1963b, p. 8]

In *Elements of Psycho-Analysis* (1963b), where Bion develops virtually the whole structure of the Grid, he refers already in the first chapter to Categories C_3, D_3, E_3, G_3, and G_4, and in Chapter VI of the same book he refers to Categories D_6, E_6, F_6, G_6, and H_6. The structure of the Grid, printed inside the cover of the book, does not include all G and H categories. It would seem, therefore, that this structure is that of the original Grid ("The Grid", 1963b). Indeed, in the later books Bion justifies not using Categories G and H, and in these, with reference to Category G, only G_2 remains (Figure 13.2):

> Suppose that at the end of the day's work the analyst wishes to review some aspect of his work about which he is doubtful. Assume further that the preoccupation centres on some phrase of the patient's. Recalling the session, the context of the statement, the patient's intonation, the analyst can place the statement in a category which, in the light of after knowledge, he thinks is correct . . . Such an imaginative exercise is closer to the activity of the musician who practises scales and exercises, not directly related to any piece of music but to the *elements* of which any piece of music is composed. Correct interpretation, therefore, will depend on the analyst's being able, by virtue of the grid, to observe that two statements verbally identical are psychoanalytically different. . . . Incidentally, the whole of the preceding discussion can be taken as an example of the use of the grid for an exercise designed to develop intuition and the capacity for clinical discrimination.

In the *Commentary* of *Second Thoughts* (1967b), Bion refers to his previous work: "This sort of experience led me to try a number of experiments in note taking, including some, perhaps the most convincing, which were intentionally subjective reports on my feelings about the day's work." He also tried a card index set up to find references to patients to scrutinize the material quickly if he should wish to be reminded of his or her psychoanalytical history: ". . . finally, I abandoned note taking altogether. . . . One reason (relevant in this immediate context) was my growing awareness that the most evocative notes were those in which I came nearest to a representation of a sensory image. . . . The notes did not make it

	Defini-tory Hypo-theses 1	Ψ 2	Nota-tion 3	Atten-tion 4	Inquiry 5	Action 6	...n
A β-elements	A1	A2				A6	
B α-elements	B1	B2	B3	B4	B5	B6	...Bn
C Dream Thoughts, Dreams, Myths	C1	C2	C3	C4	C5	C6	...Cn
D Pre - Conception	D1	D2	D3	D4	D5	D6	...Dn
E Conception	E1	E2	E3	E4	E5	E6	...En
F Concept	F1	F2	F3	F4	F5	F6	...Fn
G Scientific Deductive System		G2					
H Algebraic Calculus							

FIGURE 13.2

possible to remain conscious of the past but to evoke expectations of the future."

Bion says in *Two Papers: The Grid and Caesura* (1977b): ". . . there are invariants present in the psycho-analytic experience and in the theoretical formulation. On the correctness of this assumption the genuineness of the psycho-analysis depends" [p. 30]. In a cogitation transcribed from tape, Bion says:

> I am inclined to think that I would have to use the Grid itself at some point in this book (*The Dream*, Book I, of *A Memoir of the Future*)—as an effort of formulating or re-forming or show-ing the relationships of one aspect of it to another, with a kind of arrangement by which all these relationships were shown in a form that was different from that of the narrative of the book itself. It would display the way in which the logical or rational connections of one part with another could be formu-lated—although, of course, rational formulation is not

necessarily an adequate formulation for something that is not
really rational at all. [1992, p. 357]

The axes of the Grid

The horizontal axis

The horizontal axis relates to "uses" to which the elements in
the genetic axis are put. The horizontal axis is incomplete and
the series is extensible. . .They were devised primarily with
what I have called a K link in mind but their usefulness is
unimpaired for L and H. I may explain that K is intended to
denote the domain of learning from experience, L to denote
the domain of love in all its aspects and H the domain of hate.
[1963b, p. 8]

Column 1:

Column 1 is subtitled a definitory hypothesis. . . . Statements, to which this category is appropriate, mark that
elements previously regarded as unrelated are believed to
be constantly conjoined, and to have coherence. A statement in this column should be considered to have
significance but not meaning. [1963b, p. 9]

Column 2:

Column 2 is to categorize the "use" to which a statement,
of whatever kind . . . and however untrue. . . is put with
the intention of preventing a statement, however true in
the context, that would involve modification in the personality and its outlook. I have arbitrarily used the sign ψ to
emphasize the close relationship of this "use" to phenomena known to analysts as expressions of resistance. [1963b,
p. 9]

Statements representing the realization in such a way that
the analyst's anxiety that the situation is unknown and
correspondingly dangerous to him, is denied by an interpretation intended to prove to himself and the patient that
this is not so. [1963a, p. 18]

Column 3:

Statements that are representations of present and past realizations. An example of such a statement would be a brief summary reminding the patient of something that the analyst believes took place on a previous occasion. This corresponds to the function Freud denotes by the term *notation*. [1963a, p. 18]

Column 4:

Column 4 represents the "use" described by Freud in . . . ["Formulations on the Two Principles of Mental Functioning": 1911b], as the function of attention. . . . Statements properly regarded as appropriate to Column 4 relate to constant conjunctions that have been previously experienced and the "use" represented by Column 4 categories differs in this respect from the "use" represented by Column 1. [1963b, pp. 9–10]

Column 5:

A criticism of Oedipus, implicit in the story, is the obstinacy with which he pursues his inquiry. This aspect of curiosity may seem unimportant to the philosopher of science but it is of significance clinically and therefore worth including with Columns 3 and 4 as representing something that is more than a difference of intensity just as 4 (attention) is more than an intense 3 (notation). [1963b, p. 10]

Column 6:

The last column which I have annotated 'action' also requires comment. It refers to those phenomena that resemble motor discharge intended to unburden the mental apparatus of accretions of stimuli. [1963b, p. 10]

. . . the last category that I propose to distinguish, the statement. . . is used as an operator. . . . Functions of interpretations that fall in this category, and therefore the interpretations in this one of their aspects, are analogous to *actions* in other forms of human endeavour. For the analyst the transition that comes nearest to that of decision and translation of thought into action is the transition from thought to verbal formulations of category 6. [1963a, pp. 19–20]

The vertical axis

BETA- AND ALPHA-ELEMENTS:

The first two rows of the genetic axis may be discussed together: β-elements and α-elements are intended to denote objects that are unknown and therefore may not even exist. By speaking of α-elements, β-elements and α-function I intend to make it possible to discuss something, or to talk about it, or think about it before knowing what it is. At the risk of suggesting a meaning, when I wish the sign to represent something of which the meaning is to be an open question, to be answered by the analyst from his own experience, I must explain that the term "β-element" is to cover phenomena which may not reasonably be regarded as thoughts at all.... Ideally any meaning that the term accumulates should derive from analytic practice and from analytic practice alone. Much the same is true of the α-element except that this term should cover phenomena that are reasonably considered to be thoughts. I would regard them as elements which make it possible for the individual to have what Freud described as dream thoughts. [1963b, pp. 10–11]

β-elements—This term represents the earliest matrix from which thoughts can be supposed to arise. It partakes of the quality of inanimate object and psychic object without any form of distinction between the two. Thoughts are things, things are thoughts; and they have personality. [1963a, p. 22]

The β-element row is for the categorization of elements, like an unpremeditated blow which is related to, but is not, thought. [1977b, p. 3]

Row C:

... row C is intended for categories of thought which are often expressible in terms of sensuous, usually visual, images such as those appearing in dreams, myths, narratives, hallucinations. [1977b, p. 3]

I have regarded C category elements as being the stuff from which the scientific use of models derives. One advantage of the model is that it does not commit the psycho-analyst to the formal rigidity of a theory, but presents him with a tool which he can discard when it has served his purpose. [1967b, p. 141]

Row D:

The preconception may be regarded as the analogue in psycho-analysis of Kant's concept of "empty thoughts". Psycho-analytically the theory that the infant has an inborn disposition corresponding to an expectation of a breast may be used to supply a model. [1967b, p. 111]

Row E:

When the preconception is brought into contact of a realization that approximates to it, the mental outcome is a conception. . . . When the infant is brought into contact with the breast itself, mates with awareness of the realization and is synchronous with the development of a conception. [1967b, p. 111]

Row F:

Concepts are named and therefore fixed conceptions or thoughts. [1967b, p. 111]

Row G:

The scientific deductive system. In this context the term 'scientific deductive system' means a combination of concepts in hypotheses and systems of hypotheses so that they are logically related to each other. The logical relation of one concept with another and of one hypothesis with another enhances the meaning of each concept and hypothesis thus linked and expresses a meaning that the concepts and hypotheses and links do not individually possess. In this respect the meaning of the whole may be said to be greater than the meaning of the sum of its parts. [1963a, p. 24]

Row H:

> Calculi—The scientific deductive system may be represented by an algebraic calculus. In the algebraic calculus a number of signs are brought together according to certain rules of combination. [1963a, p. 24]

A discussion of Bion's proposals

We must recall that, when Bion discussed the definitory hypothesis, he emphasized that "Any definitory hypothesis . . . has always been recognized to have a negative function. It must always imply that something is; equally it implies that something is not. It is therefore open to the recipient to infer one or other according to his temper . . . . suppose that the inability to tolerate frustration is 'excessive': the personality may react against the statement, seeing only its negative implications and, in the extreme case, refusing to allow the statement, to him a 'no-thing' even to exist. The attempt then is to annihilate the statement in its function of definitory hypothesis" [1970, p. 16]. In the figure representing The Grid, in the cell referring to the definitory hypotheses, there are, therefore, three subdivisions: the definition itself, the negative aspects of the definition, and the annihilation of the definitory hypotheses (Figure 13.3). It is possible to indicate the negative aspects of the definitory hypotheses by creating another kind of Grid, using co-ordinate axes. In this case, we would have an abscissa with both a negative and a positive value (+1, −1) (Figure 13.4). As far as Column 2 is concerned, it is evident that a distinction must be made between a statement that is a lie, and a false statement. The liar must be certain of his knowledge of the truth to ensure that he will not trip up on it, blindly and by accident.

According to Bion, if we were to use the co-ordinate axes, Row 2 would cease to exist, becoming, therefore, −2. This would imply a more general change in the location of the columns (for example, Row 3 would be in Cell 2, and so on: Figures 13.3 and 13.4). The close relation between Columns 3, 4, and 5 (Figure 13.3) should be emphasized. We have already referred to Column 5, but we would

	Definitory Hypotheses 1	ψ 2	Notation 3	Attention 4	Inquiry 5	Action 6	...n
A β-elements	A1	A2				A6	
B α-elements	B1	B2	B3	B4	B5	B6	...Bn
C Dream Thoughts, Dreams, Myths	C1	C2	C3	C4	C5	C6	...Cn
D Pre-Conception	D1	D2	D3	D4	D5	D6	...Dn
E Conception	E1	E2	E3	E4	E5	E6	...En
F Concept	F1	F2	F3	F4	F5	F6	...Fn
G Scientific Deductive System		G2					
H Algebraic Calculus							

Column header annotations: Definition / Negative aspects / Destruction, Lie / Falsity, Obstinacy / Curiosity, Expulsion / Development

Figure 13.3

like to call attention to the fact that Bion made a distinction between obstinacy and curiosity. In the 1963 "The Grid" (Bion, 1963b), Column 5 is described as "Oedipus", and in subsequent Grids this is changed to "Inquiry". This also applies to the analyst himself/herself. It is possible, therefore, to divide the cell or place a minus sign (−5) in the co-ordinate axes.

Column 6 can also be divided. We quote:

This last category is used as an operator. The intention is primarily that the communication will enable the patient to effect solutions of his problems of development . . . . For the analyst, the transition that comes nearest to that of decision and trans-

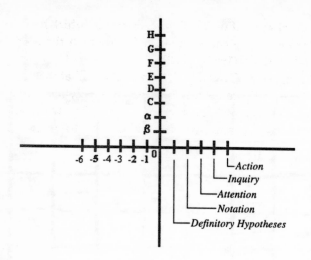

Figure 13.4

lation of thought into action, is the transition from thought to verbal formulations of category 6. [1963a, pp. 19–20]

Moreover, Column 6 can also be used to classify "phenomena that resemble motor discharge intended to unburden 'the mental apparatus of accretions of stimuli'". According to what we said, the action, if representing development, is placed in the positive abscissa, and if representing a discharge, it remains as –6 (Figures 13.3 and 13.4).

> β-elements are a way of talking about matters which are not thought at all; α-elements are a way of talking about elements which, hypothetically are supposed to be part of thought. The poet Donne has written 'the blood spoke in her cheek . . . as if her body thought!' This expresses exactly for me that intervening stage which in the Grid is portrayed on paper as a line separating β-elements from α-elements. Note that I am not saying that is either beta or alpha, but the line *separating the two* which is represented by the poet's words. [1990, p. 41]

In Figure 13.3 we have added this line.

In Figure 13.4, where we drew the geometric co-ordinates, we preferred to consider the beta-element as positive, taking into consideration Bion's definition of this element, in which he says: "This term represents the earliest matrix from which thoughts can be supposed to arise" (1963a, p. 22).

With regard to Category C, Bion suggests that: "This category will certainly require extension as psycho-analytic experience accumulates; even now it deserves a 'grid' of its own to expand it suitably for psycho-analytic use." [1977b, pp. 3–4] (Figure 13.3).

Using the Grid

CLINICAL MATERIAL

Tuesday's session

$P_{1.1}$ When I opened the door, she looked at me and smiled in a superior manner and said that she had understood that I had given her freedom: "don't come tomorrow." (Monday was a holiday. Was this mentioned in our Thursday session, or did I say: "Until Tuesday"? She was due to have a session very early on Friday morning, but she did not come).

She continued with a series of complaints about her husband, discussing his intentions. She had given him an amplifier. He wanted that very much for his birthday. But she gave it to him earlier, knowing how much he wanted it. She thought he did not appreciate it enough, didn't show the excitement she expected him to show.

$A_{1.1}$ *You are showing me, through your husband, what you thought I did to you, not appreciating you enough, not appreciating what you bring me.*

$P_{1.2}$ [Very angry] *I want you to help me in my relationship with my husband, and you say things like that. It is not true, there is no relationship between us, I can't accept this.*

$A_{1.2}$ *Why do you think I would waste your time and mine, speaking of something, if I hadn't thought that that thing was the correct thing to say? I'm not saying that my interpretation is right, but why would I have said what I said if I didn't think I was right?*

Wednesday's session

P_{2.1}   Yesterday, after the session, she went to visit her father, who, according to her, was very depressed. She attributed his depression to a visit he made to her brother on Easter Saturday, where the father saw the whole family. Even her mother's brothers were there, but not the mother herself, who is separated from her father. Returning from her father's house, she found her husband anxiously speaking to her mother's bodyguard. He was angry because the bodyguard had not put the dog's lead on, and he (the husband) had taken the dog out. *The little dog I loved so much, he ran away, the blood was all over the pavement.* As she spoke of this, it seemed she had lost her breath.

A_{2.1}   *You are talking to me through your breath—and it's almost as if you have stopped breathing—about your feelings in relation to the dog's death, and today you also mentioned the separation between your mother and father.*

P_{2.2}   She spoke of her children's reaction: the eldest was furious with his father, blaming him for the dog's death, for not having put the lead on. The second child, her favourite, was also very disturbed but did not want a fight with his father. She said that, in the children's presence, she had not wanted to let her husband perceive that she also blamed him. Then she began to talk to herself, furious with her husband: *he is guilty, I am right to be furious. That dog was a male dog, still young, was still being trained, and we were very tolerant with him. Even if he made a mess, we were very kind to him.*

A_{2.2}   *As you are speaking, I accept facts happened as you told me. But I would say there is also another meaning in what you told me.*

I would like to call your attention to the fact that it seems to me that you are saying this as the nearest way to explain something to me that you really don't know much about. Blood must remind you of something, as well as this death where there are two criminals. We are two here as well. Who is the guilty one? Me? You? What are we guilty of?

Tuesday's session

$P_{1.1}$ On trying to register it, I preferred to consider the whole event as a single statement, wishing to push onto me the feelings of unbearable memories in a pre-verbal and verbal language, with the same use of discharge. Could be Column 6, but I preferred to consider it as a false statement and therefore marked Column 2 (Afraid of catastrophic changes?). Therefore A_2.

$A_{1.1}$ Image of the disagreement with the analyst and with the patient's husband. Therefore C_4.

$P_{1.2}$ I thought she described the experience of the analytical session as a frustration, simultaneously registering it as a form of resistance to inquiry. Therefore E_2.

$A_{1.2}$ I spoke in terms of actual life, but at the same time questioning it. Therefore C_5.

Wednesday's session

$P_{2.1}$ I considered this communication to be an account of the visit to her father's house, where the father was very depressed. Could be C_1, but through the associations, there was a transformation and a pre-verbal communication "stopping breathing".

Therefore A_6.

$A_{2.1}$ I called attention to the "feeling" (emotion) (dog's death and parents' separation) and called the patient's attention to this. Therefore C_4.

$P_{2.2}$ This is an account, but based on a preconception that someone is guilty.

Therefore E_4.

$A_{2.2}$ I called attention to the story that she had told me. Therefore C_3.

But later I suggested that we should search for the meaning of the facts in terms of the model: there is blood, two criminals, and one death. Therefore C_5.

These changes are illustrated in the following Grid:

Tuesday's Session

$$P_{1.1} = A_2 \qquad\qquad A_{1.1} = C_4$$
$$P_{1.2} = E2 \qquad\qquad A_{1.2} = C_5$$

Wednesday's Session

$$P_{2.1} = A_6 \qquad\qquad A_{2.1} = C_4$$
$$P_{2.2} = E_4 \qquad\qquad A_{2.2} = C_5$$

Conclusions with the help of the Grid

I classified the patient's statements in A_2 and E_2, and later, in the second session, in A_6 and E_4. In four of the statements, two are beta, and as for the use, one is 2 and the other 6. Why is she coming to see someone she wants to attack? Why so much pre-verbal communication? Does it seem that I am a good person to come to because I am so bad, so inferior, that this gives her the security that she can do better than me? Although I ask myself what she is doing here, why is there only aggression and negation? I also registered E_2 and E_4. In E_2, despite denying our relationship, she is able to express an idea of why people go to analysis: because she expects to get some help. The analysis will help her in her relationship with her husband.

I notice that she talks to me about her father, about the depression, about the separation from her mother, about the different reactions of her children, and about the husband's position in their lives. In sum, she talks to me about her family. She does not seem to be speaking of feelings, but this is not true. She is not just speaking of her family, but, because her family means something to her, she is drawing my attention to this fact. In the Grid, E_4 is a development. I used my experience of two different sessions (Tuesday and Wednesday) that I have considered as one on the graph because I was doing an exercise and working at the same time to understand the movements of my patient in terms of thoughts or no thoughts and the uses she was making of her statements.

Some suggestions for further thoughts

We would suggest that the signs G and H be maintained in the genetic axis. They will not be final products of the verbalization of an interpretation, since, as Bion points out, for the communication to be felt by the patient it needs to go from the sophistication of Category H to Category C, which is in a visual image. Our way of working develops unattached to theories (although these theories exist within us, in our fund of knowledge) and is carried out in a state of "hallucinosis" (without memory, desire, or understanding). Knowing, also, that the material the patient gives us, even when it seems familiar to us, relates to something that is unknown both to the patient and to ourselves, we must work patiently, until there appears a specific fact, a common denominator, or the perception of a contradiction, which we can then communicate to the patient, thus obtaining perhaps a few more associations; then, still patiently, we must continue until an intuition may lead us to the perception of a model of what is being thought in the analytical relationship. We have, then, a certain security that will eventually and finally take us to verbalization. We believe that this whole process (in a state of conscious "hallucinosis") corresponds to a Deductive Scientific System. Therefore, we go through G, H, and finally C. If we were to place this interpretation, as we verbalize it to the patient, in the Grid, we would register neither G nor H. However, if, experimentally, we want to play the *game*, as Bion says, corresponding or not to what actually occurred, we will be exercising ourselves and discussing these matters. This is a type of exercise that can be carried out by one person alone or in a group. What would be the scientific conclusion we reached that took us to C?

It is essential that we should refer to some theories and the use of mathematics in Bion's work, such as the functions and factors in *Learning from Experience* (1962a), chapter 1. F(alpha) functions as a constant, due to its situation as an *unknown quantity* and to the factors being able to be replaced by theories and conceptions of a fixed value. The theory of functions makes it easier to bring together the realization with the deductive system representing it. For the use of the term "realization", Bion quotes Semple and Kneebone in *Algebraic Projective Geometry*. When Bion talks about the deductive scientific system he quotes Braithwaite in *Scientific Explanation* (1955). Elements alpha and beta are used in the same way that unknown quantities are used in algebraic calculations. The term "Vertex" is used as a substitute for point of view. There are also several references to point, line, direction, and orientation. Bion speaks in terms of physics when he says that dreams would need to be thought of as belonging to a far more widely extended C category. "Sooner or later the investigation would have to be extended to infra and ultra-sensuous areas" [1992, p. 326]. The following passage from *Attention and Interpretation* (*Ultimate Reality*) illustrates his thought about the "mathematics" needed for psychoanalysis:

> The realities with which psycho-analysis deals, for example fear, panic, love, anxiety, passion, have no sensuous background, though there is a sensuous background (respiratory rate, pain, touch, etc.) that is often identified with them and then treated, supposedly scientifically. What is required is not a base for psycho-analysis and its theories but a science that is not restricted by its genesis in knowledge and sensuous background. It must be a science of at-one-ment. It must have a mathematics of at-one-ment, not identification. There can be no geometry of 'similar', 'identical', 'equal'; only of analogy. [1970, p. 89]

Also referring to algebraic calculi, Bion says that perhaps one day mathematics could be a great help for psychoanalysis, if it was permitted, when using this type of calculi, to reach the genesis of the calculus itself through an inverse path. In *Second Thoughts*, Bion affirms that "Mathematical elements, namely straight lines, points, circles and something corresponding to what later becomes known by the names of numbers, derive from realizations of two-ness as in breast and infant, two eyes, two feet and so on" [p. 113].

Bion raises the hypothesis that Euclid's Theorem and Freud's discovery of the Oedipus complex, together with Oedipus' myth and Sophocles' version, are similar in that both intend to find solutions for conflicts and problems that are, simultaneously, a manifestation and a tentative solution. Oedipus' myth in itself involves the issue of the knowledge in which a question is raised, asking for a reply. Which was the question proposed by the

Sphinx? Bion emphasizes "its" (i.e. the Sphinx') question. Tradition says that the question was: "What is it that walks on four feet in the morning, on two feet by midday and on three by early evening?" And the answer was: "Human beings, because they crawl on all fours when babies, they walk on their two feet most of their life, and they use a stick in old age." Bion suggests that this answer should be re-evaluated. To support his argument, he refers to a proposition called "Pons Asinorum" (1.5) from Euclid's first book. Bion says that we are used to relating the term "isosceles triangle" to the mathematical sense of the term—that is, a triangle having two equal sides (indeed, Euclid's proposition refers to the isosceles triangle as a triangle having two sides equal). But the Greek term may be translated as "a thing with three knees having legs equal", and knees, in primitive Greek literature, are frequently associated with genitalia. Consider Euclid's Proposition 1.47 (also called "Pythagoras' Theorem"), the popular name for which is "The Bride's Theorem", according to Heath's *The Thirteen Books of Euclid's Elements* (1956, p. 417): this name was originally used for a right-angled triangle with 3:4:5 sides. Plutarch gives a fanciful and oedipal description of it: the perpendicular would be the male, the base the female, and the hypotenuse the offspring of the two; in the 3:4:5 triangle the first, 3, is the first odd number and is perfect; 4 is the square of the even side 2; and 5 is partially similar to the father and partially to the mother, being the sum of 3 and 2. And why are we interested in all this? Much could be said about Bion's hypotheses—for example, when we speak of the oedipal current that extends from the primordial evolution to the most advanced calculi. Bion suggests, for instance, that thanks to the elaboration of scientific methods, we are learning more, but, simultaneously, calculi are being produced that are impregnated with the impulse to escape from oedipal material and archaic reminiscence. Can the calculus, once realized, produce an equipment able to investigate adequately the problem that gave origin to the calculus in the first place? Can the calculus, which represents an attempt at abstraction as an escape from an oedipal situation, be elaborated to explore this situation? Is there already a type of calculus that does exactly that? Can the Oedipus conflict be solved by a mathematical experiment? Then, the inner world would be explored by a calculus that would be interested in its origin.

Still from *Cogitations*, we would like to mention the following passage:

> In psycho-analysis it is assumed that a theory is false if it does not seem to minister to the "good" of the majority of mankind. And it is a commonplace idea of good. The whole idea of "cure", of therapeutic activity, remains unscrutinized. It is largely determined by the expectations of the patient though this is questioned in good analysis (as I know it). But in nuclear physics a theory is considered to be good if it aids the construction of a bomb that destroys Hiroshima. Too much of the thinking about psycho-analysis precludes the possibility of regarding as good a theory that would destroy the individual or the group. Yet there will never be a scientific scrutiny of analytic theories until it includes critical appraisal of a theory that by its very soundness could lead to a destruction of mental stability, e.g. a theory that increased memory and desire to a point where they rendered sanity impossible. [1992, p. 378]

We quote this because we find it of great importance in our psychoanalytic work (for the Grid too, working alone or in groups).

Let us consider the last lines of this paragraph. Our interpretation is: with no memory and no desire, we can achieve a mental stability and scientific scrutiny, being either a psychoanalyst or physicist, deciding at each moment what is better in our relation with a patient or with mankind.

Bion's work: an outline

> There is much more continuity between intra-uterine life and earliest infancy than the impressive caesura of the act of birth allows us to believe.
>
> Freud, *Inhibitions, Symptoms and Anxiety* (1926d [1925])

Caesura is a pause in the interior of a long sentence, after an accentuated syllable. In music, it is also an element of rhythm.

Bion's work is extensive. The different Caesuras are here condensed.

1

1 (1943) Bion and Rickman: "Intra-group Tensions in Therapy"
2 (1946) "The Leaderless Group Project"
3 (1948) *Experiences in Groups, I–IV*
4 (1948) "Psychiatry at a Time of Crisis"

2

1 (1950) "The Imaginary Twin"
2 (1952) "Group Dynamics: A Review"

3

1 (1953) "Notes on the Theory of Schizophrenia"
2 (1955) "Development of Schizophrenic Thought"
3 (1955) "Differentiation of the Psychotic from the Non-Psychotic Personalities"
4 (1957) "On Arrogance"
5 (1958) "On Hallucination"
6 (1959) "Attacks on Linking"

4

1 (1962) "A Theory of Thinking"
2 (1962) *Learning from Experience*
3 (1963) "The Grid"
4 (1963) *Elements of Psycho-Analysis*
5 (1965) *Transformations*

5

1 (1966) "Catastrophic Change"

2 (1967) "Commentary" in *Second Thoughts*

3 (1967) "Notes on Memory and Desire"

4 (1970) *Attention and Interpretation*

6

The papers and books below are classified according to the presentation forms:

CONVERSATION WITH BION

1 (1973) Bion in São Paulo

2 (1974) Bion in Rio de Janeiro

3 (1974) Bion in São Paulo

4 (1976) Four Discussions with Bion (Los Angeles)

5 (1977) Bion in New York

6 (1978) Bion in São Paulo

CONFERENCES

1 (1967–1968) Bion with Argentineans

2 (1971) *The Grid* (Los Angeles)

3 (1975) *Caesura* (Los Angeles)

4 (1975) Conferences in Brasilia

5 (1976) "Evidence" (paper)

6 (1976) Borderline personality disorders:

I "Emotional Turbulence"

II Addendum: "On a Quotation from Freud"

7 (1979) "Making the Best of a Bad Job" (paper)

INTERVIEWS WITH BION

1 (1974) Interview by Rio Colleagues

2 (1978) An Interview with W. R. Bion—John S. Peck

SEMINARS WITH BION

(Bion preferred to call these Clinical Seminars, rather than Supervision)

THE ROLE OF THE GRID IN BION'S WORK   199

1 (1967–1968) Bion with Argentineans

2 (1973) Bion in São Paulo

3 (1974) Bion in Rio de Janeiro

4 (1974) Bion in São Paulo

5 (1975) Bion in Brasilia

6 (1978) Bion in São Paulo

7

THE TRILOGY

1 (1975) *A Memoir of the Future I: The Dream*

2 (1977) *A Memoir of the Future II: The Past Presented*

3 (1979) *A Memoir of the Future III: The Dawn of Oblivion*

8

1 (1981) *A Key to A Memoir of the Future*—Compiled by W. R. Bion and F. Bion

2 (1982) *The Long Week-end (1897–1919) (Part of a Life)*

3 (1985) *All my Sins Remembered*

4 (1987) *Clinical Seminars and Four Papers*

5 (1992) *Cogitations*

CHAPTER FOURTEEN

What is thinking—
an attempt at an integrated study
of W. R. Bion's contributions
to the processes of knowing

Paulo Cesar Sandler

> One thought alone occupies us; we cannot think of two things
> at the same time. This is lucky for us according to the world,
> not according to God.
>
> Pascal, *Pensées*, 145

This study makes use of two of Bion's functional models of the
mental apparatus—the "digestive" model and the "reproductive"
one—in order to move towards an integrated model of thought
processes. Perhaps with the development his observations allowed
for we are now in a condition to examine some actual processes
underlying the intercourse between an analyst and his (her) patient.

"Feeding" and "reproduction" are the psychic, immaterial
facts that occur, in the sense that life itself is being actively maintained and continues to be so. They are counterparts in psychic
reality of some facts of material reality, food being provided and
sons and daughters being born. They occur in the mind of the
"*two-body psychology*" of the analytical setting (Rickman, 1950).

They are not sensuously apprehensible, concrete facts. There is no sexual intercourse; it is not a sexual fact, and no meals are served, but the patient is nourished in the sense his mother nourished him when he was a baby and life is renewed in the exercising of femininity and masculinity by both members of the analytic pair. Analysis itself happens, with increments in approximations to the many O's of the patient. "*Real analysis is real life*" (Bion, 1977a, p. 80), and it happens during the analytic session in its transient character in the same sense that a creative couple may give rise to sons and daughters.

We consider thinking as a term that has some counterparts in reality: a method used for the apprehension of reality when this apprehension goes beyond the use of the sensuous apparatus; there is a "de-sense-ifying" of raw sensuous data that comprises reality, the action of alpha-function (Bion, 1962b, p. 6). Milk becomes breast, through the creation of alpha-elements whose O is "nourishment". Mother's sexual apparatus transforms the raw concrete data coming from the spermatozoon into some kind of energy during its symbiotic relationship with the ovum, in the prototype of the container/contained (Bion, 1962a, 1963a) relationship that repeats itself in a later stage between mother and baby. It is also considered that dream-work is an unconscious fact in thinking and in the apprehension of reality. It allows the differentiation between psychic reality and sensuous apprehensible pseudo-realities.

Processes of knowing and knowledge

Thinking is intrinsically intertwined with knowledge. Freud's and Bion's psychoanalytic developments of Hume's, Kant's, and Nietzsche's epistemology allow us to discriminate between pretensions of getting *knowledge* and *coping with processes of knowing* (Sandler, 1994, 1997).

When one aims at getting *knowledge*, one is also involved in:

• Final answers.
• Possession of truth (absolute truth).

• Achievement of something "positive"; thinking is directed towards satisfaction, for "knowledge" is completeness-seeking—it abhors the "negative" frustration of knowledge.

• The belief in sequential and linear relationships of cause and effect.

• The construction of doctrinaire bodies that constitute scholasticism—in other words, the adoption of Canons (or Paradigms).

• Spotting no links between the person who knows and the object known except as regards the use of the sensuous apparatus, or, in other words, believing in the non-interference of the observer in the phenomena observed.

• Aiming at explanation and understanding.

One may contrast some features of the *process of knowledge*:

• An absence of aims (*"la réponse est le malheur de la question"*, a quotation much loved by Bion from Maurice Blanchot); aims are replaced by attempts at observing ontology, or genetic development.

• An acceptance of the lack of final answers; a tolerance of paradoxes during an unending process of knowing.

• An attempt to achieve a sense of truth: the process of knowledge is a method of perceiving that the loved object and the hated object—*or the known object and the unknown object*—are the one and the same object.

• It is "negative"—that is, it tolerates frustration and does not seek complete satisfaction.

• There are no mandatory sequential and linear relationships, and hence no belief in cause and effect; it looks for the *"selected fact"* (Bion, 1962b) and *"invariances"* (Bion, 1965); it describes evolutions and tries to describe processes of *"being"* (without ever achieving those descriptions).

• There are no moral codes of judgement. "Right" and "wrong" are considered products of mind, not Nature-dependent observable facts. Right and wrong rationales are replaced by the observation of falsity and truth (or hallucination and reality). "Forgetting", in the sense of having been learned by experience and stored in the unconscious, is taken into consideration. "Must" is replaced by "need", "desire" is at least partially replaced by "possibility".

• It uses Organons—that is, instruments—and does not adopt Canons.

• Empiricism is regarded in its post-Kantian terms, as developed by Schopenhauer, Darwin, Nietzsche, Freud, Einstein, and Heisenberg. It is a sensible intuition based on preconceptions that are Nature-dependent and development-dependent—in other words, preconceptions that seek realizations that never wholly match them. This incomplete matching allows for the formation of conceptions. The experience of no-breast allows for the inception of thought processes—thinking in the absence of the object (Bion, 1962b). Sensuous apparatus is a port of entry to data that are transformed into thoughts and dream-work. The experience therefore concerns the sensuously apprehensible facts appertaining either to material reality (Freud, 1900a, p. 620) or to psychic reality, which is non-sensuous; it does not split them and does not deny any one of them either.

• It makes attempts towards lifelike, transient (Freud, 1916a [1915]) apprehensions and comprehension, as opposed to understanding and explanation (Bion, 1967b, 1970).

• Notice is taken of the interference of the observer in the phenomena observed.

• It uses a *"language of achievement"* (Bion, 1970, pp. 73n, 125; 1975, pp. 203–204). The "axioms" thus obtained are linked to need and possibility, determined by choice and chance, and nature-dependent.

A process of knowing is ever on the move. Its movement is characterized by a constant paradox that includes *what is known and what is unknown*, or PS↔D in Bion's quasi-mathematical notation of Klein's formulation of the two positions. "Knowledge" thus obtained is never *final*; there are no doctrines or schools sprouting from it. It looks for selected facts (Poincaré, quoted by Bion, for example, in *Learning from Experience* (1962a) and *Cogitations* (1992), pp. 72 and 18, respectively) and invariances (Bion, 1965), and therefore it respects transcendence and its dynamic balance↔imbalance with immanence, without splitting them. There are neither paradigms nor canons. There are some transient, fleeting moments of expression of transcendences, or "invariances"—evolution in O (Bion, 1965).

The main consequence of giving precedence to the idea of processes of thought is the development of the hypothesis that thoughts exist without a thinker to think them. The processes of thinking and perhaps even the development of an ability to think are imposed on the mind. It is a developmental need that is due to the existence of thoughts. For example, such thoughts as "wheel", "passionate love", "motherhood", "Oedipus", "Planck's constant", already existed, albeit in a non-sensuous or very primitive, larvate or cystic form—"floating in reality as it is"—a long time before someone was available to think them. The clinical relevance of this hypothesis is that thoughts without a thinker also exist in the analytic room, waiting for the creative couple to think them. Thoughts are epistemologically previous to thinking (Bion, 1962a, 1962b, 1963a). Bion never claimed originality for this hypothesis, despite the opinion of some authors (such as Meltzer, 1978, and Thorner, 1981). As Freud with Oedipus, so it can be said that Bion used this hypothesis in an original way. Hints of it, albeit stated as an absurd, can be found in Descartes' work (Descartes, 1637). What I think we owe to Bion is the unearthing and pursuing of this clue in a practical way—psychoanalysis itself, outside the field of philosophy—something that suggests that what we call "thinking" and "knowledge" perhaps cannot be confined to theoretical and philosophical limits.

Psychoanalytical research has illuminated how pretensions to knowledge and abhorrence towards coping with transient processes of knowing appertain to the realm of hallucination. In contrast, coping with processes—necessarily incomplete—of knowing appertains to the realm of human nature and its relationships with the real world and real, Nature-dependent facts. This is necessarily incomplete; it is a transient live fact, in perpetual motion, evolving if and when life exists. Bion made some suggestions: that the whole body of psychoanalysis could be a *"vast paramnesia"* to *"fill the void of our ignorance"* (Bion, 1976c, 1976e); also, that we should stop *"investigations in psycho-analysis"*, *"but in the psyche it betrays"* (Bion, 1975, p. 122). The insight could be linked to the perception of *"trains of thoughts already available"* to the patient (Bion, 1975, p. 204). *"Paramnesias"*, *"investigations in psycho-analysis"*, correspond to *knowledge*. *"The psyche it betrays"* and *"already available trains of thoughts"* correspond to *processes of knowing*.

The "non-explanation factor" stems from "an ability to tolerate paradoxes" (Sandler, 1996). The tolerance of paradoxes is possible in many ways, and one of them is the use of intuition coupled with the dialectical method: thesis, antithesis, and synthesis. Or mother, father, and son/daughter, or, PS↔D. Tolerance of paradoxes is embedded in seminal key concepts in our science, which were intuitively formulated through the use of antithetical pairs: the two principles of mental functioning (the conscious awareness of reality being the synthesis), the life and death instincts (synthesis: life itself); love and hate (synthesis: the creative parental couple); PS↔D (synthesis: mental life itself); psychical reality and material reality (synthesis: human being), container/contained; in its various expressions, synthesis is mother/baby, the creative couple, analyst and analysand, binocular vision, to quote a few examples.

Processes of knowing, especially dream-work, are dependent on an epistemological function of the mind. This is a function that strives to reach reality, although the fulfilment of this goal is impossible, for O is unknowable. Thinking processes are factors in the various expressions of the epistemophilic instinct that promotes the K link—the artistic, mathematical, and psychoanalytical functions of the mind, which may have appeared phylogenetically and ontogenetically in this order. These functions strive to express fleeting glimpses of partial aspects of O.

Knowing, thinking, and psychoanalysis: the value of the negative

Freud-like, Bion was seemingly able to integrate some most outstanding contributions stemming from the Renaissance and from the Enlightenment and Romantic periods with psychoanalysis, furthering the development of the knowledge of *"facts as they really are"* (Bion often quotes this phrase of Samuel Johnson) and the study of the vicissitudes, obstacles, and difficulties created by this same human being in order *not to know what "facts really are"*: the field of –K, some *transformations*, such as rigid, projective, and in hallucinosis (Bion, 1965). Knowing and thinking are inseparable from the perception of reality and its vicissitudes.

Freud unburied the *relevance of the Oedipal triangle—in itself an antithetical pair followed by synthesis—*in the same way as he realized *the existence of a principle.* Poets such as Shakespeare and Goethe were able to convey it implicitly in poetical form; musicians such as Bach and Beethoven, in a musical form. *For lack of a better name, Freud called this principle the "Reality Principle"* and bestowed a practical use on it. Its hallmark is a "frustration-factor". This realization was doomed to remain stubbornly outside the reach of Science, whose silly infancy insists on being "positive"—that is, pleasure-seeking, satisfaction-fulfilling. The "no-breast" aspect of reality was and is continuously denied. "I Think", "I Know", "I discovered", "I have", "The solution" seemed to be preferable to "I think that I think", "I am and I also am not" (to put up with a paradox), "I know and I do not know", "I think and I hallucinate", "I hate and I love". When one experiences what "No" is all about, one may realize—in oneself—the evolving "Yes". Psychoanalysis describes *the names of our lies* (Marques[1]), through the formulation of names such as "transference", "narcissism", "projective identification", among many others. Perception of those lies may be a way for the person to become "what he or she is in reality" as Nietzsche, Freud, and Bion insisted many times. The fact that psychic reality comprises psychic non-reality still befuddles some authors (such as Arlow, 1996).

Is it possible to get an inner, vivid and experienced apprehension of processes of thinking starting from the vertex of their absence? In analytical practice, this means the possibility of hallucinating during an analytical session and experiencing the

---

[1] Dr. Miguel Marques, personal contribution during a course on the apprehension of Psychic Reality held in 1994 in Sociedade Brasileira de Psicanalise de São Paulo.

expression of the psychotic personality—especially those expressions appertaining to PS and the lack of an ability to experience (PS↔D). This is the "*stamping ground for the wild asses*" referred to by Bion in *A Memoir of the Future* (1975, Book 1, p. 9). Conscious awareness of no-reality created by human mind, "*to turn the unconscious, conscious*" at its highest pitch, the field of –K or "minus", "negative" broadly speaking, yield to the evolving experience (being, transformation in O) of reality.

Transference and projective identification: mindlessness?

Are "transference" and "projective identification" epistemological errors linked to the lack of concern about truth and reality? (1992 [circa 1960], pp. 125, 247). Patients attribute to some people the same feelings, ideas, desires, and perhaps realistic ideas that were due to significant figures of their historical past, long gone and now appertaining to the realm of memory and hallucination. Patients under "transference" are not able to deal with reality, to face it—even the most elementary of realities, as, for example, that the analyst is not their father. The person cannot think and discriminate; probably it was not a mere coincidence that Bion proposed to regard transference as a rigid transformation—the *rigor mortis* of thought processes? Projective identification as observed by Klein, is an unconscious omnipotent phantasy that makes its "owner" believe that he has the power to split off and thereafter expel undesired ideas, wishes, feelings, thoughts, or whatever. Once felt as appertaining to the outside, external milieu, this phantasy completes its cycle with the omnipotent feeling that such undesired feelings and ideas ought be "inoculated" into someone else (primarily the Mother). Both transference and excessive projective identification in adulthood are expressions of failures in thought processes—in Bion's terms, the field of minus K and the transformations in hallucinosis. Freud was acutely aware of the hallucinated nature of transference, and Klein also stressed the "*phantastic nature*" of projective identification (Freud, 1912b, p. 108; Klein, 1946, p. 298).

"Breast" is a "real reality". To perceive it, some babies may have difficulties in working through two commonly seen approaches:

(a) the "naively realistic" approach, splitting and denying its immaterial character;

(b) the "naively idealistic" approach, imagining the breast as its own creation,

thus repeating ontogenetically the fumbling infancy of epistemology. Perhaps epistemology itself, still divided by the following dilemma, is also trapped in the fumbling psychotic infancy of all individual minds (Bion recommends studying the mental state of the philosopher of science—1992, p. 7).

(a)   The baby may fall into what in philosophy is regarded as "naive realism"—as pointed out by Cassirer, Hartmann, and Bachelard, among others—which is an excessive reliance on the sensuous apparatus. Naive realism produced a formidable confusion in philosophy due to a reaction against what is deprecatingly called "empiricism" and, in the end, attacks against reality itself, seeing it as a product of the human mind. Bion was able to integrate Pascal's, Hume's, and Kant's work in such a way that this pitfall was avoided in modern psychoanalysis. A detailed exposition of this subject is to be found in Sandler (1997). One concludes that what was apprehended through this comparatively short-range method is reality itself. The baby splits off psychic reality from material reality and privileges the latter; it corresponds to the "enforced splitting" described by Bion in Chapters 5 and 6 of Learning from Experience (1962a). This approach originates from an excessive leaning towards the sensuously apprehensible aspects of the breast. Psychic reality loses its psychic features and is replaced by a state of mind that is neither awake nor asleep, neither alive nor dead—thoughts are reified and turned into concrete entities (Bion, 1962b, p. 10; Sandler, 1990, 1997b). Development is hampered; adults who follow this path come to be a kind of mosaic of psychotic, neurotic, infantile, and pseudo-adult aspects, without integration and coherence between fragmented aspects. Things-in-themselves cannot cohere to the extent that "they" constitute closed, isolated "worlds". They are not "link-able" objects; alpha-elements, in the sense of Parthenope Bion Talamo's "Lego" blocks (Bion Talamo, 1995), cannot be formed. Bion coined dozens of metaphors that convey this state of mind, as, for example, "*The mind that is too heavy a load for the sensuous beast to carry*" (Bion, 1975, p. 45).

(b)   In the second case, the baby insists in dealing with the breast as if it were a bunch of projections. Intolerance of frustration means that such a baby tries to introduce its pre-conceived breast into the real breast, transforming it, in his mind, into a non-reality that can reach a point of no-return (a special kind of Tpβ that constitutes a deformation, as described by Bion, 1965, p. 12). This kind of baby, like the hallucinated "adult", refuses to deal with the real breast. He does not allow reality to be as it really is, but tries to make sure it will be what it is desired to be. He cannot introject the real breast, since it is enviously and greedily hated, trying to be superior to the breast. I shall not dwell on the vicissitudes of the mother–baby relationship, taking the reader's acquaintance with Mrs. Klein's descriptions for granted.

Hallucination prevails in both cases. In (b) the mind's products are privileged, and faeces are overvalued in a paranoid–schizoid fashion and dealt with as if they were thoughts and reality itself. The person inflicts a pseudo-mental life on himself which *grows*, inflationary, cancer-like, but cannot *develop* for it has no limiting factor (the No-breast, frustration) nor any mating with this limiting factor, reality itself. We will return to this point.

In (a) the baby and the adult produce a manic overvaluing of concrete properties. In both cases, the baby cannot put up with the paradox first described by Winnicott (1969) that the breast was created by him as well as already existing. In the subjectivistic approach that characterizes "*naive idealism*", the baby thinks it created the breast and denies that it already existed; in the first case, the baby stifles its mental life. The non-sensuous spectrum of psychic reality is, accordingly, almost extinguished. The baby feels that what exists is the external breast and nothing more than that. The expressions of these vicissitudes of development of thinking appear in later ages in many guises. For example, the naive idealism that mistakes the products of the mind with reality creates the belief in the existence of charismatic, mystic, messianic leaders, gurus, geniuses, nationalism, ownership of absolute truth, "idealism", and a contempt towards Science up to the point of denying that the latter can exist outside ideologies. It also created the idea that the world or reality itself does not exist at all beyond what we see. This is a pseudo-objectivistic approach. It expresses itself in greedy tycoons and politicians, and also in sheer delinquency—lack of concern towards life, people, and truth. In Science, it produced "positivism". This lack of concern for life expresses itself through dismissal or contempt towards Motherhood and Fatherhood, and lack of interest in symbiotic relationships and in collaborative links with oneself and with other people.

Some extensions made possible through Bion's contributions

Bion proposed an analogical model of thinking processes—namely, the functioning of the digestive apparatus. This model allowed for some synthetic metaphors, that convey the functioning of the mental apparatus used in thinking, such as *"truth is the food of mind"*. His research has led to some insights about the transformation of concrete sensuously apprehensible stimuli into non-concrete, immaterial, psychic facts (this is the operation of *"alpha-function"*—Bion, 1962a, 1962b), in the same way that concrete food is transformed into immaterial energy (ATP—adenosine tri-phosphate—where matter and energy meet in the human body). Its counterpart in the great universe is Einstein's $E = mc^2$.

I propose to fit Bion's concept of container/contained, in the sense of the exercising of masculinity and femininity and the basic creative act—namely, the parental couple and its intercourse—into the framework of the alpha-function model and the digestive apparatus model in order to enable us to have some glimpses of the thought processes and the processes of knowing as they appear during an actual analytic session. Does a psychic ability to be intuitively penetrated, without confusing a breast with a penis, exist? Is the spermatozoon a material reality that has a counterpart in psychic reality that can be called a "thought without a thinker"—

waiting for a thinker who will think it— the ovum is then a material reality that has as its psychic reality counterpart the thinker
who will think the spermatozoon? In this primeval, inchoate area,
one cannot separate matter from energy, psychic from material. I
propose to regard as non-separate facts, made separate by effects
of rational discourse and splitting processes in the mind, psychic
and material, father, mother, and the reproductive system. Could
"the thought" thus "created" be a counterpart of sons and daughters?

Some links between the "digestive and reproductive systems model" and the thinking processes

The digestive system is a highly developed and effective system
that ensures a useful splitting between blood (living, perpetual
movement, energy, manifestation of life instincts) and faeces
(dead, immovable, expression of death instincts). This splitting
must occur from the point of view (vertex) of the living body. We
are not stating that faeces are waste *per se*, or "absolute waste". We
are not dealing here with absolute truths, for faeces, once expelled,
may collaborate with the life cycle, albeit in a transformed way, in
the sense that Freud described the fusion of death and life instincts. Bion's model allows us to compare hallucinations to faeces,
and the capacity to hallucinate with some of the functions performed by the mental apparatus in the same sense that the
production of faeces is a function of the digestive apparatus. Hence
we may consider that the *human capacity to hallucinate* differs from
its *products*—namely, hallucinations—in the same sense that faeces
differ from the human capacity to digest food.

The capacity to hallucinate, hand in hand with the capacity to
think, is present all the time, day and night, much like a hand or a
coin with two faces where one may grasp their nature of "coin-
ness" or "hand-ness" by observing either one of the faces. The
simultaneous observation of both faces is impossible to the sensuous eye.

If the preconception of a breast does not find a realization, it is
doomed to remain pure hallucination. The same outcome would

occur if, when the baby hallucinates, it found an exact realization matching the hallucination.

We simultaneously *create thoughts and produce hallucinations* from the raw material coming from the environment through the senses. To create is regarded here as linked to a creative couple; to produce is a "homo-", solitude-ridden act. I propose to regard the capacity to hallucinate as having a relevance to thinking in a way that is analogous to the relevance counterpoint has to musical language. The capacity to produce faeces is a counterpoint to the capacity to produce glycogen and ATP—energy for the body; the capacity to hallucinate is a counterpoint to the capacity to think and to dream. A basic difference between real thoughts and hallucinations is that the latter, like faeces, are purely individual productions that do not require a pair; their "dead" quality stems from their "homo-" quality. They are all the same—faeces. A person can claim ownership and authorship of his faeces as well as of his hallucinations; little children usually do this. Thoughts are a particular form of apprehension and transformation of something that already exists—thoughts without a thinker claim a thinker to "marry" them. Thoughts, unlike hallucinations, demand a link—in this case, with reality itself. It is both an individual transformation and something that has already existed, appertaining to the realm of Platonic forms or O.

Talking and the creative couple

One may observe *what is happening* when the two members of the analytic couple talk to each other—the emotional experience that casts specific links—the uses and functions of what is being said. *What is happening and links* may be the clue to furthering the insertion of the reproductive system model into a broader framework that includes alpha-function and the digestive system model.

Clinical experience allows for the hypothesis of using the digestive apparatus model and the reproductive system model in a binocular way. During an actual session of analysis, the analyst will pay attention to content and to the function of what is being said, felt, and done. *I am proposing a description of a state of mind*

where the two basic facts of life—nourishment and reproduction—have
psychic counterparts that function simultaneously and have expressions
in the area of thinking and knowing, including the very earliest method of
knowing something, the basis of introjective and projective identifica-
tions. One may try not to separate them, and one may also try not
to blend them hastily to a point of such an intermingled confusion
that forms the basis of some unconscious phantasies—for example,
the confusion between a penis and a breast. Food for the mind is
simultaneously food for life—sperm—and the analyst, irrespective
of his or her physical sex, may exert at least to some extent his or
her feminine qualities in order to be "drilled" or "penetrated" by
what the patient says. To do this, his or her analysis must be
extensive enough, up to the point of working through feminine
and masculine aspects. I suspect that this is one of the many manifestations of the bisexuality of the human being observed by Freud
(1905d), which must be dealt with during an analytic session. To
be penetrated by the patient's talk is to exercise a female function;
to furnish a view or an interpretation is to exercise male potency.

Thoughts without a thinker, reality itself, will be allowed to be
"penetrated"—and the thinker will think them, the way the ovum
is penetrated by a spermatozoon, and some still unknown facts,
probably at the quanta level, will occur. Something creative happens. At a given moment the patient says something. What the
patient says may be considered as a masculine thrust. Intuition—
feminine intuition—and the ability to care—perhaps the most
synthetic way love manifests itself—are put into play. The analyst
may say something after this true insemination. In order to say this
"something" which has been intuited through the use of the analyst's femininity, the masculine traits must now be exerted. This
"something" will in turn inseminate an *"inseminable"* patient who
is minimally able to use his very same feminine and masculine
qualities. A new being is born—the intercourse between the two
members of the pair.

One must not be too stuck to PS if one is to cope with reality as
it is—to allow "inoculation" by reality itself. A very silent patient
who confused a penis with a breast "saw" a special helmet in his
head, with a sliding roof, that could be made to work each time the
analyst, obviously seated behind him, uttered a word. He felt the
analytic intercourse as a homosexual attack and transformed his

hallucinated experience into a visual image, the "anti-analyst helmet". When the helmet was being "seen" by this patient, before its
existence was put into words, it was pure hallucination. Once the
image had been described to the analyst, who was inseminated by
it, a session was amenable to be dreamt, and hallucination (faeces)
turned to be a shared dream—the verbal formulation: "anti-analyst helmet", the session itself. The analyst's alpha-function
digested part of the patient's former beta-element (the visual image of an incomprehensible strange helmet) that made some
scattered facts coherent—homosexual fears, the analytical session
itself, and so on.

Thinking and coping with reality

Thinking encompasses unconscious processes; nothing can be conscious if it has not been turned unconscious. This is Bion's amend-
ment to Freud's theory of the unconscious. His now classical
examples appear in *Learning from Experience* (1962a) and *Cogitations* (1992): the learning of walking and the constant conjunctions
involved in the learning of words such as Dad. No K link can
evolve without the obtruding of H and L links (Bion, 1962a, 1963a).

The inception of thinking occurs to the extent one is able to
cope with the No-breast. No-breast is experienced if there is a
minimum ability to tolerate the frustration and the pain that things
are what they are and not what one wishes they were. The breast is
the prototype of this truth. This is also the prototype of hatred
towards reality, depending on greed, envy, and intolerance of frustration. Moral codes are born here, for one attempts to impose
what one feels *must be* instead of coping with and dealing with
what *is*, the very imposition of feelings the person makes on himself and on others being a manifestation of PS (or omnipotence of
thinking, as described by Freud in *Totem and Taboo*, 1912–1913).
Why should the universe adapt itself to our feelings, demands, and
even scientific laws, asks Bion in *A Memoir*? In the same sense,
years earlier, he had noticed that some patients become "*baffled*"
when events follow the "*laws of Natural Science*" and not the laws
of this person's "*mental functioning*" (Bion, 1956). The breast is

never what one demands it should be or expects it to be, even if those expectations may prove to be reasonable. The presence of memory and desire hampers thinking from its inception onwards.

Sense of truth

Thinking is furthered when the *sense of truth* allows one not to fall back on occupying the paranoid–schizoid position wholly and therefore one is able not to cling tenaciously to judgemental values of "right" or "wrong". {Right *or* wrong} is the outcome of one who loses the sense of truth. One tries somewhat desperately to replace real thinking by rational or imitative (delusion) rules of {right *or* wrong} when one cannot perceive that truth *and* falsehood appertain to the realm of reality and hallucination.

The tolerance of the first paradigmatic paradox furnished by the real object that is at once loved and hated furnishes a model for the human being. This means that one can be penetrated by reality *as it is*—by facts *as they are, to some extent*. One cannot know its ultimate truth, but one can intuit some truthful aspects of real life, expressions of O. Gradually one is able to build up faith that reality itself exists despite its ultimate unknowableness.

The analytic couple and the process of thinking

The K link and the digestive/reproductive model

As in the container/contained relationship, the basis of all emotional experiences, thinking is an emotional experience whose counterpart in reality is the basic creative couple, the sexual parental couple. The analytic couple provides an opportunity for experiencing links and emotional events. As far as thinking is concerned, we may consider the parts to be related: (a) the patient with the analyst; (b) the patient with him (her) self or internal reality and (c) the patient with common sense (external reality), paving the way to his or her commonsensical apprehension of reality. These three relationships can be linked in at least two ways.

Genetically speaking, the K link as described by Bion (1962a, 1963a) at the intrapsychic level stems from one's daily and nightly dream-work, primitive projective identification and introjective identification as methods of communication with mother and formation of objects, allowing for preconceptions (protophantasies in the sense described by Freud) mating with *frustrating* realizations (Bion, 1962a)—in short, our realistic perceptions of internal and external reality. The K link would be achieved at its most developed level under a symbiotic relationship. There is a real relationship and a real, evolving (life-instinct) inroad into the unknown; an offspring or real thoughts appear.

The parasitic and commensal relationships lead to pseudo-thinking, to transformations in hallucinosis, and/or to rational constructs; in philosophical terms, idealism/subjectivism from the former and rationalism/positivism—concrete "thinking"—from the latter. The K link cannot install itself in the parasitic and in the commensal relationships; there is a "homo-" intercourse or no intercourse at all. The person cannot hear the other person (usually there is no regard for "otherness"); the person cannot even hear him (her) self. There's an unreal, static, ever-repeating, false, imitative (Philips, 1989) pseudo-relationship, producing psychomas, wasteful and destructive as are cancers in the physical realm.

To have concern for the presence of another person in the room expresses itself through real talking. If the digestive–reproductive model is valid, we may note symbiotic, commensal, and parasitic links when observing the talk and its functions in a specific case. "Talking", "hearing", and "listening" occur, along with their opposites appertaining to the field of minus K: no-talking disguised as talking as a manifestation and medium of projective identification (Bion, 1956, 1957a), not-hearing, not-listening. "Hearing" is here regarded as a purely sensuous act; to listen may be regarded as encompassing the former as well as words, feelings, emotions, and the appearance of the most basic needs—instinctual needs. The activity of "listening" and the link is not only with the on-looker—it also has to do with the person who talks: it is an intra-psychic relationship between the person and him- (her-) self.

The person who is really able to speak will be able, to some extent, to be intuitively penetrated, "femininely" penetrated, by his or her own needs. Both thinking processes that start from inchoate states and those able to entertain second thoughts, cogitations, reflections, and the regard for truth are inner, mostly unconscious "speeches" of a person with him- (her-) self. I do not propose to regard thinking processes on this level as either purely material or purely immaterial fact; there is no such thing, except in the realm of our limited possibilities of the apprehension of real facts. For example, there are people who cannot even know that they must drink some given quantities of liquids; in the end, they produce kidney stones. One cannot say that they were able to talk with themselves and to think. There are people who cannot listen to other forms of this *inner voice*, which indicates one's needs and possibilities, not only one's desires and idealizations. One may search for one's own abilities and know them, one must work, one must look for a mate, or one must take care of a sibling. During analysis, an occurrence, which is as common as it is overlooked, is that patients utter words, but they cannot hear what they say. Many times no interpretation is needed at all, but only a helping invitation to hear what he or she is saying. For example, a person may say, "Oh, I came here because the physician sent me—he said, you have nothing at all, go and see a psychiatrist." Among those people, many of them cannot hear that they are pointing to their depression or sense of helplessness at not having themselves at their disposal. In truth, they "have nothing", for they cannot count on their true self. What happens when a person cannot hear what he or she says and thus produces a split between him and himself? A common finding is the idea that pain may be avoided.

Sometimes, in thinking processes that are not "homo-", thus providing a counterpart of the symbiotic relationship in the area of thought, the person can "marry" with reality itself. If the person is an artist, he or she can marry with a certain medium. The paradigmatic situation of the baby with the breast is a "hetero-" relationship. In this case, the baby yields to being penetrated by nourishment. "Nourishment" is another area where psychic reality and material reality are married and yet are not intermingled, preserving their own "identities", in a paradox that cannot be resolved outside the realm of splitting, denial, and projective identification. Nourishment and thinking, like music and life, like a real analysis, are ever-renewed, ever-new experiences, each time they occur. To think is a lifelike experience; at its most compacted, explicit and extreme form, the supremely creative parental intercourse—it has no memory and no desire; like O, it is unknowable, but it simply happens to be—or does not happen. One may live the moment, may perceive the moment, and may try to profit from it after *realizing* it, to the extent to which this is possible.

Conclusion

The prototype of real thinking may be seen with the aid of a dual model: it is a basic creative situation—namely, the psychic counterpart of parental intercourse and of the basic intercourse between mouth and breast. Thinking is born when the baby can apprehend what a breast and nourishment are all about. Its first mo(ve)ment, like an overture, happens to be when the baby can think in the absence of the object—that is, when it experiences the No-breast. The adagio, a second mo(ve)ment, occurs when the baby is able to apprehend breast and nourishment as separate entities that are the one and same entity, without splitting them— in other words, not splitting material reality from psychic reality and not confusing them either, in the same sense as in a real marriage, where the partners are united but are able to preserve their individualities in a paradox that demands tolerance. In this sense, "thinking" might be regarded as the mind's counterpart of an emotional experience of recognizing the supreme creativity of the parental couple as well as the caring and loving attitude and action of the nourishing breast.

Both the reproductive system and the digestive system have counterparts in psychic reality, and they may therefore be used as models of the processes of thinking and knowing. Knowing may be compared with having sons and daughters.

The analytic couple that is able to think also gives expression to this original creative couple, for the analyst is inseminated by each patient's free associations and vice versa. One is able to accept one's own femininity, being penetrated by breast and reality itself as nourishment; one is able to accept one's own masculinity, being able potently, prodigally, to act *into* this reality in order to perform a "marriage with reality". I suspect that Freud and Bion regarded this as "modification in reality". As a result, Oedipus, the son, is born—the son is "A Thought". It is New and it is also Not-New. It was not created by a hallucinated mind, but by a mind that was able to penetrate and to be penetrated by a Natural Reality—O. In this sense, Thinking may be regarded as Mind's perennial presentation (to itself) of the parental creative couple and its outcome, the sibship.

Thinking allows a marriage of the person with his or her inner reality, instinctual needs, and real possibilities and limitations— the person as he or she really is. With the aid of thinking processes one is able to reach some partial knowledge of who one is in reality. To know, to think, to live, and to love are inseparable facts, made separate by failures in thinking.

CHAPTER FIFTEEN

The various faces of lies

Elizabeth T. de Bianchedi, Claudia Bregazzi, Carmen Crespo, Elsa Grillo de Rimoldi, Silvia Grimblat de Notrica, Delia Saffoires, Adela Szpunberg de Bernztein, Alicia Werba, & Rosa Zamkow

> If we add something to the truth, we will take something away from it.
>
> Luigi Pirandello

> It may, in general, seem astonishing that the urge to tell the truth is so much stronger than is usually supposed. Perhaps, however, my being scarcely able to tell lies any more is a consequence of my occupation with psychoanalysis.
>
> Sigmund Freud, *The Psychopathology of Everyday Life* (1901b)

This chapter is the fruit of passionate discussions, in the setting of a study group on Bion's ideas, co-ordinated by Dr. Elizabeth T. de Bianchedi, on the topic of truth, falsities, and lies, in answer to Bion's invitation to think about these human phenomena, which so frequently appear in our everyday life, and of course also in our clinical practice.

"What is truth? said jesting Pilate (according to Sir Francis Bacon), and would not wait for an answer" says Bion in the second paragraph of his article *Caesura* (1977b). He continues: "We prob-

THE VARIOUS FACES OF LIES

ably cannot wait for an answer, because we have not the time. Nevertheless, that is what we are concerned with—inescapably and unavoidably—even if we have no idea of what is true and what is not. Since we are dealing with human characters we are also concerned with lies, deceptions, evasions, fictions, phantasies, visions, hallucinations—indeed, the list can be lengthened almost indefinitely" [Bion, 1977b, pp. 41–42].

We want to discuss here some of the difficulties, contradictions, dilemmatic situations, and problems with which the Bionian concept of the lie and his formulations about the mental functioning of the liar present us.

We will begin with some definitions. According to the Ferrater Mora *Philosophical Dictionary*, a *falsity* is the lack of truth or of authenticity, a lack of harmonization between words, ideas, and things. In logic, falsity is the term contrary to truth: if by "truth" one understands the correct fit between a thought and reality, "falsity" is its unsuitability. The *lie* is a formulation or expression opposite to what one knows, believes, or thinks. To lie is to induce into error, to falsify, to pretend or disguise something, making it look—by external signs—like something else; it is also to break a pact, to fail to keep one's word.

In the first part of his work (until 1965), the opposition Bion sets is between truth and falsity (Bianchedi, 1993). In that period, the concept of truth applied by him seems to be the Aristotelian (like the one we quoted from the Dictionary), where truth is defined as the correspondence between a statement and that to which the statement refers, the reality it names. It seems to be a "common-sense" truth, related to the concept of the "selected fact". The opposite of truth is a falsity. Later on, near the end of *Transformations* (1965), Bion's concept of truth has become a different one, especially when he refers it to "transformations in O" (obviously different from "transformations in K"). This concept of truth is a more Platonic/Kantian version, which sees O, the truth, as the ultimate, unknowable, infinite reality. Any formulation of *this* truth, made by a human being, will necessarily be a falsity. In this new context, falsities are the only way the human mind has of stating and communicating truth—in relation to unknowable truth, which could be intuited—and which exists independently of the thinker. The emotional contact with truth becomes a falsity in the thinking/publishing mind. The container (the human thinking mind formulating its experiences) necessarily transforms this true content, achieved in at-one-ment with O, into a falsity. From this vertex, falsities (not as they are understood in common language, or in Bion's first formulations) are basically K transformations of the truth. However, in this chapter we do not wish to discuss philosophical problems but, rather, investigate the importance of these phenomena in mental development and in psychoanalytical practice.

Bion has stated that the growth of the mind and of the group is in correlation with the capacity to think about emotional experiences. In this conception, love of truth is essential. The feeling of truth allows the mind to learn from experience; on the other hand, hatred of truth and its corollary, the lie, starve and/or poison the mind. In *Learning from Experience* (1962a), Bion gives a beautiful description of the mother's mind and her reverie, meaning by this function her capacity to contain the baby's realistic projective identifications and detoxify them before returning them. He suggests that the human infant receives the communication of the mother's true feelings, not through her words (falsities in the sense we mentioned previously), but through her behaviour and emotions. Truth, like food and love, are essential for the growth of both members of this primary link.

Taking these different formulations into consideration, we can consider the concept of "falsity" as a hinge concept between truth and lies. A formulated thought—a falsity—can become a lie, depending on its nature, use, and quality, and whether the link between container and contained, thought/emotion and thinker, is commensal, symbiotic, or parasitic. In the commensal link, both are related without implying each other—truth "is there", although it has not yet been discovered. In the symbiotic link, the truth and the thinker are in touch and modify each other, both growing through their inter-relationship. In the parasitic link, one destroys the other. The first of these three links is associated with a truth about to be intuited, the second with "falsities", and the last with lies.

A falsity undoubtedly acquires many tones and degrees as it moves farther away from truth. Bion (1970) speaks of the nature and degree of this estrangement, this formulation being of the essence of Bion's thoughts, because it includes the notion of movement or translation.

The lie is obviously a complex phenomenon. Bion speaks of lies throughout his works, giving the topic a whole chapter in *Attention and Interpretation* (1970) and referring to it often in *The Grid* (1977b). However, there are a number of questions we want to pose here.

The many dilemmatic situations of lies

For Bion, the lie is a particular transformation of the truth, used in various inter-related senses. Among these, we can mention falsities known to be such—for example, the use of the formulation " . . . we'll meet at sunrise", which (scientifically) is known as a false one, but is nevertheless used and understood in common language. Bion (1970) calls this a commensal relationship between the mind (container) and the formulation (content), which usually does not harm nor poison the mind of the one stating it nor the one listening/understanding it. Then there are myths, fabulous concoctions, social lies, "little white lies", compassionate lies, hypocrisy, "lying to oneself", defensive lies (sometimes used to save one's life), those related to perversions, and those due to omniscience (an omnipotent mental state, which also generates a vast assortment of lies, although those who maintain this mental attitude would swear by the "truth" of their prejudices), and so on. What, then, is a liar?

Is a liar someone who has once told a lie? But is there anyone who has *never* told one? Perhaps only a baby, because he still has no language—if, as Bion (1970) holds, the existence of a thinker/speaker is absolutely necessary for the lie. Is a liar someone who uses this mental functioning only occasionally, or someone who does so usually? And someone who lacks truth in analysis, who does not associate freely, what is he? A patient who cannot yet make contact with his truths, because of shame, repression, fear, or inhibitions? Again, there can be no patient who has not at least once either refrained from mentioning something he was thinking about or feeling, hidden something, said the opposite to his thoughts, or concealed an association during the psychoanalytic session. Should we consider him a lying patient? Or is the lying patient someone who *usually* lies to the analyst, in order to evoke/induce certain ideas in him or promote certain interpretations—an aspect of the reversal of perspective described by Bion (1963a)?

In the following comment on the various dilemmatic situations with which the lie and the liar present us, our numerical order does not imply degrees of greater or lesser importance, being only a tentative classification.

First dilemmatic situation:
lies and Lies

One of the first problems we met was Bion's permanent oscillation between two kinds of formulations described as lies: on the one hand, those that are a defensive strategy to evade a painful situation (the mechanisms of defence); on the other, those destined to denude not one's own mind, but basically that of the receptor, of the possible contact with truth. Therefore, to widen the conceptualization on this topic, we are going to differentiate the "lie" (with a small letter), related to defence mechanisms, from the "Lie" (with a capital letter), specifically related to conscious and denuding lying. We will use this mode of expression in the rest of this chapter.

In practice, it is essential to discriminate one from the other, since they have different motivations and depend on different functioning and states of mind. Obviously, they also imply different kinds of links: the lie, as a defensive strategy in the face of a threat of a catastrophic change, puts the mind into a paradoxical situation, since it confronts the problem of accepting the truth with the risks this implies—that is, emotional turbulence; or to choose the lie, which starves the mind at the cost of its integrity but guarantees its equilibrium.

For Grotstein (1981), the difference between falsities and lies is in the latter's use of psychotic mechanisms, which include disavowal; Meltzer (1978), analysing Bion's work, considers that lies (which for Meltzer also include hallucinations) are *always* defensive, and he places them on Row 2 of the Grid—something that Bion (1963a) also did, but later on (1977b) rejected. For Bléandonu

(1990), the psychotic patient and the liar attack the bases of psycho-analysis by destroying free association. Whereas the psychotic patient does so unconsciously, the liar falsifies associations on pur-pose.

We find that as analysts we do not yet have clear enough theo-ries to account for these different phenomena. One option would be to circumscribe the term "Lie" to those statements that imply or produce, in the one who tells it and/or in the one to whom it is told, a denudation of true feelings, an un-learning of what had already been learned, an un-thinking of what had already been thought, an un-linking of what had been linked. If we accept this option, then the Lie is a product of the psychotic part of the per-sonality, suffusing the non-psychotic aspects with morality/superiority. And lies—products of normal defence mechanisms, as is the case in normal and/or neurotic personalities—would there-fore not be included.

As for placing lies and Lies into the Grid, there are a number of problems, some already visualized by Bion himself. He first (1963a) put falsities, defence mechanisms, and lies all into Column 2; in *The Grid* (1977b) he found Column 2 inadequate for all these formulations. He himself then suggested that: "Column 2, like Row C, requires an expansion into a 'grid' of its own", and others (among them Meltzer, Bianchedi, and Sor, some members of the PCC in California, and so on) have thought about the possibility of constructing a Negative Grid in order to include Lies and other psychotically based formulations. Another possibility would be to place defence mechanisms into Column 2, and Lies into Column 6. This is still an open problem.

Second dilemmatic situation:
Lies, the contact with truth, and symbolic functions

In order to Lie, one previously has to have been near, or directly in touch with, the truth—in order not to stumble into it by accident. But for a Lie an audience is also necessary, someone who listens to it and believes/values it, as Freud also said about jokes (1905c). Obviously, the, Liar has to have had sufficient development of alpha-function—the function that produces symbols and allows for formulation/publication in linguistic terms. It is of course also true that, in order to put a discovered truth (discovered in at-one-ment with O) into words, a *thinker* (capable of thinking and publishing it) is also necessary: if he does publish it, it will be through a transformation in *K*, and therefore a falsity. A thinker is therefore also necessary for the formulation of a truth—a point that Bion did not state explicitly.

One of our questions refers to the destinies of the mental functioning of the Liar, who has reached sufficient development to have contact with truth. Grotstein (1995) refers to this problem when he says that the psychotic and the liar are closer to O and confuse it with K, whereas the normal and the neurotic individuals confuse K with O and are never really in touch with O—with the exception of geniuses or mystics. Liars and/or psychotics, says Grotstein, have lacked an adequate passage through the paranoid-schizoid and depressive positions and therefore confuse our sense of external reality with the "thing-in-itself" without an adequate imaginary or symbolic disguise.

Another possible way of thinking about this could be related to Meltzer's (1986) ideas about lies and hallucinosis, in an effort to apply these concepts to the type of Lies we are considering. Meltzer holds that the dream image generated by alpha-function *is* produced (an image in which the sense is trapped), but this mode of functioning, in face of the risk of the emergence of some not accepted thought, could be reverted half-way to produce a train of lies and false representations ("reversed alpha-function"). For Meltzer, this would be like covering symbols that have begun to be formed with a cloak of lies; these symbols have not been destroyed but are only disguised and therefore are potentially available to knowledge.

Third dilemmatic situation: the "creativity" of Lies

The Liar is sometimes (always?) creative in his constructions. How can this creativity be related to the Lie, the poison of the mind? We can draw a connection here with Meltzer's (1986) thoughts about the construction of primal lies or *false symbols*: "Examination of the techniques of the pamphleteer and pornographer, the demagogue and the propagandist, suggest that what looks like high intelligence is in fact a compound of speed and negativism that 'dazzles' the mind and interferes with rational honest thought". We can therefore stress that the true symbol requires time for its processing, and that speed interferes with and dazzles it, impeding the possibility of access to thought and truth.

Another possible solution to this problem is to think about it in relation to the characteristics of the link: if we consider that only the symbiotic link generates a conception of something new, then the existence of creative Lies (lies?) must be the result of a symbiotic link. But the un-truthful aspect of these creations makes us suggest a "– symbiotic link" (minus symbiotic link), tainted by –K. The symbiotic link aids integration in an ever-evolving complexity implicit in growth and development, in the context of a PS↔D relationship, and we think that a "– symbiotic link" can be thought of as the growth of cancerous cells, as Bion states in Chapter 13 of *Attention and Interpretation* (1970)—pulverizing truth and fragmenting the contained and the container.

Fourth dilemmatic situation:
social lies

The social aspect of the lie is also very important and poses a series of problems. On the one hand, very "creative" lies, like some philosophical or theological writings, have apparently—Bion speaks of this problem in his "parable of the liar" in *Attention and Interpretation* (1970)—saved humanity from succumbing to the anxieties related to knowing about one's own limitations and finitude/mortality. For example, the resistance of the Establishment in the face of the truth of certain scientific theories—those of Copernicus, Galileo, Darwin, and Freud, among others—have prevented a social catastrophic change, modulating their later acceptance. In these situations the social lie does not seem to be poison for society—it looks, rather, more like a passport to its survival. The container (society) is not prepared to receive the truth, and a period of time is necessary to develop one that can assimilate it. This type of situation has been thoroughly explored by the methodologist T. Kuhn in his book about *The Structure of Scientific Revolutions* (1970).

However, in the story/myth Bion (1977b) makes of the burial in Ur, the belief in the lies of religion, magic, and so on brought whole groups to their death. Social lies, then, save the group while poisoning the individual (Bianchedi, 1996).

This could also be linked with the *use* of ideas. If their use is *fanatical* (Sor & Senet de Gazzano, 1993), it can also be destructive of the group or groups. To put these Lies into action can lead to the extermination of whole populations, as occurred during the Inquisition, in several genocides, and in the Holocaust.

Fifth dilemmatic situation: structure or mental state?

Another of the (already very many) questions we pose, because of the co-existence in the mind of truthful and lying functioning, is whether it is possible to speak of a lying mental state, or whether it would be more correct to consider it a structure of the kind described as "perversion of thinking". Another possibility is to think that lying is a mental state, that can occur in any psychopathological condition as well as in a normal mental structure.

We do believe that the lie–Lie, being a human product, is part of our mental functioning. But the sometimes imperative need of the Liar to fall back on this kind of functioning can fix it in a rigid structure, which estranges him irreversibly from real or honest contact with the truth.

Sixth dilemmatic situation: analysability of the Liar

Can a lie be analysed? We believe it can. Can a Liar be analysed? Melanie Klein seems to have thought that he could not, but Bion (*The Grid*, 1977b) believes it is possible, as does Edna O'Shaughnessy (1995). We have not yet reached an answer, but the following discussions may help us to approach one. Bion's ideas allow us to reflect about the difference between one situation and the other. The decision to accept being in analysis puts the individual into the (dangerous) position of knowing that *it* (psychoanalysis) is a domain especially designed for the search of and commitment to truth. It is as if through analysis, or through the analyst, it were possible to distinguish everything that (as through a contrasting medium) signals that which is not associated with truth.

One would have to investigate the motives that bring a Liar to analysis. One of these might be a certain discomfort (an ego-dystonic situation) with his Lying aspects, recognized as such by other parts of his personality. Perhaps an indicator of analysability could be the degree to which a person wants analysis to endorse his Lies, or hopes to question them and change them.

We also wonder: if coming close to truth or making contact with it is food for the mind and changing it into Lies a poison, then who is the victim of this poison? The one who expresses them, or the one who listens/receives them? Does the Lying patient poison his own mind or that of the analyst? Or both? From a psychopathological point of view, we consider the Lie a perversion of thought. Analysts are beginning to consider the lie (in its various forms) as having a status between neurosis and psychosis (as Freud did with sexual perversions). At first, Freud (1905d) saw neurosis as the negative of perversions; later on (1924e) he considered perversions as more related to psychotic mechanisms (disavowal) but with an adequate, ego-syntonic relation to reality.

How can the analyst (working in good faith, and therefore assuming that his patient communicates the possible truths of his thoughts, feelings, and so on) realize that his patient is a Liar? Sometimes a long process is necessary to reach this conclusion. There are, however, some indicators that can be recognized as emotional countertransference reactions (in the wider sense of this term as formulated by Paula Heimann, Racker, Blejer, and so on) of the psychoanalyst, like feelings of a lack of understanding, incoherence, perplexity in hearing certain narratives, ethical conflicts in the face of the content of the patient's material, feelings of risk of complicity with the patient, and so forth. The greatest risk is obviously that the analyst, not being aware of the situation, falls into collusive corrupt or perverse pacts with his patient, never discovering or revealing the Lie to himself or to the patient.

Clinical vignettes

We have selected some clinical vignettes that, we believe, induce dilemmatic situations in the analyst.

Julius

Similarly to the patient described by Bion (1970), Julius was for a number of years usually at least 20 minutes late to his sessions—a fact he explained in various ways, always mentioning his difficulties which the journey to the office (he lives out of town . . .) and the time of his sessions imposed on him. On the other hand, when he *was* in session, he was a collaborative patient, capable of making connections with his conflicts and feelings and making evident progress in his analysis. His coming late was persistently interpreted by his analyst, who understood that the difficulties in using his sessions completely was fundamentally related to very deep fears of dependence and severe separation anxieties. The interpretations given him about the possible meanings of his coming late are uncountable. In spite of the fact that Julius partially changed his behaviour, when his coming late re-appeared, it was always followed by the same excuses, with no possibility that he could himself think about the relationship between coming late and his inner world. It was necessary for the analyst to become able to discover that the patient, in these repetitive episodes, was acting out a Lying aspect of himself, expressed in the fact that time and time again, year after year, he would express different versions of the same reasons, failing to recognize the analytic work done and his understanding of these attitudes.

In our understanding, what in the beginning of Julius's treatment might have been understood as a defence of the acknowledgement of his resistances, degenerated later into Lies. By his "excuses", the patient left apart a psychic reality of which he already had ample experience, denuding his mind of any content that could connect him with the truth of his emotions and destroying the significance of the analyst's interpretations. Only after having painfully analysed this aspect of his personality was there a striking change in his behaviour. Arriving late once again, he came to the session very much disturbed, telling the analyst that at the time of his session—having turned off the alarm clock—he had had an obvious transferential dream, one that highlighted very primitive phantasies related to his "symptom". In the dream, *he was in the house of the analyst, who showed up in a night-gown. He felt very uncomfortable and inadequate in this situation.*

Martha

Martha, 19 years of age, lied about the economic situation of her family at the beginning of her psychoanalytic treatment. Her parents complied with this lie, stating that they were in a very precarious economic situation. They said that the grandmother had to have an operation, and if Martha started a treatment of more than twice a week, they would not be able to pay for the operation. Implicitly, this meant that the choice was between either a psychoanalytic treatment of their daughter or the grandmother's life. The analyst was convinced this was true, and Martha began her treatment twice a week. During the analysis, it became evident that, instead, her family was in a very high economic situation. This Lie was based on the supposition that the analyst would take advantage of this fact if she knew of their real monetary power. When the analyst detected this situation (through indirect data), she felt anger about the attack that had been made at her, anger that interfered with her thinking capacity. During the treatment, different versions of the same Lie appeared, for example hiding acquisitions of material goods (i.e. a new car, the place they were going to go for vacations, etc.). These misunderstood situations sometimes generated "counter-actings" in the analyst, like accepting partial payments or allowing temporary debts.

During the tenth year of analysis, when this Lying situation had already been cleared up and the analyst knew the real economic situation of the family—because the patient no longer hid it—Martha came to a session saying that since the previous one *I have felt drowned in a cloud of dust or flies, which did not let me pay attention to any of the things I had to do in my job.* She linked this with a lie she felt compelled to tell her sister-in-law. The sister-in-law's father had died two days earlier, and she was very depressed. The patient told her sister-in-law that after returning from the wake the telephone rang, . . . *and, you know, I couldn't tell her that it was my father who had called, I told her it was my mother. I couldn't tell her because . . . . if she had lost her father, how could I tell her that my father was calling me? And while I was speaking to her I became more and more confused, and I was in a big mess, everything was getting mixed up. This is what happens to me . . . . I can't show what I have.* Martha questioned the lie she had told her sister-in-law. She connected this with the Lies she had told during the first years of her treatment. At this time of the analytical process she could perceive what happens to her head when she hides what she "has", lying and changing the truth. It is similar and yet different from what used to happen when this aspect was projected into the analyst, provoking confusion and anger in her. Actually, she could partially contain this in her mind, with awareness of the confusion into which she fell.

Laura

Laura, 41 years of age, called for an interview the day she learned of the (unexpected) death of her therapist. She did not state a clear motive for needing help; she described herself as crammed with external pressures, which she felt she had to fulfil, *because she was thus educated.* These pressures were fundamentally economical ones—she said that she had serious debts—and the need to start a parental lawsuit against the father of her third son. She said that there had been *many close deaths in her life,* mentioning that of *her father* (whom she described as a dishonest professional), *two pregnancies of her mother, her grandmother, J. F. Kennedy, and Martin Luther King.* She said that her therapist's death had brought her no internal conflict.

It did not take the analyst long to realize that the above-mentioned supposed debts were in reality the result of fraudulent activities of the patient, who had used (and perhaps was still using?) money her clients gave her for investments, believing she would return it in the future. The analyst was also aware—because this had been said by Laura and was then disavowed—that the actual swindles did not end there. Having been married, she had had a three-year-long love affair with the husband of her cousin, a man who carried out criminal operations in important financial centres.

The analyst suggested continuing having psychotherapeutic interviews until the economic situation of the patient would be clearer—the patient was only now seriously intending to look for a job—and when Laura's expectations in reference to a treatment were also more clear. During the interviews the analyst asked herself a great number of questions. The patient seemed to her to be someone who was severely disturbed, with a dishonest and psychopathic structure, and at double risk: an internal and an external one. Laura was someone who had hurt others and also herself, and may continue doing it. However, the analyst also saw her as someone burdened with all this, and willing to change. She asked herself: is this repentance and willingness to change true, a lie, or a Lie? Having at the same time realized the degree of the economical and emotional disaster the patient suffered and caused, she wondered whether she was not being called on to be an accomplice, maintaining a treatment and accepting fees with money of dubious provenance. On the other hand, she felt that psychotherapeutic sessions could be a certain anchor, which could partially protect Laura from falling into a destructive spiral.

Balint's patient

A patient came to the consultation. He was about to begin analysis but had not made up his mind. He had already seen some other analysts. He told a long, complicated, rich narrative, with details about what he felt and suffered. The analyst listened but did not understand. He asked the patient to come to another interview. The patient continued with his story, exaggerating it. The analyst still did not understand. What the patient was telling him were things as credible as any others, but the problem was that they did not harmonize.

The analyst said: "It's curious, you tell me many interesting things, but I must tell you that I don't understand anything of your history." The patient relaxed, smiled, and said: "You are the first sincere man I have found: I have already told all these things to a number of colleagues of yours, who immediately saw the evidence of an interesting and refined structure. I told you all this as a test, to see whether you were, like the others, a quack and a liar."

The analyst describing this episode is Balint, who mentions this case in his book *Primary Love and Psychoanalytic Technique* (1952). We believe that the emotional reaction of the analyst, of (a) not understanding, (b) the acknowledgement of not understanding, and (c) the awareness that the different elements of the story do not harmonize is an exquisitely receptive answer in the face of lying material.

Some questions related to the clinical vignettes

- Does the consistency of Lies change and become lighter during analysis?
- Does the Lie, for these patients, have the same imperious need that objects have for the perverse patient?
- Is the Lie a successful realization of the individual, which allows him to evade suffering pain?
- Should we deepen the interplay of the identifications that remit to a primitive superego needed by the Lie?
- Is it a mode of communication of patients, using realistic projective identification (Bion, 1962a)—with real effects in their analysts—like the attacks psychotic patients make on ego functions, with a mixture of arrogance and omnipotence?
- What, if anything, is the artificial character of the Lie symbolizing?
- Is Lying a way of preventing psychosis?

We want to finish this paper with Bion's phrase, mentioned in the ninth and last of his *Roman Seminars*, on 17 July 1977:

> Our capacity to say the truth dies through the lies we tell others.

We completely share his opinion.

REFERENCES

Allen, W. (1998). The Kugelmass episode. In: *Collected Prose* (pp. 345–360). London: Picador.

Alves, D. B. (1989). A consciência da soledade. Paidea II. In: *Revista Brasileira de Psicanálise*: 23–29.

Anderson, R. (Ed.) (1992). *Clinical Lectures on Klein and Bion*. London and New York: Tavistock/Routledge.

Andrade, C. D. (1983). *Poesia e Prosa*. Rio de Janeiro: Ed. Nova Aguiar.

Arendt, H. (1971). *The Life of Mind, Vol. I*. New York: Harcourt Brace Jovanovich.

Aristotle (360 BC). *Metaphysics* (ed. by W. D. Ross). In: *The Great Books of the Western Hemisphere*. Chicago, IL: Encyclopaedia Britannica.

Arlow, J. (1996). The concept of psychic reality—how useful? *International Journal of Psycho-Analysis*, 77: 659.

Association Française de Psychiatrie (1991). *W. R. Bion, une théorie pour l'avenir*. Paris: Éditions Métailié.

Auden, W. H. (1940). Atlantis. In: *Collected Shorter Poems, 1930–1944*. London: Faber & Faber.

Bachelard, G. (1938). *A Formação do Espírito Científico (contribuição para uma psicanálise do conhecimento)*. São Paulo: Contraponto, 1996.

Balint, M. (1952). *Primary Love and Psychoanalytic Technique* [reprinted London: Karnac Books, 1986].

Barale, F., & Ferro, A. (1992). Negative therapeutic reactions and microfractures in analytic communication. In: L. Nissim & A. Robutti (Eds.), *Shared Experience: The Psychoanalytic Dialogue* (pp. 143–165). London: Karnac Books.

Baranger, M., & Baranger, W. (1961–62). La situacion analitica como campo dinamico. In: *Problemas del campo analitico* (pp. 128–164). Buenos Aires: Kargieman, 1969.

Berlin, I. (1956). *The Age of Enlightenment*. New York: Meridian , 1984.

Bezoari, M., & Ferro, A. (1990). Elementos de un modelo del campo analitico: los agregados funcionales. *Revista de Psicoanalisis, 47* (5/6): 847–861.

Bezoari, M., & Ferro, A. (1992a). El sueño dentro de una teoria del campo: los agregados funcionales. *Revista de Psicoanalisis, 49* (5/6): 957–977.

Bezoari, M., & Ferro, A. (1992b). From a play between "parts" to transformations in the couple. Psychoanalysis in a bipersonal field. In: L. Nissim & A. Robutti (Eds.), *Shared Experience: The Psychoanalytic Dialogue* (pp. 43–65). London: Karnac Books.

Bezoari, M., & Ferro, A. (1996). Mots, images, affects. L'aventure du sens dans la rencontre analytique. *Revue Canadienne de Psychanalyse, 4* (1): 49–73.

Bianchedi, E. T. de (1993). Lies and falsities. *Journal of Melanie Klein and Object Relations, 11*: 30–46.

Bianchedi, E. T. de (1996). "Narcissism and social-ism". Unpublished paper presented at the First Italian Congress of the IIPG, Taormina, Italy (July).

Bianchedi, E. T. de (1997). From objects to links: discovering relatedness. *Journal of Melanie Klein and Object Relations, 15*: 227–234.

Bion, F. (1981). Talk in the Memorial Meeting to Dr. Wilfred R. Bion. *International Review of Psycho-Analysis, 8*: 5.

Bion, W. R. (1956). Development of schizophrenic thought. In: *Second Thoughts*. London: Heinemann Medical Books, 1967 [reprinted London: Karnac Books, 1987].

Bion, W. R. (1957a). On arrogance. In: *Second Thoughts*. London: Heinemann Medical Books, 1967 [reprinted London: Karnac Books, 1987].

Bion, W. R. (1957b). Differentiation of the psychotic from the non-psychotic personalities. In: *Second Thoughts*. London: Heinemann Medical Books, 1967 [reprinted London: Karnac Books, 1987].

Bion, W. R. (1959). Attacks on linking. In: *Second Thoughts*. London: Heinemann, 1967 [reprinted London: Karnac Books, 1987].

Bion, W. R. (1962a). *Learning from Experience*. London: Heinemann Medical Books [reprinted London: Karnac Books, 1984].

Bion, W. R. (1962b). A theory of thinking. In: *Second Thoughts*. London: Heinemann Medical Books, 1967 [reprinted London: Karnac Books, 1987].

Bion, W. R. (1963a). *Elements of Psycho-Analysis*. London: Heinemann Medical Books [reprinted London: Karnac Books, 1984].

Bion, W. R. (1963b). The Grid. In: *Taming Wild Thoughts* (ed. by Francesca Bion). London: Karnac Books, 1997.

Bion, W. R. (1965). *Transformations*. London: Heinemann Medical Books [reprinted London: Karnac Books, 1984].

Bion, W. R. (1967a). Notes on memory and desire. *Psychoanalytic Forum*, 2 (3): 271–280 [reprinted in: E. Bott Spillius (Ed.), *Melanie Klein Today, Vol. 2: Mainly Practice* (pp. 17–21). London: Routledge, 1988. Also in: *Cogitations, Extended Edition*. London: Karnac Books, 1994.

Bion, W. R. (1967b). *Second Thoughts*. London: Heinemann Medical Books, 1967 [reprinted London: Karnac Books, 1987].

Bion, W. R. (1968). *Lectures and Seminars in APA*. Buenos Aires: Argentina.

Bion, W. R. (1970). *Attention and Interpretation*. London: Tavistock Publications [reprinted London: Karnac Books 1984].

Bion, W. R. (1973). *Bion's Brazilian Lectures 1*. Rio de Janeiro: Imago Editora. Also in: *Brazilian Lectures*. London: Karnac Books, 1990.

Bion, W. R. (1974). *Bion's Brazilian Lectures 2*. Rio de Janeiro: Imago. Also in: *Brazilian Lectures*. London: Karnac Books, 1990.

Bion, W. R. (1975). *A Memoir of the Future, Book I: The Dream*. Rio de Janeiro: Imago. Also in: *A Memoir of the Future*. London: Karnac Books, 1991.

Bion, W. R. (1976a). *Clinical Seminar Recorded in São Paulo*. Private copies.

Bion, W. R. (1976b). Emotional turbulence. In: *Clinical Seminars and Four Papers*. Oxford: Fleetwood Press, 1987. Also in: *Clinical Seminars and Other Works*. London: Karnac Books, 1994.

Bion, W. R. (1976c). Evidence. In: *Clinical Seminars and Four Papers*.

Oxford: Fleetwood Press, 1987. Also in: *Clinical Seminars and Other Works*. London: Karnac Books, 1994.

Bion, W. R. (1976d). Interview with A. G. Banet Sr. In: *Group and Organisation Studies*, 1 (3): 268–285.

Bion, W. R. (1976e). On a quotation from Freud. In: *Clinical Seminars and Four Papers*. Oxford: Fleetwood Press, 1987. Also in: *Clinical Seminars and Other Works*. London: Karnac Books, 1994.

Bion, W. R. (1977a). *A Memoir of the Future, Book 2: The Past Presented*. Rio de Janeiro: Imago Editora. Also in: *A Memoir of the Future*. London: Karnac Books, 1991.

Bion, W. R. (1977b). *Two Papers: The Grid and Caesura*. Rio de Janeiro: Imago Editora Ltada [reprinted London: Karnac Books, 1989].

Bion, W. R. (1978). *Four Discussions with W. R. Bion*. Perthshire: Clunie Press [reprinted in: *Clinical Seminars and Other Works*. London: Karnac Books, 1994].

Bion, W. R. (1979a). Making the best of a bad job. *Bulletin British Psycho-Analytical Society*, February 1979. In: *Clinical Seminars and Four Papers*, 1987. Also in: *Clinical Seminars and Other Works*. London: Karnac Books, 1994.

Bion, W. R. (1979b). *A Memoir of the Future, Book 3: The Dawn of Oblivion*. Strathclyde: Clunie Press. Also in: *A Memoir of the Future*. London: Karnac Books, 1991.

Bion, W. R. (1980). *Bion in New York and São Paulo* (ed. by F. Bion). Strathclyde: Clunie Press.

Bion, W. R. (1982). *The Long Week-End 1897–1919: Part of a Life* (ed. by F. Bion). Oxford: Fleetwood Press [reprinted London: Karnac Books, 1991].

Bion, W. R. (1985a). *All My Sins Remembered* (ed. by F. Bion). Oxford: Fleetwood Press [reprinted London: Karnac Books, 1991].

Bion, W. R. (1985b). *Seminari Italiani* (ed. by F. Bion). Rome: Borla.

Bion, W. R. (1987a). *Clinical Seminars and Four Papers* (ed. by F. Bion). Oxford: Fleetwood Press. Also in: *Clinical Seminars and Other Works*. London: Karnac Books, 1994.

Bion, W. R. (1987b). "Supervisão clínica em grupo realizado em São Paulo" (transl. into Portuguese by J. A. Junqueira de Mattos). Unpublished.

Bion, W. R. (1990). *Brazilian Lectures*. London: Karnac Books.

Bion, W. R. (1992). *Cogitations, extended edition* (ed. by F. Bion). London: Karnac Books, 1994.

Bion, W. R. (1994). *Clinical Seminars and Other Works*. London: Karnac Books.

Bion, W. R. (1997). *War Diaries*. London: Karnac Books.

Bion, W. R., & Bion, F. (1981). *A Key to A Memoir of the Future.* Perthshire: Clunie Press. Also in: *A Memoir of the Future*. London: Karnac Books, 1991.

Bion Talamo, P. (1987). Perché non possiamo dirci bioniani. *Gruppo e Funzione analitica, 3*: 279–285.

Bion Talamo, P. (1995). Talk. In: *Bion's Writings Around the World*. Mimeograph, San Francisco: IAC.

Bion Talamo, P. (1997a). Bion: A Freudian innovator. *British Journal of Psychotherapy, 14* (1): pp. 47–59.

Bion Talamo, P. (1997b). Sleep as a way of (mental) life. In: S. Alhanati & K. Kostoulas (Eds.), *Primitive Mental States* (v. 1: *Across the Lifespan*, pp. 91–104). Northvale, NJ: Jason Aronson, 1997.

Bion Talamo, P. (1997c). The clinical relevance of "A Memoir of the Future". *Journal of Melanie Klein and Object Relations, 15*, 2, 1997, pp. 235–241 [Paper given at the XXXIX I.P.A. Congress, San Francisco, 31 July 1995. Panel: Bion's Contributions to Psychoanalytic Theory and Technique, reported in *International Journal of Psycho-Analysis, 77* (1996): p. 575].

Bléandonu, G. (1990). *Wilfred R. Bion. La vie et l'oeuvre, 1887–1979.* Paris: Dunod. English edition: *Wilfred R. Bion. His Life and Works, 1887–1979*. London: Free Association Books, 1994.

Bonasia, E. (1988). Death instinct or fear of death? Research into the problem of death. *Rivista di Psicoanalisi, 34*: 272–315.

Bonasia, E. (1992). Séparation et angoisse de mort. *Revue française de Psychanalyse, 5*.

Borgogno, F. (1990). Introduction to the Italian edition of E. Bott Spillius (Ed.), *Melanie Klein Today*. London: Routledge, 1988.

Borgogno, F. (1992). Evoluzione della tecnica psicoanalitica. Un omaggio a Paula Heimann. *Rivista di Psicoanalisi, 38* (4): 1046–1071.

Borgogno, F. (1993). Intorno a *Memoria del Futuro* di W. R. Bion. *Rivista di Psicoanalisi, 40* (1, 1994): 71–80.

Borgogno, F. (1994). Leggendo "Nascita alla vita psichica. . . ." In: A. Ciccone & L. Lhopital (Eds.), *La nascita alla vita psichica*. Rome: Borla.

Borgogno, F. (1995). "Parla il campo": immagini e pensieri. In:

Eugenio Gaburri (Ed.), *Emozione e interpretazione*. Turin: Bollati Boringhieri, 1997.

Borgogno, F. (1998). *I Seminari Milanesi di Franco Borgogno: Sandor Ferenczi*. Quaderni del Centro Milanese di Psicoanalisi Cesare Musatti, 2. Monza: La Tipografia Monzese.

Bott Spillius E. (Ed.) (1988). *Melanie Klein Today, Vols. I & II*. London: Routledge.

Braithwaite, R. B. (1955). *Scientific Explanation*. Cambridge: Cambridge University Press.

Cassirer, E. (1906). *The Problem of Knowledge: Philosophy, Science, and History since Hegel* (transl. by W. H. Woglow & C. W. Hendel). New Haven: Yale University Press, 1950.

Castermane, I. (1996). Uma experiência interior. In: *O Correo da unesco* (pp. 32–35). Rio de Janeiro: Ed. Fundação Getúlio Vargas.

Corel, A., Faimberg, H., & Wender, L. (1982). La psychanalyse en Argentine. In: *Histoire de la psychanalyse*. Paris: Hachette.

Corrao, F. (1981). Bion: il modello trasformazionale del pensiero. In: *Orme, Vol. 1*. Milan: Raffaello Cortina Editore, 1998.

Corrao, F. (1986). Il concetto di campo come modello teorico. In: E. Gaburri (Ed.), *Emozione e interpretazione*. Turin: Bollati Boringhieri, 1997.

Corrao, F. (1989). Morfologia e trasformazione dei modelli analitici. *Rivista di Psicoanalisi, 35* (3): 512–545.

Corrao, F. (1998). *Orme, Vols. 1 & 2*. Milan: Raffaello Cortina Editore.

Descartes, R. (1637). Discourse on the method of rightly conducting the reason and seeking for truth in the sciences. In: E. S. Haldane and G. R. T. Ross (Eds.), *The Great Books of The Western Hemisphere*. Chicago, IL: Encyclopaedia Britannica.

Eco, U. (1979). *Lector in fabula*. Milan: Bompiani.

Eigen, M. (1997). A bug-free universe. *Contemporary Psychoanalysis, 33* (1): 19–41. Also in: *Toxic Nourishment* (pp. 57–83). London Karnac Books, 1999.

Emde, R. N. (1989). *The Infant's Relationship Experience: Developmental and Affective Aspects*. In: A. J. Sameroff & R. N. Emde (Eds.), *Relationships Disturbances in Early Childhood. A Developmental Approach*. New York: Basic Books.

Faimberg, H. (1981). Une des difficultés de l'analyse: la reconnaissance de l'alterité. *Revue Française de Psychanalyse, 45* (6): 1351–1367.

Faimberg, H. (1985). Le téléscopage des générations. In: R. Kaës, H. Faimberg, M. Enriquez, & J.-J. Baranes, *La Transmission de la vie psychique*. Paris: Dunod, 1993.

Faimberg, H. (1989). Sans mémoire et sans désir: à qui s'adressait Bion. *Revue Française de Psychanalyse, 53*: 1453–1461.

Faimberg, H. (1992a). The countertransference position and the countertransference. *International Journal of Psycho-Analysis, 73*: 541–547.

Faimberg, H. (1992b). L'énigme que pose le transfert. In: J. Laplanche et al., *Colloque International de psychanalyse* (pp. 211–221). Paris: Presses Universitaires de France.

Faimberg, H. (1996). Listening to listening. *International Journal of Psycho-Analysis, 77*: 667–677.

Faimberg, H. (1997). Misunderstanding and psychic truths. *International Journal of Psycho-Analysis, 78*: 439–451.

Faimberg, H., & Corel, A. (1989). Repetition and surprise: a clinical approach to the necessity of construction and its validation. *International Journal of Psycho-Analysis, 71* (1990): 411–420.

Ferenczi, S. (1932). The clinical diary of Sandor Ferenczi (ed. by J. Dupont). Cambridge, MA: Harvard University Press, 1988.

Ferrater Mora, J. (1958). *Diccionario de Filosofa*. Buenos Aires: Editorial Sudamericana.

Ferro, A. (1991). From Raging Bull to Theseus: the long path of a transformation. *International Journal of Psycho-Analysis, 72*: 417–425.

Ferro, A. (1992). *La tecnica nella psicoanalisi infantile. Il bambino e l'analista: dalla relazione al campo emotivo*. Milan: Raffaello Cortina Editore.

Ferro, A. (1993a). From hallucination to dream: from evacuation to the tolerability of pain in the analysis of a preadolescent. *The Psychoanalytic Review, 80* (3): 389–404.

Ferro, A. (1993b). The impasse within a theory of the analytic field: possible vertices of observation. *International Journal of Psycho-Analysis, 74* (5): 917–929.

Ferro, A. (1993c). Zwei Autoren auf der suche nach Personen: Die Beziehung, das Feld, die Geschichte. *Psyche, 10* (47): 951–972.

Ferro, A. (1995). El dialogo analitico: mundos posibles y transformaciones en el campo analitico. *Revista de Psicoanalisis, 4*: 773.

Ferro, A. (1996a). "A sexualidade come genere narrativo." Paper presented at "Bion en Saõ Paulo: ressonances" (14 November).

Ferro, A. (1996b). Carla's panic attacks: insight and transformations. What comes out of the cracks: monsters or nascent thoughts? *International Journal of Psycho-Analysis, 77*: 997–1011.

Ferro, A. (1996c). Los personajes del cuarto de analisis: que realidad? *Revista Madrid, 123*: 133–142.

Ferro, A. (1996d). *Nella Stanza d'Analisi. Emozioni, Racconti, Trasformazioni*. Milan: Raffaello Cortina.

Freud, S. (1900a). *The Interpretation of Dreams. S.E., 4–5.*

Freud, S. (1901b). *The Psychopathology of Everyday Life. S.E., 6.*

Freud, S. (1905c). *Jokes and Their Relation to the Unconscious. S.E., 8.*

Freud, S. (1905d). *Three Essays on the Theory of Sexuality. S.E., 7.*

Freud, S. (1911b). Formulations on the two principles of mental functioning. *S. E., 12*: 213–226.

Freud, S. (1911c [1910]). Psycho-Analytic Notes on an Autobiographical Account of a Case of Paranoia. *S.E. 12.*

Freud, S. (1912b). The dynamics of transference. *S.E. 12.*

Freud, S. (1912–13). *Totem and Taboo. S.E. 13.*

Freud, S. (1915b). Thoughts for the times on war and death. *S.E. 14.*

Freud, S. (1915c). *Instincts and Their Vicissitudes. S.E. 14.*

Freud, S. (1915e). The unconscious. *S.E. 14.*

Freud, S. (1916a [1915]). On Transience. *S.E., 17.*

Freud, S. (1917d [1915]). A metapsychological supplement to the theory of dreams. *S.E. 14.*

Freud, S. (1919h). The uncanny. *S.E. 17.*

Freud, S. (1920g). *Beyond the Pleasure Principle. S.E., 18.*

Freud, S. (1924e). The loss of reality in neurosis and psychosis, *S.E. 19.*

Freud, S. (1925h). Negation, *S.E., 19*: 237.

Freud, S. (1926d [1925]). *Inhibitions, Symptoms and Anxiety. S.E., 23.*

Freud, S. (1927c). *The Future of an Illusion. S.E. 21.*

Freud, S. (1927e). Fetishism. *S.E. 21.*

Freud, S. (1933b [1932]). *Why War? S.E., 22*

Freud, S. (1940 [1938]). Splitting of the ego in the process of defence. *S.E. 23.*

Freud, S. (1941f [1938]). Findings, ideas, problems. *S.E. 23.*

Freud, S. (1950a). The origins of psycho-analysis. *S.E. 1.* Letter of 6 December 1896 to Fliess.

Freud, S., & Andreas-Salome, L. (1912–1936). *Letters.* London: Hogarth, 1972.

Gaburri, E. (1997). Introduzione. In: *Emozione e interpretazione*. Turin: Bollati Boringhieri.

Green, A. (1973). On negative capability. *International Journal of Psycho-Analysis, 54*: 115.

Green, A. (1975). The analyst, symbolisation and absence in the analytic setting. *International Journal of Psycho-Analysis, 56*: 1–22. Also in *Private Madness*. London: Hogarth, 1986 [reprinted London: Karnac Books, 1997].

Green, A. (1992). Book reviews: "Cogitations". *International Journal of Psychoanalysis, 73*: 585.

Green, A. (1996). Has sexuality anything to do with psychoanalysis? *International Journal of Psycho-Analysis, 76*: 871.

Greenberg, J., & Mitchell, S. (1983). *Object Relations in Psychoanalytic Theory*. Cambridge, MA: Harvard University Press.

Grotstein, J. S. (1978). Inner space: its dimensions and its coordinates. *International Journal of Psycho-Analysis, 59*: 55–61.

Grotstein, J. S. (Ed.) (1981). *Do I Dare Disturb the Universe? A Memorial to Wilfred R. Bion*. Beverly Hills, CA: Caesura Press [reprinted London: Karnac Books, 1986].

Grotstein, J. S. (1995). Bion's transformations in O, the "thing-in-itself" and the "real": toward the concept of the "transcendent position". Unpublished paper given at the 39th IPA International Congress in San Francisco, CA (July), in the panel, "Bion's Contributions to Psychoanalytic Theory and Technique".

Grotstein, J. S. (1996). Bion's "transformation in O", "the thing-in-itself", and the "real": toward the concept of the "transcendent position." *Journal of Melanie Klein and Object Relations, 14* (2): 109–142.

Grotstein, J. S. (1997). "Fearful symmetry" and the calipers of the infinite geometer: Matte-Blanco's legacy to our conception of the unconscious. Matte-Blanco today I: Mainly clinical (Special Issue). *The Journal of Melanie Klein and Object Relations, 15* (4): 631–646.

Grotstein, J. S. (1998). The numinous and immanent nature of the psychoanalytic subject. *Journal of Analytical Psychology; 43* (1): 41–68.

Grotstein, J. S. (in press). *Who Is the Dreamer Who Dreams the Dream?* Hillsdale, NJ & London: The Analytic Press.

Hampson, N. (1968). *The Enlightenment. An Evaluation of Its Assumptions, Attitudes and Values.* London: Penguin Books, 1990.

Hartmann, N. (1960). *A Filosofia do Idealismo Alemão.* Lisbon: Fundação Calouste Gulbekian, 1983.

Hawking, S. (1988). *A Brief History of Time.* New York: Bantam Books, 1989.

Heath T. L. (1956). *The Thirteen Books of Euclid's Elements* (2nd edition). New York: Dover, 1956.

Hegel, G. W. F. (1817–1820). *Philosophy of Mind* (ed. by W. Wallace & A. V. Miller). Oxford: Oxford University Press, 1971.

Heidegger, M. (1931). *Being and Time* (3rd edition, transl. by J. Macquarrie & E. Robinson). San Francisco, CA: HarperCollins, 1962.

Heidegger, M. (1968). *What Is Called Thinking?* (transl. by F. Wieck & G. Gray). New York: Harper & Row.

Heimann, P. (1989). *About Children and Children-No-Longer* (ed. by M. Tonnesmann). London: Tavistock/Routledge.

Herbert, P. M. (1993). *The Life of the Buddha.* San Francisco: Pomegranate Artbooks, 1992.

Hesse, H. (1970). *Demian.* Rio de Janeiro: Civilização Brasileira S.A. New York: Bantam, 1965.

Honegger, M. (1976). *Science de la Musique.* Paris: Bordas.

Hume, D. (1748). *An Enquiry Concerning Human Understanding.*

Jones E. (1953). *The Life and Work of Sigmund Freud.* New York: Basic Books.

Jung, C. G. (1916). *The Transcendent Function* (transl. by A. R. Pope). Privately printed for the Students' Association, C. G. Jung Institute, Zurich, 1957.

Kant, I. (1783). *Prolegomena to Any Future Metaphysics that Can Qualify as a Science* (transl. P. Carus). Chicago and La Salle, IL.: Open Court, 1996.

Kant, I. (1787). *Critique of Pure Reason* (trans. by N. Kemp Smith). New York: St. Martin's Press, 1965.

Keats, J. (1817). Letter to George and Thomas Keats, 21 December 1817. In Hyder Edward Rollins (Ed.), *The letters of John Keats 1814–1821.* London: Oxford University Press, 1958.

Klein, G. S. (1976). *Psychoanalytic Theory: An Exploration of the Essentials.* New York: International Universities Press.

Klein, M. (1932). *The Psycho-Analysis of Children.* London: Hogarth

Press and the Institute of Psycho-Analysis, 1959 [reprinted London: Karnac Books, 1998].

Klein, M. (1946). Notes on some schizoid mechanism. In: *Envy and Gratitude, and Other Works*. London: Hogarth Press, 1975 [reprinted London: Karnac Books, 1993].

Klein, M. (1948). On the theory of anxiety and guilt. In: *Developments in Psychoanalysis*. In: *Envy and Gratitude, and Other Works*. London: Hogarth Press, 1975 [reprinted London: Karnac Books, 1993].

Klein, M. (1975). Infantile anxiety situations reflected in a work of art and in the creative impulse. In: *Love, Guilt and Reparation and Other Works*. London: Hogarth Press, 1975 [reprinted London: Karnac Books, 1992].

Kuhn, Thomas S. (1970). *The Structure of Scientific Revolutions* (second ed.). Chicago, IL: Chicago University Press.

Lacan, J. (1966). *Écrits*. Paris: Seuil.

Lachmann, F. M., & Beebe, B. (1996). Three principles of salience in the organization of the analyst–patient interaction. *Psychoanalytic Psychology, 13*.

Laplanche, J. & Pontalis, J.-B. (1983). *The Language of Psycho-Analysis* (trans. D. Nicholson-Smith). London: Hogarth [reprinted London: Karnac Books, 1988].

Liberman, D. (1970). Linguistica, interaccion comunicativa y proceso psicoanalitico [Linguistics, communicative interaction, and psychoanalytic process]. Buenos Aires: Nueva Visión, 1971–72.

Lichtenberg, J. D. (1983). *Psychoanalysis and Infant Research*. Hillsdale, NJ: The Analytic Press.

Matte Blanco, I. (1975). *The Unconscious as Infinite Sets*. London: Duckworth Press [reprinted London: Karnac Books, 1998].

Matte Blanco, I. (1981). Reflecting with Bion. In: J. S. Grotstein (Ed.), *Do I Dare Disturb the Universe? A Memorial to Wilfred R. Bion* (pp. 489–528). Beverly Hills, CA: Caesura Press, 1981 [reprinted London: Karnac Books, 1988].

Matte Blanco, I. (1988). *Thinking, Feeling, and Being: Clinical Reflections on the Fundamental Antinomy of Human Beings*. London and New York: Tavistock/Routledge.

Mattos, J. A. J. de (1997). Transference and counter-transference as transience. Paper presented at the International Centennial Conference on the Work of W. R. Bion, Turin, Italy (July 16–19).

McDougall J. (1995). *The Many Faces of Eros*. London: Free Association Books.

Meltzer D. (1973). *Sexual States of Mind*. Strathclyde: Clunie Press.

Meltzer, D. (1978). *The Kleinian Development, Vol. 3: The Clinical Significance of the Work of Bion*. Strathclyde: Clunie Press. New edition: *The Kleinian Development*. London: Karnac Books, 1998.

Meltzer, D. (1980). "The diameter of the circle" in Wilfred Bion's work. In: *Sincerity and Other Works: Collected Papers of Donald Meltzer* (ed. by A. Hahn) (pp. 469–474). London: Karnac Books, 1994.

Meltzer, D. (1982a). Interventi in allucinazione e bugia. *Quaderni di Psicoterapia Infantile, Vol. 13*. Rome: Borla.

Meltzer, D. (1982b). Un'indagine sulle bugie: loro genesi e relazione con l'allucinazione. *Quaderni di Psicoterapia Infantile, Vol. 13*. Rome: Borla.

Meltzer, D. (1984). *Dream Life*. Strathclyde: The Roland Harris Education Trust.

Meltzer, D. (1985). Three lectures on W. R. Bion's *A Memoir of the Future* (with Meg Harris Williams). In: *Sincerity and Other Works: Collected Papers of Donald Meltzer* (ed. by A. Hahn) (pp. 520–550). London: Karnac Books, 1994.

Meltzer, D. (1986). *Studies in Extended Metapsychology: A Clinical Application of Bion's Ideas*. Strath Tay, Perthshire: Clunie Press.

Meotti, A. (1978). La filosofia dell'induzione. In: Meotti, A. (Ed.), *L'induzione e l'ordine dell'universo*. Milan: Edizioni di Comunità.

Meotti, A. (1981). A Bionian hypothesis on the origin of thought. *Rivista di Psicoanalisi 37* (3–4): 425–435.

Molesworth, Mrs. (1877). *The Cuckoo Clock*. London: Macmillan [reprinted 1938].

Money-Kyrle R. (1955). An inconclusive contribution to the theory of the death instinct. In: *New Directions in Psycho-Analysis*. London: Tavistock Publications [reprinted London: Karnac Books, 1993].

Nietzsche, F. (1888). *Ecce Homo—How One Becomes What One Is* (trans. by R. J. Hollingdale). London: Penguin Classics.

O'Shaughnessy, E. (1995). Minus K. Paper presented at the XXXIX IPA Congress in San Francisco. *International Journal of Psycho-Analysis*.

Ogden, T. (1994). The analytic third: working with intersubjective clinical facts. *International Journal of Psycho-Analysis, 75*: 3–20.

Pascal, B, *Pensées* (ed. by W. Trotter). In: *The Great Books of the Western World*. Chicago, IL: Encyclopaedia Britannica, 1994.

Peirce, C. S. (1931). *Collected Papers, Vols. I–VIII* (ed. by C. Hartshore & P. Weiss). Cambridge, MA: Harvard University Press.

Philips, F. (1989). Imitation et hallucination en Psychanalyse. *Revue Française de Psychanal. 53*: 1293.

Planck, M. (1949). Scientific autobiography (ed. by F. Gaynor). In: *The Great Books of the Western World*. Chicago, IL: Encyclopaedia Britannica, 1994.

Popper, K. R. (1958). *The Logic of Scientific Discovery*. London: Hutchinson.

Pritchard, F. H. (1925). *Fifty Stories from Uncle Remus*. London: George G. Harrap [reprinted 1948].

Rickman, J. (1950). The factor of number in individual- and group-dynamics. In: *Selected Contributions to Psycho-Analysis*. London: Hogarth Press, 1957.

Ricoeur, P. (1970). *Freud and Philosophy: An Essay on Interpretation* (transl. by D. Savage). New Haven, CT: Yale University Press.

Rorschach, H. (1921). *Psychodiagnostics: A Diagnostic Test Based on Perception*. Bern: Huber (transl. & English ed. by P. Lemkau & B. Kronenberg, ed. by W. Morgenthaler). New York: Grune & Stratton, 1942.

Sameroff, A. S., & Emde, R. N. (Eds.), *Relationship Disturbances in Early Childhood. A Developmental Approach*. New York: Basic Books.

Sander, L. (1962). Issues in early mother–child interaction. *Journal of the American Academy of Child Psychiatry, 1*: 141–166.

Sandler, P. C. (1988). Introdução. In: W. R. Bion, *Uma Memória do Futuro*. Rio de Janeiro: Imago Editora.

Sandler, P. C. (1990). *Fatos: a tragédia do conhecimento em psicanálise*. Rio de Janeiro: Imago Editora.

Sandler, P. C. (1994). "The differentiation between system and totalities: passion and enthusiasm"; "Reinhold, Beck, Maimon, and Bion: the return of the mind"; "The space–time 'O'"; "Fichte: glancing 'D', rapid return to 'PS'"; "Schelling and Freud: rescue of the mind (D)". Lectures on "The Apprehension of Psychic Reality" at Sociedade Brasileira de Psicanálise de São Paulo and at Nucleo de Psicanálise de Curitiba. Rio de Janeiro: Imago Editora.

Sandler, P. C. (1996). "Hegel, Melanie Klein and Bion: unequalled romantics"; "The absolute"; "Putting up with paradoxes"; "'NO' revisited: dialectics"; "The absolute, dialectics and psycho-analysis as the search of truth about oneself". Lectures on "The Apprehension of Psychic Reality" at Sociedade Brasileira de Psicanálise de São Paulo and at Nucleo de Psicanálise de Curitiba. Rio de Janeiro: Imago Editora.

Sandler, P. C. (1997). The apprehension of psychic reality: extensions of Bion's theory of alpha-function. *International Journal of Psycho-Analysis, 77*: 43.

Semple & Kneebone (1949). *Algebraic Geometry*. Oxford: Clarendon Press.

Sor D., & Gazzano, M. R. (1993). *Fanatismo*. Santiago de Chile: Editorial Anank.

Speziale-Bagliacca, R. (1984). Em-mature e l'enunciato del non-agire. Da "Lo sviluppo kleiniano" di Meltzer alcune riflessioni sulla memoria e il desiderio. *Rivista di Psicoanalisi, 30* (1): 143–155.

Speziale-Bagliacca, R. (1991). *On the Shoulders of Freud: Freud, Lacan, and the Psychoanalysis of Phallic Ideology*. New Brunswick, NJ: Transaction Books.

Speziale-Bagliacca, R. (1997). *Colpa*. Rome: Astrolabio.

Stern, D. N. (1985). *The Interpersonal World of the Infant*. New York: Basic Books [reprinted London: Karnac Books, 1998].

Stern, D. N. (1995). *The Motherhood Constellation*. New York: Basic Books [reprinted London: Karnac Books, 1998].

Symington, J., & Symington, N. (1996). *The Clinical Thinking of Wilfred Bion*. London & New York: Routledge.

Thorner, H. A. (1981). Notes on the desire of knowledge. *International Journal of Psycho-Analysis, 62*: 73.

Tucker, W., & Tucker, K. (1988). *The Dark Matter: Contemporary Science's Quest for the Mass Hidden in: the Our Universe*. New York: William Morrow.

Vallino D. (1997). Il campo psicoanalitico e il giardino segreto: una metafora per lo sviluppo del pensiero vivente. In: E. Gaburri (Ed.), *Emozione e interpretazione*. Turin: Bollati Boringhieri.

Webb, R. E., & Sells, M. A. (1997). Lacan and Bion: psychoanalysis and the mystical language of "unsaying". *Journal of Melanie Klein and Object Relations, 15* (2): 43–264.

Wilkinson, E. M. (1969/1993). Goethe. In: *Encyclopaedia Britannica*. Chicago, IL: Encyclopaedia Britannica.

Williams, M. H. (1985). The tiger and "O": a reading of Bion's *Memoir of the Future*. *Free Associations, 1*: 33–56.

Winnicott, D. W. (1969). The use of an object. *International Journal of Psycho-Analysis 50*: 711. Also in: *Playing and Reality* (pp. 86–94). London: Tavistock, 1971.

Winnicott, D. W. (1987). *The Spontaneous Gesture. Selected Letters* (ed. by F. R. Rodman). Cambridge, MA: Harvard University Press [reprinted London: Karnac Books, 1999].

INDEX

Abalos brothers, 15
absolute:
    as O's *nom de plume*, 133
    truth: *see* truth(s), absolute
abstraction, 85, 105, 112, 118, 119,
    195
achievement:
    language of, 8, 203
    man of, 132
acting:
    in, 92
    out, 30, 113, 121, 150, 230
action(s):
    as corresponding to evacuation,
        112, 113
    in Grid, 112, 183, 188
adequate interpretations, 75
adequate objects, 149
adequate role for patient played by
    analyst, 149
aesthetic experience of not knowing,
    affectionate, 4
Ainsworth, M., 174

algebraic calculations, 194
algebraic calculus(i), 186, 194
Allen, W., 93
alpha:
    -beta-ization/alphabetization, 6,
        67, 92, 105
    lack of, 5–6
    element(s), xxii, 23–25, 34, 36, 44,
        92, 94–96, 101–105, 116, 120,
        128, 184–186, 188, 194, 201, 209
    function, 34, 36, 37, 43, 50, 92, 94,
        95, 97, 101, 102, 115, 118, 120,
        121, 135, 177, 184, 193, 201, 210,
        212, 214, 225, 226
    reversed, 226
    metafunction, 105
    myth-making as essential function
        of, 177
Alves, D. B., xiii, 3–4, 27–44
analysability, 115–116
    of Liar, 228–229
analyst, function of as intellectual
    leader, 68n

Index compiled by Silvio A. Merciai.

analytic process, 7, 36, 44, 70, 151,
    232
Ananke, 129, 135
Andreas-Salome, L., Freud's letter to,
    81
animism, 47
annihilation, 159, 186
    threat of, 114, 123
    or baby's fear of dying, 120
anxiety(ies), 194, 227
    analyst's, 24, 44, 150, 182
    castration, 4, 46
    death: *see* death, anxiety(ies)
    depressive, 103
    and difficulties suffered by Bion's
        mother, 11
    evacuation of, 118
    fear of end as primary cause of, 47
    lying in deepest layers of
        primordial mind, 120
    nameless, 84, 85
    paranoid, 30
    patient's, 44, 81
    prey–predator, 134
    psychotic, 46, 47
    realistic/real, 4, 46
    separation, xiv, 37, 42, 230
    stirred by decisions, 41
apprehension(s), 203
    of common sense, 37, 215
    inner, 206
    of processes of thinking, 206
    of reality, 201, 212, 215, 217
        psychic, 35, 41
    of selected fact, 36
Aristotle (Aristotelian), 9, 45, 49, 131,
    140, 175, 221
arrogance, 125, 234
at-one-ment, 194, 222, 226
ATP (adenosine-tri-phosphate), 210,
    212
attack(s), 49, 167
    against analyst, 67
    on common sense, 175
    on conscious; on inner and outer
        reality and mental apparatus,
        49
    on curiosity, 25

on ego functions, 234
on furthering of thinking–feeling
    processes, 25
on life, 95
on links: *see* link(s)
by patient, 148, 153
on reality, 208
sponsored by death instinct, 141n
attention, 121, 179, 183
    to needs and feelings of other, 61,
        63
    suspended, 84
awe, 70, 138

Bachelard, G., 208
balpha, 5–6, 102, 104, 105
Baranger, M., 84
Baranger, W., 84
basic assumption(s), 59, 117, 119–120
Beethoven, L., 206
being, process of, 202
being-in-itself [*Dasein*], 7, 130, 133,
    134
Berkeley, G., 68n, 176, 177
beta:
    element(s), 5, 92, 97, 102, 104, 111,
        112, 115, 116, 118, 119, 120, 121,
        123, 131, 143, 184–186, 188, 192,
        194, 214
    space, 111
"betalomi", 92
Bianchedi, E.: *see* Tabak de Bianchedi,
    E.
bi-logic structures, 140
binocular, 205, 212
Bion, Francesca, xiii, xxiii, 3, 11–19,
    21, 77, 108
Bion, Frederic, 11
Bion, W. R., *passim*
    All My Sins Remembered, 15, 77n,
        199
    "Arrogance, On", 197, 216
    "Attacks on Linking", 47, 65, 125,
        197
    Attention and Interpretation, 24, 38,
        45, 53, 54, 58, 58n, 109, 122,
        125, 126, 132, 136, 186, 194, 198,
        203, 222, 223, 227

Bion in New York and São Paulo, 22, 23, 26, 74, 77, 96, 144n

Brazilian Lectures, 22, 74, 76, 198, 199

Clinical Seminars and Four Papers, 22, 74, 95, 199

Clinical Seminars and Other Works, 22, 74, 95

Cogitations, xiii, 4, 12, 16, 21, 23, 35, 38, 58, 63–72, 73, 74, 92, 101, 111, 115, 124–125, 132, 138, 160, 161, 166–171, 175–177, 182, 194, 196, 199, 204, 207, 208, 214

"Development of Schizophrenic Thought", 197, 214, 216

Elements of Psycho-Analysis, 58n, 92, 96, 101, 125, 132, 136, 165, 180, 182, 183, 184, 185, 186, 188, 189, 197, 201, 204, 214, 216, 224, 225

"Evidence", 198, 205

Experiences in Groups, 169

Four Discussions with W. R. Bion, 22, 198

"Grid, The", 8, 178–199, 225

"Interview with A. G. Bonet Sr.", 48

Learning from Experience, 47, 58n, 92, 101, 125, 136, 179, 193, 197, 201, 204, 208, 210, 214, 216, 222, 234

Long Week-End 1897–1919: Part of a Life, The, 58, 144, 199

Memoir of the Future, A, xiii, xvi, 7, 14, 34, 44, 62n, 75, 96, 109–110, 126, 142, 144n, 155–163, 172, 181, 188, 199, 201, 203, 205, 207, 209, 214

"Notes on Memory and Desire", 21, 22, 38, 58n, 82, 198

"Quotation from Freud, On a", 205

Second Thoughts, 58n, 125, 165, 166, 172, 180, 185, 198, 203

Seminari Italiani, 56, 74, 77–78

Taming Wild Thoughts, 16

"Theory of Thinking, A", 47, 92, 97, 125, 165, 197, 201, 202, 203, 204, 208, 210

Transformations, 54, 58n, 92, 97, 101, 125, 132, 165, 197, 202, 204, 206, 209, 221

Two Papers: The Grid and Caesura, 58n, 110, 113, 181, 184, 189, 198, 220, 221, 223, 224, 225, 228

War Diaries, 15

works of, in *International Journal of Psychoanalysis*, 58n

Bionian analysts, 2–3, 56n, 57–58, 108, 152, 153

Bion's Legacy to Groups, v, 12

Bion Talamo, Parthenope, v, xiii–xiv, xvi, 1–9, 15, 17–19, 20–26, 56, 56n, 58, 59, 61, 62, 63, 63n, 64n, 71n, 74n, 76, 108, 209

bizarre object: *see* object(s), bizarre

black holes, 123

Blanchot, M., *La réponse est le malheur de la question*, 25, 74n, 122, 202

Bléandonu, G., 224–225

Blomfield, O. H. D., 129n

body, part of, inner, 115

Bonasia, E., xiv, 4, 45–55

Borgogno, F., v, xiv, 1–9, 56–78

Bowlby, J., 174

Braithwaite, R. B., 194

branchial cleft, 111

breast(s), 34, 119, 120, 121, 123, 141, 185, 194, 201, 208, 209, 210, 211, 213, 214, 217, 218, 219

absent, 144

-feeding, 35

no-, 203, 206, 209, 214, 218

thing-presentation of, 118

Bregazzi, C., 220–235

Brer Fox & Brer Rabbit, 20, 22

Buber, M., 72

Buddha: *see* clinical vignettes, Case B

caesura, 196

of act of birth, 41, 110, 196

between mother's womb and child, 110

in Bion's work, 9, 197–199

calculus(i), 186, 194, 195

Calvino, I., 5, 90

Cantor, G., 131

capacity(ies):
   for accepting loss, 89
   of analyst:
      for being "in tune" at different
         stages of analysis, 61
      to concentrate on present
         situation, 24
      for not jumping to conclusions,
         26
      to offer himself to patient as
         container, 69
      to remember patient, 23–24
      to respond fully to calls for help,
         70
   for attaining subordination to
      group, 167
   of being able to share own
      examination of reality, 168
   for clinical discrimination, 180
   to contain baby's realistic
      projective identifications and
      detoxify them before returning
      them, 222
   for cooperation, 162
   for dialogue, 74
   for discrimination of real from
      false, 38
   to experience O, 132–133
   to hallucinate, 211, 212
   for identification, 110
   to know and to think, 146, 147, 154,
      176, 211, 212, 222, 231
   of learning from own experience,
      168
   to love, 149, 162
   mental, needing to be nourished,
      77
   for mourning, 135
   narrative, 103, 105
   negative: see negative capability
   for protection, 160, 162
   to recognize truth, 113
   to represent, 116, 123
   for reverie, 69, 93, 102, 118, 120–121
   to say truth, 235
   for sympathetic concern for
      individual, 12
   to synthesize one's own sensory

      perceptions, 168, 176
   to think emotions, xxi
   for thinking and linking, 125
   of unconscious to be potentially
      interpretable, 115
Caro, J., xxi
Cassirer, E., 208
Castermane, I., 42
catastrophe, infantile, 135
catastrophic change, 4, 48, 49, 60, 191,
   224, 227
   and fear of death, 54–55
cause(s):
   and effect, linear relationship of,
      202
   primary, of anxiety, fear of end as,
      47
   memory, desire, and
      comprehension as causes of
      opacity in psychoanalytic
      work, 39: see also memory and
      desire
chaos:
   absolute, as infant's proto-
      experience of O, 141
   and complexity, 141
   as organized by selected fact, 135
   as presentation of unconscious, 140
clinical experiences, 8, 113, 114, 121,
   135, 169–171, 212
clinical vignettes:
   Balint's patient, 233–234
   "a bloodshed", 100–101
   Case A, 50–51
   Case B (Buddha), 51–52
   Case C, 52
   charming and co-operative patient,
      79–81
   Julius, 230–231
   Laura, 232–233
   male who works in trade, 32–34
   Martha, 231–232
   "Martina's phimosis", 97–99
   "uncouth countryman and the
      mother", 99–100
   "using the Grid", 189–199
Cluny Museum, 28
Colette, S. G., 29, 30, 36

column(s) in Grid, 25, 112, 158, 182–184, 186–188, 191, 225
commensal link(s), 216, 222
commensal relationship(s), 216, 223
common sense (CS), 8, 34, 35, 36, 37, 38–42, 62n, 68n, 131, 164–177, 215, 221
communications from patient, conscious or unconscious, 24, 48
compassion, 121, 156, 160, 162
comprehensibility, 38, 39, 41
comprehension, 5, 9, 44, 70, 203
and common sense, 38–42
and comprehensibility, 38
concept(s), xxii, 185
of *a priori*, 137
of bastion, 84
of Being, 130
of *"cura"*, 61
of empty thoughts, 185
of filter, 135
of foreclosure, 114
of person's relationship to gods, 136
of philosophical doubt, 113
of psycho-sexuality, 91
of Register of Real, 129
of stylistic complementarity of interpretation, 88
tolerance of paradoxes as embedded in seminal key concepts in psychoanalysis, 205
see also Ananke; balpha elements; breast; common sense; container/contained; dream; drive; envy, primary; falsity; invariance; lie/Lie; memory and desire; *Nachträglichkeit*; negative; O; object; personality, psychotic part of; position, depressive; position, transcendent; publication/public-ation; reality, brute; reality, psychic; representation; thing in itself; truth

conception(s), xxii, 185, 203, 227
concern:
for facts, 121
for individual (or patient), 12, 13, 61, 66n, 74, 216
lack of, 207, 210
concrete thinking: *see* thinking
conflict, 40, 42, 87, 175, 232
-free area of ego, 84
with group, 174
between narcissism and socialism, 175
Oedipus: *see* Oedipus
between premature and postmature parts present in same body, 160
of will, 72n
Conscious, 102, 115, 117, 174, 181, 205, 207, 214, 224
attacks on, 49
see also consciousness
consciousness, 36, 124, 126–127, 137n, 150, 173, 174
constant conjunction(s), 118, 120, 123, 132, 176, 183, 214
container/contained, 7, 47, 48, 58, 59, 60, 69, 92, 97, 105, 106, 116, 127, 128, 131, 136, 139, 142, 146, 148, 149, 201, 205, 210, 215, 222, 223, 227
acting as, 146, 149, 150
correlation(s), 172–173
affective, of "sense" of affects, 172
based on common sense, 165, 166
with common sense, 8, 34, 41, 165
between different emotions, 172, 173
with group, 41–42, 173, 175–176, 177
growth, with capacity to think about emotional experiences, 222
between ingestion of food and intestinal movements, 31
between senses/sensory perceptions, 165, 173, 176, 177
sensory, of common sense, 172

Cotard's delusion, 52
counterpoint(s), 38–44, 212
countertransference, 23, 25, 76, 85,
    147, 150, 153, 229
    reactions, emotional, 229
couple, 30, 95
    analytic, 5, 6, 26, 70, 72n, 204, 205,
        212–213, 215–218
    as human unit, 13
    incorporation as opposed to
        excorporation, 117
    "nothing" and "no thing", 114
    parental, 106, 201, 205, 210, 212–
        214, 215, 218, 219
    talking and creative, 212–214
courage:
    of Frederic Bion, 11
    lack of, 73n
    of liars, 53
    of Parthenope Bion, 18
    of Wilfred Bion, 64, 72n, 73n, 77,
        144
    of Wilfred Bion's mother, 11
Crespo, C., 220–235
Croce, B., 157
cure, 41, 196
    hope for, 22, 24
    not being permanent, 171
curiosity, v, 12, 24, 25, 26, 28, 34, 37,
    51, 183, 187

D (depressive position): see
    position(s)
Dante Alighieri, 155
Darwin, C., 203, 227
Dasein: see being-in-itself
death:
    anxiety(ies), xiv, 46–48, 51
    emotional awareness of one's own,
        50, 55
    fear of, 4, 45–55, 120
        and catastrophic change, 54–55
        transformations of, 53–54
    instinct, 4, 45–55, 129, 134, 139,
        140–141, 148, 153, 205, 211
    mental, 114
    problem of, in Freud, Melanie
        Klein, Bion, 46–48

decathexis, 143n
decision process as function of
    maturing process, 42
deductive reasoning, 45, 49
deductive system, 65, 193; see also
    scientific deductive system
defence(s):
    against difficult
        countertransference feelings,
        150–151
    against self-knowledge, 148
    depressive, 134
    in favour of making contact, 148
    function of, 135
    in psychotic, 167
    manic depressive, 130, 134
    mechanisms of, 224–225
    narcissistic, 4
    paranoid texture of, 153
definitory hypothesis, negative
    function of, 186
deity, 13, 139n
denial, 46, 49, 52, 112, 113, 114, 218
dependence:
    fears of, 230
    feelings of, 56
depression/depressed patient(s), 24,
    44, 81, 100, 190–192, 217, 232
depressive:
    anxieties: see anxiety(ies)
    clinical depressive illness
        (melancholia), 135
    defences: see defence(s)
    experiences, 98
    position: see position(s)
Derrida, J., 140, 142
Descartes, R., 68, 112, 113, 176, 177,
    204
desire, memory and: see memory and
    desire
destruction, 7, 8, 52, 123, 167, 196
destructiveness, primary, 49
destructive process, 161
dialogics, 142
digestion:
    of balpha elements, 6, 104–105
    mental, 65, 72, 92, 94, 102, 112, 117,
        121, 124, 130

digestive apparatus/system, 31, 210, 211, 218
digestive model: *see* model
dilemmatic situation(s), 221, 223–229, 230
disorder(s):
  mental, xx
  post-traumatic stress disorder, 144
  of scattered, familiar, and apparently unrelated elements, 171
  of thought, 40
Donne, J., xxii, 188
Donnet, J.-L., 109
dread, 135, 144
dream(s):
  artificial, 110
  in four movements, 27–38
  images, 44, 226
  -like nature, 65
  -like vision, 7–8, 155–163
  patients': *see* clinical vignettes
  psychoanalysts dreaming material offered by patient, 44
  synthesizing function of, 168
  -thoughts, 34, 95, 102, 127, 177, 184
  -work, 168, 201, 203, 205, 216
  -alpha, 34, 44–45, 65
dreaming, 4, 157
  dreams, apparatus for, 105
  mind, narrative capacity of, 105
drive(s), 112, 113, 115, 117, 118, 122, 126, 131, 167, 174, 175
  emotional, 167
Drummond de Andrade, C., 27

early experiences, 120, 126
Ecclesiasticus, 13
Eckart, J., 131
ego:
  abandonment of, 132
  conflict-free area of, 84
  -dystonic situation, 229
  functions, 234
  instincts, 175
  pleasure:
    primitive, 116

purified, 119, 136
suspension of, 139
-syntonic relation to reality, 229
thoughts and judgements representing reality in, 118
Einstein, A., 162, 163, 203, 210
ejection, 117
emotion(s):
  capacity to "think", xxi
  experiences of, 7, 33, 34, 36, 41, 42, 44, 45, 71, 104, 112, 118, 121, 132, 145, 148, 212, 215, 218, 222
  inexhaustible palette of people's, 76
  linked with risk of life, 48
  missing in Bion's classical works, 61–62
  patient's utterances as dense with, 63
  slave of, reason as, 45
empirical experiences, 176
envious attacks, 67
envious hatred, 44, 209
envy, 39, 44, 49, 67, 69, 144, 173, 214
  of analyst, 23
  primary, 68
epistemological argument, 174
epistemological dimension, 130
epistemological errors, 207
epistemological function of mind: *see* mind
epistemological pilgrimage, 131
epistemological vertices, 6, 133
epistemology, emotional, 141
epitaph:
  for Bion's tomb, 26
  Moschus' *Epitaph for Bion*, 72
Eros, 47
establishment, 70, 136, 157, 173, 227
Euclid, 178, 194, 195
Eumenides, 120
evacuation(s), 105, 113, 116–118, 122–124, 128, 147, 152
  through action as most radical attempt at denial, 112
  as one way of getting rid of noxious excitations, 123

evolution:
  of analytic process, 36
  anti-, 65
  of Bion's ideas, 60
  and change, catastrophic, as linked
    by Bion, 55
  and maturation, as opposed to
    crisis, decadence, and decline,
    158
  mental, as catastrophic and
    timeless, 54
  in O, xxii, 143–144, 204: see also O
  of psychoanalysis, 57, 58
excorporation, 117
Exodus, 138

fact(s), selected, 24, 30, 36, 83, 135,
  173–174, 202, 203, 221
faeces, 157, 209, 211, 212, 214
Faimberg, H., xiv, 5, 79–90
Fairbairn, R., 81
falsity(ies), 9, 132n, 203, 220–226
fantasy(ies), 2, 26, 27, 48, 83, 115, 119,
  121
fashion, 25, 57, 64, 209
feeding, 35, 52, 120, 121, 200
feeling(s):
  of being mad, being a murderer,
    54
  countertransference, 147, 150, 153
  of depression and guilt, 40
  of inadequacy, 14
  omnipotent, 207
    and omniscient, 44
  of persecution, 81, 123
  of personal freedom and authority,
    32
  of reality/unreality, 37
  of sameness of object, 36–37
  see also concern; dependence; guilt;
    isolation; omnipotence;
    truth(s)
Ferenczi, xiv, 242, 243
  Cogitations as new Clinical Diary, 4–
    5, 56–78, 169
  work of, 63
Ferrater Mora, J., 221

Ferro, A., xv, 5–6, 91–107
fiction(s), 6, 13, 75, 109, 110, 125, 127,
  221
field, 70, 104
  emotional facts of, 92
Flora, F., 157
fragment(s), 25, 208
  of new theories, 158
fragmentation, 30
  of container and contained, 227
free will, 29, 36, 38, 40, 42
Freud, A., 155
Freud, S., passim
  Beyond the Pleasure Principle, 126
  Formulations on the Two Principles of
    Mental Functioning, xxi, 183
  Future of an Illusion, The, 47
  Inhibitions, Symptoms and Anxiety,
    41, 196
  "Negation", 116
  Psychopathology of Everyday Life,
    The, 220
  "Thoughts for the Times on War
    and Death", 46
  Totem and Taboo, 214
  "Uncanny, The", 46
  Why War, 162
frustration(s), 30, 31, 40, 41, 44, 62,
  118, 123, 173, 186, 191, 202, 206,
  209, 214
Furies, 120

God, 47, 68, 132, 133, 138, 160, 176,
  177, 200
Goethe, J. W., 206
greed, 39, 44, 144, 214
Green, A., xv, 6, 25, 62, 66n, 73n, 74n,
  76n, 108–128
Grid, xvii, 8, 25, 58, 59, 89, 96, 97, 109,
  112, 158, 178–199, 223, 224, 225,
  228
  row(s) in, 96, 97, 112, 184–186, 224,
  225
Grillo de Rimoldi, E., 220–235
Grimblat de Notrica, S., 220–235
Grinberg, L., xvii, xx–xxiii, 3, 9, 15
Griselda, 20, 25

Grotstein, J., xv, 6, 7, 129–144, 224, 226

group(s), xvi, xvii, xx, xxi, 2, 5, 8, 9, 22, 33, 34, 37–42, 56, 59, 64–68, 72, 73, 136, 156, 159, 160, 166–178, 193, 196, 197, 220, 222, 228
  experiences with, 40
  therapy, experiences in, xiv

growth, emotional, 69

guilt, 30, 31, 44, 68, 135, 190, 191

guru, Bion as, 75

H/hate, 97, 122, 131, 136, 175, 182, 205, 206, 214

hallucinosis, 193, 226
  category of eternity, 55
  conscious, 193
  system, 53–54
  transformation: *see* transformation(s)

Harris Williams, M., 144

Hartmann, H., 84, 208

Hegel, G. W. F., 8, 115, 156

Heidegger, M., 7, 130, 133, 140

Heimann, P., xiv, 4, 57, 68n, 69, 229

Heisenberg, W. K., 203

Heraclitus, 142

Hesse, H., 41

hologram, 95

hostility, 12, 40, 42, 157

Hume, D., 131, 161, 201, 208

hypercathexis, 143n

hypothesis(es):
  to be forgotten, 152
  definitory, 117, 182, 186
  emotional experience as matrix of mind, 112
  infant's feeling as though it were about to die, 47
  regarding existence of "thought without thinker", 20, 204; *see also* thought(s)
  similarity between Euclid's Theorem and Freud's Oedipus complex, 194
  of something primitive in mind, 111

of using digestive apparatus model and reproductive system model, 212
  see also beta-element(s); wish-fulfilment, hallucinatory; unconscious

'I', experiences of, 115

Id, 115

idealization(s), 59, 61, 69, 217

identification(s), xiv, 5, 85, 87, 88, 110, 162, 178, 194, 234
  introjective, 213, 216
  primary, 132n
  projective, xxi, 93, 114, 116, 120, 134, 135, 179, 206, 207–210, 213, 216, 218, 222, 234

ideogram, 35

ideograph, 127

imaginative conjecture, 143–144

imaginative exercise, 180

imaginative reverie, 69

immortality, 40, 46

inadequacy:
  of analyst, 150
  of attention, 35, 63
  of interpretation, 74–75
  of objects: *see* object(s)
  of praxis, 158
  of psychoanalytic theory, for understanding and analysing psychotics, 109

incorporation, 82, 88, 117

independence:
  of Bion's theoretical and technical positions, 5, 108
  of external fact, of observers, 169

independent way of mind, 2

Indra, 128

induction, 161, 173

infant:
  emotional experience of, 128
  proto-experience of O of, 141

infra-sensuous areas, 194

inner experience, 42, 43
  destructive, 120

inoculation by reality, 213

inquiry, 130, 158, 159, 183, 191
  in Grid, 187
insight(s), 14, 18, 30, 41, 113, 126, 205,
  210
  experience of, 43
  institutionalization, 60
  integrating experience, 36
intercourse:
  between analyst and patient, 213–
  214, 216
    underlying process of, 200
  between mouth and breast, 218
  and parental couple, 210, 213, 218
  sexual, 33, 201
International Centennial Conference
  on Work of W. R. Bion, v, xiv,
  xvi, 1–2, 3, 6, 15, 17, 26, 56, 77n,
  108
Internet, xvi, 2
intimacy, emotional, 66
Introduction to the Work of Bion, xvii,
  xxi, 15
introjection, 44, 47, 92, 116, 117, 120,
  151, 209
  re-introjection, 111, 120, 147, 150,
  151
intuition, xxi, xxii, 3, 9, 18, 24, 35, 36,
  37, 38, 39, 41, 42, 44, 72, 126,
  131, 136, 139, 144, 152, 172, 176,
  180, 193, 203, 205, 210, 213, 217
intuitive process, 35, 36, 42
invariance(s), 4, 48, 49, 202, 204
invariants, 181
isolation, 11, 42–44, 56, 73

jargon, in representation of
  psychoanalytic experience, 4,
  18, 57, 70
Johnson, S., 206
Jones, E., 46
jouissance, 119
Joyce, J., 2, 91, 155
Jung, C. G., 137
Junqueira de Mattos, J. A., 142n

K/knowledge, 5, 9, 38, 39, 41, 44, 65,
  69, 116, 122–123, 127, 131, 132n,

136, 137, 139, 142, 147, 148, 153,
  156, 182, 194, 201–205, 206, 214,
  215–218, 221, 222, 226
  –K, 65, 67, 114, 122–123, 206, 207,
  227
Kant, I., 7, 9, 25, 53, 110, 114, 121, 131,
  137–138, 143, 185, 201, 203, 208,
  221
Keats, J., 85, 113, 122
King Lear (Shakespeare), 39–41, 121
  Cordelia, 39–40
  Edgar, 121
  Goneril, 39
  Kent, 39–40
  Regan, 39
  Tom, 121
King, E., 15
King, K., 15
Kipman, S.-D., 60n
Klein, M., xvii, xxi, 4, 6, 7, 25, 29, 36,
  46–48, 51, 58, 59, 65, 76n, 81,
  107, 109, 120, 122, 129, 131, 132,
  134, 138, 139, 144, 146, 147, 148,
  155, 174, 179, 203, 207, 209, 228
Kleinian:
  analysts, 7, 47, 58–59n, 64, 108, 109,
  146, 147, 152
  Bion as "Kleinian", 5, 16, 58–59
  "cause", 65–66
knowledge as independent category,
  122

L/love, 9, 14, 15, 86, 122, 131, 136,
  149, 160, 175, 182, 194, 204, 205,
  206, 213, 214, 219, 222
L'enfant et les sortilèges, 29
Lacan, J,. 88, 112, 114, 129, 130
Laplanche, J., 88
learning, 157, 225
  from experience, 41, 42, 153, 168,
  182, 203, 222
leisure, 13
Liberman, D., 88
lie(s), 4, 9, 50, 53, 54, 55, 113, 126, 186,
  206, 220–235
life, emotional, 30
link(s), 41, 114, 120, 131, 136, 168, 175,

185, 209, 210, 211, 212, 215, 216, 222, 224, 225, 227
    attack on, 67
    lack of, 81
    primary, 222
    see also H/hate; K/knowledge; L/ love
linking function, 120, 175
    un-linking, 225
listening, 4, 5, 60, 61, 65, 79, 83, 84–85, 216, 223
    to listening, 5, 79–90
    to silence and to interpretations, 85–87
logic, 45, 76, 87, 140, 185, 221
    bivalent, 140
Luzuriaga, I., xv, 7, 145–154

Madame Bovary, 93
Maizels, N., 138
Marlowe, C., 142
Marques, M., 206
Mary, Queen of Scots, 142
mathematics, xxi–xxii, 118, 131, 140, 161, 193, 194
maturing process, decision process as function of, 42
Matte Blanco, I., 7, 140, 141
Maugham, W. S., 133
meaning, inner, 37
megalomania, 167
Meltzer, D., xv, 59n, 62, 76n, 103, 144, 224, 225, 226
memory(ies):
    conscious searching for, 22
    and desire (without), xxii, 22, 23, 24, 25, 39, 41, 42, 44, 59, 69, 70, 82–84, 89, 139, 146, 156, 163, 164, 178–179, 193, 196, 215, 218: see also understanding
    game, 101–102
Mendeleev, D. I., 178
mental activity, 112
mental apparatus, 49, 183, 188, 200, 210, 211
mental attitude, 223
mental batteries, 13

mental behaviour, 154
mental change, 55
mental contents, 114, 147
mental counterpart, 97
mental death, 114
mental freedom, 2
mental growth, 43, 54, 69
mental health, 9, 53
mental laziness, 63
mental life, 103, 205, 209
mental mechanisms, 171
mental outcome, 185
mental pain, 160
mental process, 35, 41, 42, 112, 137n
mental resistance, 62
mental space, xxii, 69, 93, 122
mental stability, 178, 196
mental stamina, 13, 18
mental state(s), 93, 102, 120, 147, 165, 208, 223, 228
mental structure, 228
mental substance, xxii
mental suffering, 156
mental symptoms, 124
mental systems, 148
mental universe, 69
Meotti, A., xvi, 7–8, 155–163
Merciai, S. A., v, xiv, xvi, 1–9, 15, 20, 56–78
Messiah, 13
metapsychology, 47, 132, 134, 144
Milner, M., 81, 85
Milton, J., 155
mind:
    conscious, 24
    epistemological, 205
    psychoanalytic function of, 205
model(s):
    digestive and reproductive systems model, 9, 200, 211–212, 215–218
    double limit, 117
Molesworth, Mrs., 20
Mona Lisa della Gioconda, 7, 133
Money-Kyrle, R., 47
monism, xxii
Montaigne, M. E., 55

Moore, G. E., xxii
mortality, 47, 52, 227
mother(s), 11, 17, 29, 30, 31, 33, 48, 50,
    54, 66, 68, 80, 87, 99, 100, 110,
    118, 119, 120, 121, 128, 149, 157,
    176, 190, 192, 195, 201, 205, 209,
    211, 216, 222, 232
Mr. Kugelmass, 93
mystic(s), 7, 126, 134, 136, 142, 158,
    161, 210, 226
mysticism, 6, 48, 133, 134
myth(s), 4, 36, 52, 53, 96, 124, 177,
    184, 223, 228
    and primordial, 128
    myth-making, 177
    Oedipus, 128, 194

Nachträglichkeit, 5, 87–89
naive idealism, 208–209
naive realism, 208
nameless anxiety: *see* anxiety(ies)
nameless dread, 135, 144
nameless O, 135
narcissism/narciss-ism, 39, 42, 64,
    164, 167, 170, 174–177, 206
    primary, 167
narration, 33, 105
narrative(s), 36, 37, 68, 69, 91, 93, 94,
    95, 96, 97, 181, 184, 229, 233
    derivatives, 101–105
Nebbiosi, G., xvi, 8, 164–177
negation, 116–117, 192
Negative, the, 6, 66, 108, 115, 123,
    124–125, 153, 165, 186, 202,
    205–207, 229
negative capability/capacity, 5, 24,
    79–90, 113, 122, 173
negative Grid, 225
negative hallucination(s): *see*
    hallucination(s)
negative linking, 114
negative work of negative, 108–128
negativity, 119, 122
neo-Kantian, 25
neurotic(s), 7, 46, 47, 109, 113, 117,
    126, 127, 153, 208, 225, 226
Newton, I., xxii
Nietzsche, F., 201, 203, 206

nightmare(s), 110
no-breast: *see* breast(s)
no-me, 54
non-concrete, 210
non-differentiation, 69
non-explanation, 205
non-hypocrisy, 72
non-interference, 202
non-knowledge, 65
non-linear complexity, 134
non-linearity, 135
non-metabolized beta-elements, 104
non-reality, 206, 209
non-sense, 177
non-sensuous, 203, 204, 209
non-separate, 211
non-sequential reading, 3
non-symbolized experience, 121
non-unified subject, patient as, 87
non-verbal sense, taste as, 35
notation, 121, 178, 179, 183, 203
no thing, 6, 53, 114–116, 119, 144, 186
not knowing, 4, 85, 89
noumenon(a), 131, 137, 143
nourishment, xxiii, 201, 213, 217, 218,
    219

O, xxii, 6, 7, 48, 49, 52, 53, 54, 94, 96,
    97, 110, 122, 129–144, 173, 201,
    204, 205, 207, 212, 215, 218, 219,
    221, 222, 226, 228
object(s):
    absence of, 53, 203, 218
    bad, 73n, 123, 146, 149, 150
    bizarre, 117, 123
    death of, 54
    of desire, 47
    dynamics, 92
    external, 47, 116
    good, 146, 149, 150, 151
    inadequate, 149
    internal, xxi, 7, 93, 95, 96, 142, 145,
        149
    persecutory, 123
    presentation, 118
    psychoanalytic, 55, 131, 132, 139,
        140
    relationship, 111

role of, 120–121
unknowable, 122
whole, 149
objective experience, 131
obstinacy, 183, 187
Odyssey, 70
oedipal experience, 128
Oedipus, xiv, xxi, 25, 33, 46, 128, 175,
     183, 187, 194, 195, 204, 206, 219
Ogden, T., 140
omnipotence, 24, 44, 75, 128, 134, 144,
     207, 214, 223, 234
omniscience, 41, 44, 75, 122, 223
ontogenesis, 111
Orestes, 120
O'Shaugnessy, E., 228
Other, emotional-affective
     relationship with, 96
"ozone layer", emotional and
     epistemic, 133

paradox, 9, 111, 144, 202, 203, 205,
     206, 209, 215, 217, 218
paranoid–schizoid position: see
     position(s)
parasitic:
     liaison, 34
     link(s), 216, 222
     relationship(s), 216
Pascal, B., 200, 208
Peirce, C. S., 129
penis, 210, 213
penumbra of association(s), 119, 121
personality(ies):
     normal or neurotic, 113, 225
     psychotic part of, 4, 48, 49, 50, 52,
          53, 113, 225
Petrini, R., xvi–xvii, 8, 164–177
phantasy(ies), 2, 12, 91, 92, 93, 94, 99,
     104, 106, 131, 167, 207, 213, 216,
     221, 231
Philosophical Dictionary, 221
phylogenesis, 111
pictogram(s), emotional, 92, 101
pictograph(s), 95, 102, 121, 123, 127
pictorial image(s), 35, 123
Pilate, 220
Pirandello, L., 220

Plato, 9, 48, 131, 142, 212, 221
play, symbolic, concrete and
     primitive form of expression
     in, 147
pleasant experience followed by
     tasty one, 101, 103
pleasure, 119, 206
     anticipation of pleasure and pain,
          97
     ego, 116, 119, 136
     –unpleasure principle, 39, 111, 116,
          129, 139
Plutarch, 195
Poincaré, J. H., 131, 203
point of view, emotional, 49, 150
Pollaiolo, xvii, 77
Pontalis, J.-B., 88
Pontes Miranda de Ferreira, R. B.,
     xvii, 8–9, 178–199
Popper, K. R., 49
position(s):
     analyst's, when listening to patient,
          5, 8, 61, 70, 79–90, 107, 124, 170,
          171
     countertransference, of analyst, 85
     depressive/D, xxi, 30, 36, 37, 129–
          130, 133, 134, 135, 137, 138, 140,
          151, 152, 203, 226
     –K: see K/knowledge
     paranoid–schizoid/PS, xxi, 36, 37,
          92, 97, 105, 129, 133, 134, 135,
          137, 153, 203, 205, 207, 213, 214,
          215, 226, 227
     transcendent, 6–7, 129–144
Pound, E., 155
preconception(s), xxii, 26, 131, 137,
     139, 185, 191, 203, 211, 216
     inherent, 131
preconscious, 72, 117
presentation:
     thing-, 117, 118, 121
     word-, 117, 118
prêt-à-porter hallucinosis
     transformations of culture, 52
price to be paid, emotional, 36
primordial mind, 6, 108–128
Pritchard, F. H., 20
prodigality, 43–44

projection(s), 48, 117, 120, 123, 146,
148, 160, 209
proto-emotional tensions, 102
proto-experience of O, 141
proto-phantasies, 216
PS↔D, 7, 92, 97, 105, 109, 129, 134,
135, 136, 144, 185, 203, 205, 207,
227
psychic experience, 126
psychic reality, 29, 35, 38, 43, 137, 172,
200, 201, 203, 205, 206, 208, 209,
210, 211, 217, 218, 230
psychoanalytic experience, 4, 5, 25,
43, 57, 60, 61, 68, 71, 74, 85, 90,
121, 126, 127, 151, 162, 181, 189,
191
"psychomas", 216
psychosis, 49, 53, 109, 114, 135, 167,
229, 234
psychotic anxiety, 46, 47
psychotic aspects, 7, 46, 208, 225
psychotic defences, 52
psychotic failure, 119
psychotic fragments, 159
psychotic infancy of all individual
minds, 208
psychotic mechanisms, 224, 229
psychotic part of personality: see
personality(ies)
psychotic patient(s), xiv, 49, 52–53,
109, 113, 117, 123, 149, 151, 167,
225, 226, 234
psychotic personality, 207
psychotic positions, 134
psychotic qualities, 153
psychotic time, 55
publication/public-ation, 164, 168,
169, 226
Pythagoras' Theorem, 195

Ravel, M. J., 29
reaction(s), emotional, 23, 234
reality:
brute, 129, 135
coping with, 214–215
inner, 9, 49, 219
principle, 206
psychic: see psychic reality

representations of, 118
ultimate, 53, 122, 130, 131, 133, 136,
139, 142, 194
realization(s), 2, 68, 128, 132, 134, 182,
183, 185, 193, 194, 195, 203, 211,
212, 216, 218, 234
reasoning, process of, 24, 25
reintrojection, 111, 120, 147, 150, 151
religion(s), 4, 52, 53, 133, 159, 160,
228
repression, 114, 115, 119, 124, 223
resistance(s), 62, 113, 119, 169, 182,
191, 230
of Establishment in face of truth of
certain scientific theories, 227
to psychoanalytic treatment, 4, 54,
55
retroactivity, 87–89
revelation, function of, 176
reverence and awe, 70, 138
reverie, 13, 102
of analyst, 65, 69, 93, 103, 120–121
maternal, 47, 118, 120, 222
Rorschach, H., 95, 178
Rudra, 128
Russell, B., xxii

Sacerdoti, C., 15
sacrifice, 128
Saffoires, D., 220–235
Samarkand, 142
Sandler, P. C., xvii, 9, 200–219
Sartre, J. P., 130
satisfaction, experience of, 84
scenario, emotional, 61
Schopenhauer, A., 203
Schreber case, 109, 114, 143n
scientific character of psychoanalysis,
xvi, xxii, 6, 37–38, 130, 152, 178,
185, 194, 195, 196
scientific deductive system, 6, 125,
126, 185, 186, 193, 194
scientific mind as scientific
instrument, 124–125
scientific/pseudo-scientific theories,
52–53, 110, 227
self, xxii
inner, 145

object as being not separated
    from self of baby in beginning,
    123
postnatal, 159
reluctance to feel entire self called
    to trial during analysis, 63
true, 217
sense(s):
    of affiliation, 67
    of attunement, 70
    common: see common sense/CS
    of discipline, 75
    of external reality, 226
    of freedom, v
    of helplessness, 217
    of humour, 17
    of inferiority and frustration, 62
    "new", 24
    perceptions, 102, 169
    receptor, inner, 139
    of release, 14
    of truth, 166, 202, 215
sensible experience, 165
sensuous apparatus, 201, 202, 203,
    208
sensuous apprehensible pseudo-
    realities, 201
sensuous background, 194
sensuous beta-elements, 115
sensuous data, 201
sensuous experience, 111, 119, 121
sensuous images, 184
sensuous mind too heavy for
    sensuous beast, 96, 209
sensuous psychic reality as non-
    sensuous, 203–204
sensuous subjective, 168, 170
separation:
    anxieties, xiv, 37, 42, 230
    from Establishment, 136
    between persecutory object and
        persecuted subject, 123
sexuality, 175
    as narrative genre or dialect in
        consulting-room, 5–6, 91–107
Shakespeare, W., 39, 85, 206
Shelley, P. B., 72
sick syllogism, 4, 45–55

silence(s), xx, 23, 25, 42–44, 74, 83, 89,
    100, 150
    listening to, 84–87
sincerity, 72
social component, primary, 167
social lies, 223, 227–228
socialism/social-ism, 39, 64, 164, 167,
    170, 174–178
solitude, 42–44, 212
    awareness of, 32, 36, 37, 41
Sophocles, 194
Sor, D., xvii, 225
space, inner, 117
speech, 128
    of person, inner, 217
spermatozoon, concrete raw data
    from, 201
Speziale-Bagliacca, R., 67n, 107
Sphinx, 195
Spitz, R., 141n
splitting, 20, 116–117, 124, 135–136,
    149, 170, 204, 207, 208, 211, 217,
    218
stage-directing, function of, 105
starvation of truth, 165
state(s):
    emotional, 22, 76, 147
    inner, 73n
statement(s), 41, 53, 71, 79, 110, 115,
    146, 179–180, 182–183, 186, 191,
    192, 221, 225
Steiner, J., 151
stimuli, concrete sensuously
    apprehensible, transformation
    of, 210
storm, emotional, 76–77
strange attractor, 135
structure, emotional, 50
subjectivity, 64, 65, 134, 141, 170, 171
subjectivization, primary, 135
Superego, primitive, 234
symbiotic link(s), 216, 222, 227
symbiotic relationship(s), 201, 210,
    216, 217
symbol(s), 5, 7, 102, 122, 127, 134,
    139, 178, 225, 226, 227
symbolic disguise, 226
symbolic function(s), 114, 225–226

symbolic play, 147
symbolic representation(s), 178
symbolization, process of, 114
Symington, J., 58n, 73n, 144n
Symington, N., 58n, 73n, 144n
Szpunberg de Bernztein, A., 220–235

Tabak de Bianchedi, E., xvii, 9, 15,
    132n, 220–235
Talamo, Patrizia, v, 17, 19
Talmud, 110, 135
technique(s):
    psychoanalytic, xiv, xv, 21, 35, 47,
        145–154, 156, 171, 227
    theory of, xv, xvi, xx, xxii, 7, 26
terror, 45, 49, 54, 76, 113–114, 135
texture, 153
Thanatos, 46–47
therapeutic, 54, 66, 156, 162, 196
thing in itself, 53, 110, 121, 122, 137,
    142–143, 208–209, 226
thinking, 9, 112–114, 200–219
    abstract, 118
    apparatus for, 49, 92, 95, 103, 105,
        111, 115, 119
    attacks on furthering of thinking–
        feeling process, 25
    best possible conditions for, 26
    concrete, 114, 216
    as confused with psychic activity,
        112
    as difficult but extremely
        important, 109
    as digestion of mind, 112
    as new function, 96
    of nothing, 113
    painful nature of, 12
    perversion of, 228
    theory of, xxii, 109, 114, 119
    transition from concrete to abstract,
        111
thought(s):
    fragments of, 157
    process of, 9, 25, 26, 200, 203, 204,
        205, 206, 207, 210, 211, 215, 217,
        218, 219
    without thinker, xxii, xxv, 111, 112,
        113, 125, 204, 210–211, 212, 213

Tolstoy, L., 157
transcendence(s), 7, 130, 132, 134,
    135, 136–137, 137–138, 142,
    204
transcendentalism, 131, 136, 137–138
transcendent position: see position(s)
transcendingness, 137
transference, 92, 95, 99, 104, 151, 153,
    206, 207–210
transformation(s), 4, 5, 43, 48, 49, 95,
    107, 116, 120, 121, 128, 137, 141,
    156, 191, 210, 212, 223
    of beta (or balpha) elements into
        alpha elements, 92, 93, 105,
        111–112, 120
    of fear of death, 53–54
    hallucinatory, 4
    in hallucinosis, 52, 53, 54, 206, 207,
        216
    in K, 137, 221, 222, 226
    in O, 54, 97, 129–144, 207, 221
    process of, 49
truth(s):
    absolute or ultimate, 53, 55, 122,
        128, 130, 131, 136, 139, 142, 201,
        210, 211, 215
    emotional contact with, 221
    experience of, 173
    fear of dying and sacrifice of truth,
        45–55
    as food of mind, 210
    hatred of, 222
turbulence, emotional, 38, 92, 93, 136,
    224
Tustin, F., 113

ultimate being, experience of, 130
ultra-sensuous areas, 194
unconscious, xiv, xvi, 5, 23, 24, 25, 43,
    48, 66, 67, 71, 83, 85, 86, 87, 88,
    92, 102, 115, 117, 126, 131, 132,
    137, 140, 174, 201, 203, 207, 213,
    214, 217
    process of, 214
understanding, 34, 37, 57, 62n, 87,
    121, 131, 141, 142, 162, 203, 223,
    229, 234
    aiming at, 202

without memory, desire or, xxii, 24, 139, 193
undigested facts, 92, 94, 102, 104, 121
Unicorn, 28–29
unknowable, 110, 122, 129, 130, 140, 205, 218, 221
unknown, 37–38, 41, 43, 69, 81, 84, 85, 97, 112, 130, 161, 182, 184, 193–194, 202–203, 213, 216
unutterable experience, 43
Ur, 228

Vedas, 128
verbalization, 2, 35, 48, 94, 114, 117, 184, 188, 191, 192, 193, 214
vertex(ices), 6, 41, 91, 97, 100, 106, 107, 127, 133, 138, 153, 194, 206, 211, 222
Verwerfung, 114
voice, inner, 217
    ineffable, 140

void, inner, 114

war, experience of, 48, 162
Werba, A., 220–235
wild asses, 75, 207
wild thought(s), 2, 57, 75, 207
Winnicott, D. W., 4, 57, 65, 66, 67, 81, 109, 123, 176, 209
wisdom, converting experience into, 13
wish-fulfilment, hallucinatory, 118–120
womb, 110, 128
working-through, process of, 70
world:
    emotional, 63
    inner, 126–127, 195, 230

Young, G. W., 19

Zamkow, R., 220–235